A FACE FROM
URANUS

A FACE FROM
URANUS

Correspondence Between

Tedd Burr and Henry Bellamann

1943-1945

Edited by
Lenny Pinna

ECCLESIA

Published by Ecclesia Arts, LLC, Johnstown, PA.

Registration with WGA Registry: Number 2045191, March 12, 2020, A Face from Uranus: Burr and Bellamann letters

Copyright © 2022, Registration: TXu 2-340-922, October 10, 2022 A Face from Uranus: Correspondence between Tedd Burr and Henry Bellamann 1943-1945

ISBN 979-8-9871213-0-6 (Hardcover)
ISBN 979-8-9871213-1-3 (Paperback)

Subjects: LGBTQ, gender identity, psychology, literature, performance history, World War II

Classification: LGBTQ/social science

Print book interior designed by Patricia Oman
Cover design, Lenny Pinna, Patricia Oman

Cover photograph provided by Amber and Adrienne Slane

Nevertheless, psychologists tell us that we are prone to remember the more pleasant aspects of life and with these I do prefer to deal. Let the morbid and the "bloody" real wait to be bound in black leather when I am cold and still in eternity. Rather then, I should like to cry, "Here I am when I was. And think not too bitterly on me. I tried."

—Tedd I. Burr, 1944

CONTENTS

ACKNOWLEDGMENTS

I have been creatively working with the Burr-Bellamann letters over a twenty-year period, during which time I've received encouragement and support in many ways from many people in various locations. In Cleveland Heights, Ohio, where it all began, I'm thankful for the friends and theater colleagues who supported Tedd and me in producing our film, *Letters to Uranus: The Hidden Life of Tedd Burr*. I especially thank Jim Haviland for securing and loaning me a high-quality digital video camera, and for sound editing; Gisella, video editing; David, post-production. I am grateful for my family of friends—Scott, Christine, Shahin, Patrick, Bonnie R., Felicita— for their love and support of my life and creative work. I also thank Dobama Theatre and the Cedar Lee Theatre in Cleveland Heights, and the Cleveland Film Festival for including *Letters to Uranus* as part of the emerging digital video format back in 2000.

In the San Francisco Bay Area, I thank the staff of Chez Panisse for their encouragement; Alice Waters and Jen for the use of the café for the first reading of the film script *In the Name of Jamie Wakefield*, in which staff became actors; Clare, Julien, Steve C., Chris M., and Esteem for believing in me and the story; customers, Gilbert, Ellen, Marian, Art, and Mary B. for their support; Liz H. and Charles F. for legal advice; writers Janet and David Peoples for supporting my work in its infancy, giving me the confidence to continue; my son Matthew and my friend Robert F. for script feedback. I'm thankful for supportive LGBT communities—The Billy Club and Sundance Saloon; Spiritual communities—Gay Buddhist Fellowship, Integral Yoga, Biodanza, and Soul Motion's community of conscious dancers for supporting my whole being; my family of friends—Michael, Carol, Sharon, Claude, Cherry, Alzak, Freeman, Terri, and Bryan—for their ever-present support of my life; and my sister and brother-in-law, Laurie and Dave, for their constant love and support. I owe an enormous amount of thanks to my dear friend Ralph Thomas, who has believed in me for the past twenty years; his loyal support for my life, creative work and particularly this book has been invaluable.

ACKNOWLEDGMENTS

I am thankful for recent colleagues, collaborators, and supporters: Max Freedman for guiding my approach to the media industry; Stacy Dymalski, who advised me to self-publish, guiding me with her book, *The Memoir Midwife: Nine Steps to Self-Publishing Your Book*; Professor Susan Stryker, who guided my thinking about archiving the original letters; Professor Rachael Price for our collaborative Bellamann discussions; Mike McCuistion for his personal support and permission to use *Kings Row* material. I owe immense thanks to Patricia Oman for her book design, copy editing, and expertise in the publishing process; and Renee Williams for preparing the manuscript for publication. I wish to acknowledge the Kingdom of Callaway Historical Society in Fulton, Missouri for their *Kings Row*/Bellamann information, and I am grateful to Jennifer Ford, Greg Johnson and the entire staff of the University of Mississippi Archives and Special Collections for their assistance with Bellamann research and for including the original Burr-Bellamann letters in their Special Collections.

I am indebted to Professor Harry Bayne for his dissertation on Henry Bellamann, and for all of the information and materials he has generously shared with me. The numerous details he contributed to our discussions inspired me to envision *In the Name of Jamie Wakefield* as a much larger dramatic narrative—as a potential Limited TV Series.

—Lenny Pinna

INTRODUCTION

I think it is fairly rare to have access to both sides of a complete correspondence of letters between two people, especially when that correspondence comprises approximately one hundred long letters written at the height of World War II between a nineteen-year-old androgynous boy living in Bellevue, Ohio and a sixty-year-old best-selling author living at the Ansonia Hotel in New York City. How I became aware of the existence of such letters, and how I came to possess them, is quite a serendipitous story in itself.

One wintry evening in early February 2000, I visited the home of an actor friend, seventy-five-year-old Tedd Burr, who resided in Cleveland Heights, Ohio. Tedd, now deceased, was an androgynous figure with creamy skin and long, silky white hair. He had purposely dressed for the occasion that evening, wearing a long, faded rose-colored gown with long diaphanous draped sleeves. He announced that he had worn the very same garment as a costume when he had played Mendy, an opera queen, in a production of Terrence McNally's play *The Lisbon Traviata* at Dobama Theatre in Cleveland Heights.

As a relative newcomer to Cleveland, I began to notice Tedd around the Cleveland theater scene because of his distinctive look—long, pure white hair pulled back tightly with a braided low bun resting on the nape of his neck, the same style my paternal grandmother had always worn. Tedd and I met when we were both cast in Dobama Theatre's production of Terrence McNally's *A Perfect Ganesh*. At age 35, I was considered the "youngster" of the cast, performing with three legendary actors of the Cleveland community theater scene—Dorothy Silver, Margie Dodrill and Tedd Burr. Tedd and I developed a friendship during the rehearsals, and after the production was over, I began visiting him from time to time at his home. A few years later, as a theater director, I cast Tedd in two of my productions: As Tiresias, the blind wise man in Sophocles's *Oedipus Rex*, which was the inaugural production of my new theater company, Ecclesia; and as Adam/Hymen in the Cleveland Public Theatre's outdoor production of Shakespeare's *As You Like*

It. For several years, I continued to visit Tedd periodically at his home to converse about theater, film, and arts in general.

I visited Tedd that wintry February evening in 2000 because he had given me a play to read—*The Ladies of the Camellias* by Lillian Groag—to see if I thought there were any possibilities of my producing or directing it. At the outset of our discussion, I told him that I thought he was perfect for the part of the stage manager, Benoit, a character described as "somewhere between the ages of seventy and a hundred!" We both laughed, but for different reasons. I was merely teasing him; his laugh was more self-reflective for he saw himself playing one of the play's two leading women characters—the historically famous actresses Sarah Bernhardt or Eleanora Duse. "That's why I dressed for you," he said, disclosing the reason he had costumed himself for the evening. A light-hearted discussion arose about him always identifying with female roles. "But, I've got to stop doing that," he said with a chuckle. "Whenever I read a play, I've got to start paying attention to the *old men's* roles!" His comic delivery was perfect.

Before we began our serious discussion of the play, Tedd wanted to report on his recent theater outings, etc. This prologue was a sort of ritual at the start of our discussions. As Tedd got older, he was afraid he'd forget something, so he took to writing down notes ahead of time. He began recounting his recent activities, starting with a play he had seen at Case Western Reserve University based on letters between Olga Knipper and Anton Chekhov, which then triggered his remembrance of an older play based on letters between Mrs. Patrick Campbell and George Bernard Shaw. "They never really consummated their relationship," he said with a grin, "however, the character of Mrs. Patrick Campbell was the last role my favorite actress, Katharine Cornell, ever played."

Tedd looked down at his little cheat sheet. "Oh, yes!" He proceeded to tell me about an old movie he had recently seen on the Turner Classic Movies channel. He built up the movie's importance by describing how he had rushed home after attending the Chekhov play, "not even sticking around after to socialize," because he needed to be home in time to record this old film on his new VCR! He proclaimed the name of the film with dramatic gravitas and near worship: "Kings Row!" I sensed how much the film meant to him, but I thought he associated it with the nostalgia of his youth.

Moments later he mentioned the name Dr. Henry Bellamann, the author of the novel on which the film was based, causing him to further digress. He recounted a story about recently walking by a neighboring Baptist church that was getting rid of old books; he happened to notice an encyclopedia from 1946, and for some reason he brought it home. He felt the need to state a disclaimer: "Now I don't go around picking up things from other people's trash, but tell me if this was the finger of God, because there in the Bs was a picture of Henry Bellamann with his biographical information. What do you think of that?" A moment passed. I didn't know what to think. I assumed that I was supposed to be in listening mode. "Would you like to see it?" he asked. "I don't mean to bore you with it ..."

By now, I was well accustomed to Tedd's frequent side excursions, but I did not know yet that this conversation was building to an important revelation. "No, no, you can tell me about it," I said. He retrieved the encyclopedia and found the page with Henry Bellamann's picture. He read the entire biographical entry with relish and adoration. He read the last sentence slowly: "he was working on the sequel to *Kings Row* when he died on June 16, 1945 from a coronary thrombosis...." His eyes stilled into a look of deep remembrance. "June the sixteenth, I shall never forget that day when his widow sent me a telegram to tell me that Dr. Bellamann had passed." A moment of silence passed before I thought, "Wait. What did he just say?"

Tedd quickly closed the heavy book with a clap, stood up and changed gears. "Well that's enough of that!" he said. "Don't want to be morbid. I think we should talk about *The Ladies of the Camellias*, don't you?" He put away the encyclopedia, and we began our intended discussion of the play and who would play the lead roles. It wasn't long before Tedd began to reminisce about old actresses and their period styles of acting. He segued into stories of old classic movies and famous actresses. He stood and imitated Norma Shearer's overly expressive hands as she fluffed her hair, then he quickly dismissed her era: "Well, that was her come down you know. By 1943, the hands were out, and her last picture was a flop." He picked up again with his love of old actresses and their style of femininity, "and then, there was Bette Davis with those eyes! Eyes, eyes, eyes are so important and can say so much."

In a moment of silence we retreated into our own thoughts. I contemplated the historical art of males playing female characters. I had had my own opportunity to play a female character—dramatically chronicling the process of a middle-aged married male transitioning to female and deciding to have gender reassignment surgery. I admitted to Tedd that I felt I had gotten much more attention playing a woman compared to playing male characters. Tedd became very quiet. "Boy do I ever know. I too was very confused as a young person, not knowing who I was, because you see I felt that I was neither fish nor foul ... just lost somewhere in between."

During the ten years I had known Tedd, I had never heard him talk about his personal life, present or past. We were definitely in new territory now. I continued to remain a silent witness, as he began to open up further, coyly asking, "Would you like to see something? I-I-I'm a little sensitive about it, but it's about what I just referred to—being neither fish nor foul." Well, of course I wanted to see! By then, I was completely hooked.

He took me downstairs to his renovated basement, where he kept shelves and shelves of opera scores, albums and cassette tapes, and then he led me to a series of framed photographs and pointed to one. "This was me at age nineteen," he said. The photograph showed a young, glamorous Tedd made up like a Hollywood starlet. I was stunned. "Tedd! You were so beautiful! You looked like ... a young Katharine Hepburn," I said. He then pointed to a framed picture of an older, stony-faced man. "This," he said, "is Henry Bellamann—the author I told you about upstairs." He confided that during the time of his confusion about his gender identity, he had reached out in desperation in a letter to Henry Bellamann, and Henry answered, commencing a two-year correspondence. He also mentioned that very early in their correspondence, he had sent Henry the very same photograph, and Henry made the comment, "Your face looks like it could have come from the planet Uranus." I was flabbergasted by the comment, yet quite intrigued. I questioned Tedd: "Uranus? He said that? Uranus?" After Tedd confirmed Bellamann's comment, I asked a follow-up question: "Do you think Dr. Bellamann was a … a latent or repressed homosexual?" Uncomfortable, Tedd pushed away from the notion. "No, no, no, I don't think so," he said. "No."

My intuition was telling me that there was something underlying Henry's "Uranus" comment. I really couldn't fathom the nature of the connection between Tedd and this author, Dr. Bellamann, so I probed further. "Tedd, was Dr. Bellamann important to you in some way?" His reply shocked me. "Important? He saved my life," he said. "I really think he saved my life! You see I waited for those letters, and took from them what I needed, so that little by little I began to be able to live in a world that for so long had frightened me."

Then Tedd disclosed more: "After Henry's death, Mrs. Bellamann sent back to me all of my letters that Henry had saved." The dots suddenly began to connect. I reflected back to the moment Tedd said that Henry's widow had sent him a telegram the very day Henry died! Thoughts and questions went off in my mind like firecrackers. How important was Tedd in Henry's life that he would receive a telegram from Henry's wife informing him of her husband's death that very same day? Why would Henry save all of Tedd's letters? How would Mrs. Bellamann know of these letters, and why would she offer to send them back? Quite perplexed, I continued to probe. "Mrs. Bellamann sent all of your letters back to you?" I asked. He nodded matter of factly. "Yes, she sent all of them back."

When he disclosed that he had saved all of their correspondence for fifty-five years, and that it was currently stored in a cardboard box in his bedroom, I held up my right hand and emphatically halted him. "STOP!" I said. "I don't want to hear another word!

I would like to come back with a camera and film you looking at the letters and perhaps reading some of them for the first time on camera." I could see that my words sent shockwaves through him. He stood like a deer caught in headlights. Suddenly, Tedd was vulnerable. I sensed his immediate concern about being exposed. This was the first time he had talked to me about his private life, and as I came to find out, I happened to be the first person to whom he had ever revealed his past. And yet he had primed this conversation with all the talk about Chekhov's and Shaw's letters and recording *Kings Row* on his VCR and dumpster-diving for an encyclopedia that contained a biography of Bellamann. Was he ready to share his story with a wider audience?

It's my turn to digress. One may wonder why I so abruptly interrupted Tedd's story and asked to film him with the letters. Although Tedd's revelation seemed to come out of the blue, it felt to me like an auspicious moment. My first inclination to capture Tedd and the letters on camera arose from circumstances that happened twenty years earlier in my life. I had attempted with a tape recorder to capture all of my Italian grandfather's life stories in chronological order so that I might one day write a play or a film script about him. At the end of two hours, I realized that I had hit the pause button instead of record. I knew that I could have gone back the next day, and he would have willingly repeated it all, but I didn't have the heart to tell him.

With Tedd, this was now an opportunity to make up for that past mistake—by again attempting to capture an elder man's extraordinary story. More importantly, I realized that I was also in some way a descendant of Tedd's lineage—a lineage that was historically kept hidden. Thus it felt even more important that I capture Tedd's story for posterity. Despite what may have seemed like an indelicate and insensitive approach to Tedd's privacy, I know truly that my intentions were emanating from an honorable place. He was my friend, and I knew I would do him no harm.

The original purpose of my visit to Tedd's home that February evening was to consider directing a project that would showcase Tedd as an actor. What I learned was that Tedd really wanted to perform a female character. I knew that he was not going to get the chance to play either Sarah Bernhardt or Eleanora Duse. As a director, I couldn't imagine Tedd in either role, not because he couldn't play a woman effectively, but because I discerned that the female characters in the play were in their forties, in the prime of their craft as actresses. They were significantly famous in their careers, alluring in their sensuality, and acutely aware of their powers. Quite simply, I thought Tedd's age would not be appropriate for casting him in either role.

Yet, when I envisioned filming Tedd in his own home, dressed in his faded rose-colored gown, I easily imagined Tedd playing himself—his own androgynous, dramatic and inherently theatrical being at the center of an artistic project. The thought of directing *The Ladies of the Camellias* completely receded in comparison to the thought of putting Tedd's very own image on the large screen as the star of his own dramatic narrative! He would be able to bring all of himself, including his recognizably feminine qualities, to his art, and his own authentic story would be much more compelling to an audience than him merely playing a female role. Potentially, his performance could have much more to say or contribute to the world of art and culture or to the gender identity issues that were beginning to emerge in mainstream America. These are some of the reasons I gave to Tedd as to why I was much more passionate about potentially filming him in his own authentic narrative than directing him as a character in someone else's fiction.

After considerable begging, Tedd overcame his strong reluctance to the idea and agreed to me filming him with the letters. Knowing me as a director, actor and friend, he let me know that he trusted me—that I was approaching the project artistically, not exploitatively. I returned a few days later with a professional camera that I had borrowed from a friend to re-enact that first evening's precipitating discussion and then to proceed naturally from where I told him to "Stop." We would continue to improvise our discussion until we found a compelling reason to pull out the box containing the letters. The idea was for Tedd to take out some of his letters to read for the first time on camera. Two and a half hours of footage was shot in mini DV in one take in real time. I edited out a half hour of short snippets and segments throughout and inserted title cards with time stamps in their place. The resulting two hours of raw footage became the feature length docu-drama, *Letters to Uranus: The Hidden Life of Tedd Burr*. With Tedd's permission, the film was previewed at the Cedar Lee Theatre in Cleveland Heights to an invited audience of friends, family and colleagues. It was subsequently selected for the 2001 Cleveland International Film Festival and the 2002 NY Independent Film and Video Festival.

While working on the film, Tedd confided in me that he had been thinking about what would happen to his and Henry's letters upon his death. He wondered if surviving family would just throw them out. A part of him seriously wondered if the letters "might be worthy of publication." After he transcribed all of the letters on his rudimentary word processor, he let me read them. I was emotionally captivated by the dramatic arc of relationship that developed between Tedd and Henry throughout the duration of their correspondence.

From the moment I finished reading their letters, I believed their story needed to be told; at the time, I wasn't sure America was quite ready for it, although it did seem possible since the independent film *Boys Don't Cry* had broken into the mainstream in 1999. I informed Tedd of my desire to make a film or TV series based on his correspondence with Henry. He was agreeable to the idea but wanted to wait awhile before putting it in writing. In 2003, Tedd had a health scare and was hospitalized for several weeks; this event prompted him to officially bequeath to me the original letters with written permission for their usage. He handed over to me three large blue envelopes—dated 1943, 1944, and 1945—containing the original letters, bundled in chronological order.

Periodically I worked on script outlines and certain scenes and would inform Tedd about my ideas. In 2005, when *Brokeback Mountain* was released to critical acclaim and commercial success, I began to think and hope that a time would come when Tedd and Henry's story could be told and appreciated. Having a background in theater and dramaturgy, I have always viewed Tedd and Henry's correspondence through a dramatic narrative lens, and still hope to one day see their story presented on screen. Even so, I believe their unique personalities, creative and critical minds, and psychologically complex relationship can be experienced quite palpably through the letters themselves.

—Lenny Pinna

ABOUT HENRY BELLAMANN

Tedd tells us quite a bit about himself in the letters, but readers might want to know a little about Henry Bellamann, the famous author Tedd writes to …

Henry Bellamann was the author of the best-selling novel *Kings Row*, published by Simon and Schuster in 1940. *Kings Row* painted a portrait of a small, Midwestern town during the horse-and-buggy era at the turn of the twentieth century. The novel was considered rather scandalous because it revealed the dark secrets underlying the veneer of an outwardly prim and proper society. Within the town's web of gossip and lies, sordid stories emerged from the shadows: homosexuality, incest, adultery, pre-marital sex, insanity, a self-righteous doctor with a sadistic vengeance, corrupt bankers, and a murder-suicide. The novel definitely upset the town of Fulton, Missouri, where Henry Bellamann was born and raised. Although the author denied that *Kings Row* was based on any particular town, the inhabitants of Fulton, Missouri easily perceived the many obvious references to real people, places, and events.

Although he became most well known as an author, Henry started out early in life as an aspiring pianist. He studied piano from an early age and after high school studied in Denver with a famous British organist, Henry Housely, who had studied at the Royal College of Music. He managed to secure a series of successive teaching positions in the South; one of them was at Tuscaloosa Female College in Alabama. That's where he met Katherine McKee Jones, another music teacher. In 1907, they married in Katherine's hometown, Carthage, Mississippi and immediately set off for Greenville, South Carolina, where they both secured teaching positions in the music department at Chicora College. They taught at Chicora for seventeen years, later moving with the College to Columbia, South Carolina. The gifted couple received much notoriety in their respective fields. As chair of the music department, Henry taught piano while Katherine taught voice. They enhanced their skills by studying abroad a few summers with master teachers in Europe.

While living in South Carolina, Henry branched out into writing—books of poetry, music reviews for the magazine *Overtones* and a popular weekly literary column for the *State* newspaper in Columbia. He became particularly interested in the emerging field of psychology and was active in the Babcock Society, which promoted Freudian psychology in America. The Bellamanns held salon gatherings in their home, where notable psychology scholars presented their papers.

In September 1924 Henry became a dean of the Juilliard Music Foundation in New York City and chair of its examining board; later, in 1926, he received an honorary doctorate in music from DePauw University and became the Dean of Music at the prestigious Curtis Institute of Music in Philadelphia. He also taught music at Vassar College in New York.

It was in 1926 that he ventured into novel writing, publishing his first novel, *Petenera's Daughter*, followed by *Crescendo* in 1928, *The Richest Woman in Town* in 1932, and *The Gray Man Walks* in 1936. Then in 1940 came the major success of *Kings Row*, bringing Henry fame and saving Simon and Schuster from near bankruptcy. Subsequently, Warner Brothers bought the rights to the novel and made the film *Kings Row*, directed by Sam Wood and starring a young Ronald Reagan, along with Ann Sheridan, Robert Cummings and Claude Rains; the film garnered an Academy Award nomination for Best Picture. Henry Bellamann went on to write two more novels, *Floods of Spring* in 1942 and *Victoria Grandolet* in 1943. It was in September 1943 that the young Tedd Burr first wrote to Henry Bellamann.

The letters between Tedd Burr and Henry Bellamann sat in a cardboard box for fifty-five years before Tedd, at age seventy-five, transcribed them on an early version of a word-processing typewriter. Tedd's first challenge was to decipher Henry Bellamann's handwriting, which is quite difficult to read. Tedd informed me that it was by the ongoing thematic context of their correspondence that he was able to discern most words. This transcription became the manuscript for this book. While transcribing, Tedd added some notes indicating helpful contextual information. I have retained those notes as footnotes and added my own, indicating which ones were written by Tedd.

In the original letters, the young Tedd Burr misspelled many words. The elder Tedd maintained many of the spelling errors in his transcription because Henry specifically referred to them with humor and criticism in his responses. I did correct tiny misspelled words to limit distractions. In transcribing the letters, Tedd also made a few typing errors, which I have corrected. In a few cases, Tedd made spelling corrections or changed some of the original phrasing; in most of these cases, I decided to go back to the original letter because the intent or style seemed more appropriate to the period or to the meaning. Thus, while I used the transcription as my starting point, the original letters were the authorities on the text. All grammar errors and misspelled words I have intentionally left are followed by [*sic*]. Words or letters that have been corrected are marked in the text by square brackets.

While comparing Tedd's transcription to the original letters, I discovered that some of Tedd's original letters are missing. Almost all the original letters after January 11, 1944 (starting with letter 50) are missing, except for letters 55, 58, and 61. I had not noticed their absence before preparing the letters for publication because for years I never really touched the original letters; I wanted to preserve their archival quality. Creatively, I always worked from Tedd's typed transcriptions. It is a mystery to me as to whether Tedd intentionally omitted them from the folders or accidentally set them aside while transcribing them. Based on the on-going conversation between Tedd and Henry in the letters, there seem to be additional letters that have not survived at all. Knowing just how methodical he was about the chronological filing of all the other original letters, my guess would be that these omissions were intentional. A family member of Tedd's recently informed me that a couple days before he died he said that he "regretted throwing out the letters." Were they the missing letters?

The letters in Tedd's transcription are supplemented in this book with a few letters held by the University of Mississippi's archives. For some reason, they were not returned to Tedd with his other letters. They were found in the personal papers of Henry and Katherine Bellamann, which were donated to the University of Mississippi in 1978. Letters 71, 93, and 111 are printed courtesy of the Archives and Special Collections, University of Mississippi.

In Tedd's transcription, the letters appear in chronological order but are not numbered. I inserted the additional letters held by the University of Mississippi in the appropriate chronological order. For convenience, I have numbered the letters.

Correspondence Between
Tedd Burr and Henry Bellamann

1943-1945

1

TEDD

161 Sheffield St.
Bellevue, Ohio

September 20, 1943

Dear Mr. Bellamann,

Hardly do I know what I am about to write, or that I should write you. Perhaps I feel some inner force compelling me to do this. Any consequence must be an adventure of the future.

I hope you shall read me out here and in what I hope may follow. Before you cast me herein away, let me tell you that I am writing on the strength of Jamie Wakefield.[1]

I feel utterly self-conscious and am exhausting myself in attempts to be and write just the proper thing in this letter. Perhaps I shall be able to forget that, and have a real chat with you. You seem so real.

Last night I read a scene between Drake McHugh and Jamie Wakefield. I fell into an utter storm for it was not of Jamie I read, but of myself.

I believe that to have such an understanding of Jamie you might be able to extend to me something, I don't know quite what.

Oh, Mr. Bellamann, my eyes sting so that I can hardly see to write. I beg of you in the name of Jamie Wakefield, if you believe you could give me courage, advice or just a listening eye, I would like to write you my story.

If you can picture Jamie waiting for a coming day (Sat., Sept. 25) which would decide his possible army induction, then know the sudden confusion within me.

In the event that this may mean anything to you, please send me an address where I might write you personally, a story of a Jamie.

Sincerely,
Tedd Burr

---

1. Jamie Wakefield, a character in Bellamann's 1940 novel *Kings Row*, described as "pretty … too pretty for a boy … He looks like a girl in love." (Tedd's note)

Sept 20
Bellevue, O

Dear Mr. Bellamann,

Hardly do I know what I am about to write, or that I should write you. Perhaps I feel some inner force compelling me to do this. Any consequence must be an adventure of the future.

I hope you shall read me out here and in what I hope may follow. Before you cast me herein away, let me tell you that I am writing on the strength of Jamie Wakefield.

First letter from Tedd Burr to Henry Bellamann, September 20, 1943.

2

HENRY

Ansonia Hotel
New York City

September 22, 1943

My dear Tedd Burr,

I was much touched by your letter. Jamie is one of my favorite people because he is one of the most misunderstood.

By all means write me—but if you are going to tell me your story, tell me the <u>whole story,</u> without reservations—just "plain so."

I must tell you that I am not a psychiatrist—but you don't need one. You probably just need understanding.

I am happy that you felt you could write to me. You may be sure I respect the motive as I respect the confidence.

Sincerely,
Henry Bellamann

First letter from Henry Bellamann to Tedd Burr, September 22, 1943.

3

TEDD

161 Sheffield St.
Bellevue, Ohio

September 27, 1943

Dear Mr. Bellamann,

Buried in the fertile loam soils of Ohio is Bellevue. It's a town of several thousands; its streets are lined with flowing maples. The sun sends dusty shoots of light through the abundant leaves to the weedy gardens neatly placed at the side of each house. It is quiet and warm everywhere. On a Sunday afternoon one either naps or trudges to a solitary theater for a matinee, after which there is the lure of a dingy ice cream parlor; all end in the walk home as cool darkness is scented with odors of frying food. Hidden in this massive world is Bellevue, and hidden in Bellevue is Tedd Burr.

These were my thoughts after I had read your letter. I had hardly dared to expect an answer, yet here it was, kind and inviting. A part of you had found a way to me, insignificant me. How proud I am, and grateful.

I was reprimanded once by someone who could not understand my concern and near worship of those I felt had achieved. I can give no explanation really. It is just that there are people who live, love, have children, and pass from the world unhearaled [*sic*], and little known. Also there are those that make a splash in life whose reverberations are felt for generations. Helplessly I turn my eyes to the latter. I seem to entwine my very thoughts in the lives of the undeniably great: composers, authors, dancers, musicians, actors, poets, artists. They comprise my interests.

How odd, when I believe deep within the chambers of my heart I long to pass unhearaled [*sic*] and unknown, living, loving, and having children.

I am trying to say two things, Mr. Bellamann; That in writing me, you have brought happiness, consequently a zest for the future; and I shall tell you my story … the whole story. I have some

7

regret that it isn't a pretty story, but "Kings Row" has instilled within me such an admiration and faith in you that I shall not hesitate in throwing open my very soul. There is so much to tell.

I was born in Bellevue, July 26, 1924. [So I am 19.][2] My mother in tears once told me, "Before your birth I had prayed my child would be a daughter. I wanted a girl so much. I was disappointed in bearing a son. It was wrong of me to make up my mind so, I should be thankful I had four sons and only one daughter. Girls have such a hard life, always pain and suffering. A boy can be so independent." In my heart lay an answer, "Could it be that any woman could suffer in being a woman as I have suffered in not being one?"

My father is an engineer on the railroad. He has provided very well for us. He is thrifty and wise, he believes a father's duty is to make his family secure, and not to shower noisy affections upon them. He has a love for the soil and now owns a farm on which we do not live. I shall always remember walking across the fields with dad, he stopped, kneeled and crumbled a clod of soil in his hand. The wind whipped a cloud of dirt about us as his eyes swept over his land to the sky. I have never felt more close to my father. Our common interests are almost non-existent and it is as if both are strangers to the other. Any relationship or companionship is wordless between us.

My mother is fat from bearing children. The love between my parents is bottomless. Because of the necessary absence of my father because of his work, my mother raised us almost by herself. My sister and myself lean heavily on her with our problems, and no matter how crushed she is, she rises to help us with our load and to pray.

Five children can inflict much pain upon a mother, and I hope I can someday offer some compensation. Your letter brought a light into her eyes that was fading … "perhaps Tedd will finally find the world he has been searching for so long." I love my mother very much.

---

2. Tedd's note

My oldest brother, Lynn, who is now in the Army, and myself have exchanged hardly a word for years. We each seem to be disgusted with the other by mere appearance and interests. He is athletic and dwells on baseball; other than this I know little about him.

Martha comes next. I feel very close to her since we have shared our adventures and thoughts. I was a sister to her through childhood until now when she is a wife and mother. I believe there shall remain a bond between us throughout our lives.

After I was born came Mark who is still in school. All of us like him; my dad and mother, because he is a born farmer; Martha and myself, because he is good looking, a typical high school kid. I want to see him get on in the world, have a better start than myself. I throw open my wardrobe to him because I want him to foster friendships with boys and girls and have a normal, full life. I don't know why I think my clothes will help.

A few years later came Jerry. He is a problem for he has a miserable disposition and a temper which we all fear may reap dire consequences in his future. He is fairly intelligent but listless. His relationship with the family is a strained one with frequent outbursts. But he is young.

My paternal grandmother now lives with us. She is feeble minded and is losing her ability of speech. Because her husband is a Marine, my sister and her little son live with us. We all would lay down our very lives for this baby.

These are the people who surround me.

When I was a child I was "full of the devil." My maternal grandmother lived with us and chose me as her favorite grandchild. I shall never forget brushing her long white hair by the hour as she read her prayer books. She died when I was eleven.

A neighbor girl took a great liking to me. She was at the age when she liked to promenade with a baby buggy. She would dress me in doll's clothes and wheel me day after day.

I don't know when I began liking the company of my sister and her girl friends to that of boys. I played with my sister entirely. A great passion of mine was dressing up in adult clothes. I was accepted by the girls but I knew that I was different from them and

I regretted it. I didn't have long hair, had to wear pants when we weren't playing, and people laughed at me.

One day a girl and I undressed and were investigating our sex differences. I suppose even then we knew the purpose that difference was put to. My aunt chanced upon us and her screams are still in my ears. I was dragged to the house and remember my mother talking to me in a darkened room. I don't know what she said, I was so mortified. The neighborhood learned of it and other kids teased me. I could never feel comfortable with that little girl who had shared that experience with me, and still I escape from having to meet her. Then through my years in school I was too self conscious to bring any question of sex to my mother to be answered. It was [as] if in the sight of everyone, I was bad.

I was the perfect student and regarded a "pet" of most teachers. Outside of school I still led a girl's "play" life and my mother hoped to end this by giving me all of it I desired ... such as silk pajamas. A baseball field was located in a vacant lot across the street from our house. If I played with the boys I tried to be good with all I had. But I could never hit the ball or catch it. My younger brother was a whiz, my older brother was embarrassed by me. When teams were picked, I was the last choice. In no time I wasn't wanted at all. I was called "sissy," and could hardly bear it. But I found myself willing to be called this if I could remain to keep score so that I might be around some of the boys ... whom I liked!

In time I turned from the ball games across the street entirely. I took piano lessons and did so well I acquired a conceit about my great abilities, developed my own theories of how to play the piano, decided that scales were useless, took lessons on and off for four years and quit. I realize now how wrong I was in this attitude for I love the piano and play continually, but being a PIANIST has slipped from me. I was also a boy soprano and having a lodge-minded aunt I sang almost nightly. I liked best to sing in church. I even had an unsuccessful radio audition [in Cleveland].[3]

------

3. Tedd's note

I fell into the clutches of a neighbor boy and our relationship consisted of the simplest of sexual excitements, but damage was being done by this I'm sure. I became slightly enamored by men, but I also admired a few girls in my class, like everyone else, I had "my girl," but never did I have a sexual desire for them nor did any girl mean anything deep to me. If I lost their affection it made no difference to me.

I was about twelve or thirteen[,] my sister was too grown to play with me as we once had and since I didn't have a knowledge of self defense was an outcast from boys and spent my life alone, my voice began to change, and I fell in love.

HE was a handsome senior I saw going to school every day. I waited for him to pass me, and if I missed him, I was dejected for hours. I was starved for the sight of him after he had graduated. On Christmas vacation when he was home from college he would ice skate on the reservoir. I learned to skate and only once did I ever feel he suspected my feeling for him. I looked up to see him watching me and a pang went through me that I feared he must feel too. I saw him less and less after that. I was miserable and lonely, thought only of him. I don't know where he is now and that love has changed. Sometimes I think it is still there, or perhaps significant of the love that might have been if I were a woman.

Other boys were telling sensual tales and talking about babies. I became disgusted and drew away from them. I fell to masturbation which I regarded as a weakness and fought to stamp out. In my sophomore year an interesting teacher opened to me a fascinating subject: literature. I began to read every spare moment I had. Up to this time I had not been able to read and comprehend.

As for singing ... One day I looked in a Cleveland paper and discovered an advertisement of the "Mets" spring season to be there.[4] I knew nothing of opera but in looking over the strange names came upon Lohengrin and Flagstad, both I knew I had heard of. I got tickets and began to devour books on opera. By the

---

4. Metropolitan Opera, New York City. (Tedd's note)

time "Lohengrin" arrived I felt very versed.[5] From that day my love of opera has never wavered. I read everything I could of it and wanted more than anything to be an opera singer. It seemed the answer to everything: to wear beautiful flowing robes and jewels, to act … (I was forever giving tragic scenes at home) … and to sing, to be among those great artists. Twice I tried singing teachers. Some people said I was a soprano, others that I was a tenor, others that I was going to be a bass. In the midst of this I sang everything operatic I could find. People advised me to let my voice change, not to sing at the present time. I couldn't resist. I would break out in a fever of song. Soon people said I was not singing, just screaming. And so my dream seemed to fade until today I feel that the one thing that might have filled my life, being an opera singer, has been closed to me forever.

In school my scholastic standing stood high. I was active in journalism and wrote a few plays and short stories. These were quite enthusiastically received. When I had an emotional upset, I usually wrote a poem. In dramatics I was voted the outstanding, all around Thespian of the year. I made records as Macbeth for the Shakespearean classes. In a bit part I stole the show of the Senior Class Play. Someone called me a faery. The Principal objected to my one day absence a year to see an opera. I took art to escape a physical education class. I wore powder and was conscious of my appearance. If I did not wear face makeup I was unhappy and things went wrong. When I did wear it, I was a different person. I was happy and free and energetic. That is what it came to mean to me. I wore it well, most people remained undecided if I wore it or not. I learned to wear it correctly, and with discreet moderation. I ushered at a movie theater, my pay being the privilege of seeing the movies as often as I chose and to study them. Walking home alone at night I learned I wanted to be a woman more than

---

5. *Lohengrin* (1848), opera by Richard Wagner (1813–1883), German composer; Kirsten Flagstad (1895–1962), Wagnerian soprano from Norway. Tedd is especially fond of Wagnerian operas and mentions them many times in his letters.

anything. I prayed but thought I was an atheist. I did two fairly successful impersonations of Carmen Miranda. I was voted into honorary societies and graduated.

For my four high school years I had a newspaper route and in those solitary walks a strange story developed in my mind and bothered me. From school I had one friend, Jeanne, who is now in nurse's training, and I told her my story idea. She begged me to write it and reluctantly I began. She has a great deal of faith in my becoming a writer. In four years I found I had barely a skeleton of a story. I began writing the summer of 1942.

That September I secured an office job at Dayton, Ohio. I was employed by the Army Air Forces of Patterson Field. No one knew my past and I seemed to start with a clean record. I liked that. I worked hard and several of the unit heads bid for my services. At first they regarded me as a conceited member of a wealthy family. After that was rectified I had some fine friendships. I wrote in my book when I could.

For several years I had used face make-up. After I had been in Dayton a few weeks I began to wear it to work. Three girls and I struck up a friendship and had fine times seeing movies and talking. I went on to great length advising them not to fall in with men, and the cruelties of men. They listened speechlessly, and I like to talk. However, I felt self conscious in their company. People noticed … little me with three attractive girls.

One day it got around to me that a man in the shops of our building wanted to date me. It was then I knew my conspicuousness and fears. I was afraid to step out into the shops. For months I fought this fear and finally was rid of it.

By this time I had worked myself up into a reliable position in the Personnel Department. I began to enjoy the attentions men showered on me and in my job I was brought into sharp contact with them. There were any number I was attracted to and was jealous when they associated with the office girls.

One day I learned that the Major I worked for referred to me openly as a faery and wished I wasn't employed in his office. But I was a good employee and continued in my advancements.

To his accusation I had an almost breathless reaction. I didn't know a scientific definition of "faery" but thought I had a pretty good idea of what he meant. I knew he had no facts to base this on. But I began to think that everyone was looking at me, laughing at me! Because of crowded living quarters I roomed with three other boys. I had little to do with them. They discussed continually their women until I often thought I would vomit … or wished I could. Several times they thought I was asleep and made remarks as to whether I was a male or a female and what they would like to do in case I was either one. After that I hardly exchanged a word with them. I was happy though, my hair was heavy and pompadour, my complexion was clearing, I was getting pretty.

The three girls I associated with broke up. One went home because she fell in love with a man who did not return that love. The second was jilted and became somewhat of a prostitute. The third, Dorothy, was a victim of a sad high school love affair and as a result was disillusioned and detested all men. It is with this last that a deep friendship was born. We both felt cut off from a normal world within ourselves and seemed to understand the other's wearied mind.

In March, 1943, I was called home for an Army examination. My world had crashed. I lived in a fever of prayer and realized that I did believe in some kind of God. It was horrible, that examination, and they rejected me when they learned I did not lay girls, and still did not admit being attracted to men. Our family doctor suggested I not return to work but take a rest. When I was a senior in school I had been ill for many weeks and had not ever fully recovered my health.

I went back to Dayton, but things had changed. My old job had been filled, but a unit chief who had much toleration for me took me into her department and after a while she valued my services very highly. I believe she spoke for me when I returned to the office because it had been rumored she had had an affair with one of the officers and I had been the only person in the office who would speak to her. I believe she was grateful. Suddenly everything broke out! I was really attractive. My face and hair made people wonder if I was a girl or boy. Everywhere I went I was met with their gazes, and many actually questioned me. Soldiers came to the office and asked about me. They watched me continually. I often changed my route of going to work because men waited for me along the way. Cars honked, men yelled and whistled at me, everywhere eyes turned on me. My whole life was a confused tension.

But I was stubborn and would not change. I felt there must be some reason for my being as I was. Perhaps God has some design for me. Something deep inside told me to carry on, to have courage, some day I would know why I had gone through this. There was a reason. There was a reason. And so I did not yield. Perhaps I could not.

I had joined the Y.M.C.A. Dramatic Players and had read for them scenes by Danny in NIGHT MUST FALL.[6] I was told my interpretation was outstanding … but there were no "Danny" parts in any of the plays they were giving and well … after all … how could they ever use me! I knew I would not ever accept a part I could not play, would be miscast in. I had seen Tallulah Bankhead in "The Little Foxes" and loved her deep voice and vibrant personality. I wanted to play Regina Giddens.[7] I disliked those actors. Here they were lost in Dayton, many I suppose had dreams of being professionals but never had gotten the opportunity. But instead of diving into drama and enjoying it, they were petty and fought among themselves until I wearied of them and thought that if all actors were like these, I wanted no part of it. One woman seemed to sight the problem I faced and tried to help me. It seems she went through much the same thing as this, but won, now is

---

6. Tedd mentions Emlyn Williams's 1935 psychological thriller *Night Must Fall*, particularly the character Danny, in many letters. The charismatic Danny is gradually revealed in the play to be a seducer and murderer.

7. Regina Giddens is the protagonist of Lillian Hellman's 1939 play *The Little Foxes*. Giddens is the steel-willed head of a wealthy southern family who will do anything to remain powerful. Tallulah Bankhead originated the role.

married and a happy mother. She talked to me strictly as if I were a man, pushed me forward, but I had no faith in her kind aid.

One evening my unit chief had dinner with me. As we left the restaurant she said she could never eat with me again. All during the meal everyone had watched me until she could hardly stand the embarrassment. I went often without dinner after that. I lacked the courage to enter a restaurant!

Dorothy was the only one who withstood these assaults with me. It made no difference to her. She, as Jeanne, had faith in my abilities to someday accomplish.

Another evening in a restaurant a man approached me and invited me to his hotel room. I fled. The same thing occurred in a theater restroom. At a bus station a drunken soldier called me a "queer." Continually I was mistaken as a lady and given a bus seat by a soldier. Waiters referred to me unsuspectingly as Madam. Several men looked at me really earnestly and deeply.

In my mind I began running, running from the life pressing down on me. I persisted in appearing as beautiful as I could! I prayed for death even more than womanhood. I thought I would go insane. I was afraid to walk down the street now.

Finally I completed my book and those who read it offered various degrees of enthusiasm. It was different. They often asked me if I had read "Kings Row." I had not. Always something arose to prohibit my reading it. But I had seen the movie as many times as I had been able to.

There came to the room where I stayed a young man assigned to the Field for a week's specialized training. He shared my bed and his second night there he made a kind of love to me. I knew I had reached my peak in being attractive and was flattered by his attentions. Reluctantly the next day I went home to Bellevue for several days leave. I rushed back and this man renewed his interest in me. That night he caressed me to him and told me how desirable and beautiful I was. "If you were only a woman," he repeated again and again. He kissed my neck and held me close. With his head in my arms I wanted eternity to descent [*sic*] on the moment. It was all I had ever wanted. Then he begged me to satisfy him. I drew away from him, this was a reminder of my shortcomings, my inability, I was not a woman! Further more, I would have no man holding such [an] act over my head. Strangely enough, it was not difficult to repulse him. He became angry and I learned he had done this kind of thing before. What a fool I had been! The next night he went out and had a woman who was one of his instructors. As he stumbled into the room and wearily went to bed ... Thank God! it wasn't necessary for him to sleep with me that morning ... he laughed about his late act. I had dry tears and "What a fool I've been!" in my heart. That morning he left. I was not sorry I had had no sex relationship with this man for it proved to me that when the Major and other men accused me in their minds, I knew they were wrong. I had fought something and felt clean and good. Whatever weakness I had, I had the courage to keep it in myself and remain respectable.

On July 17 at ten in the morning, I was coldly informed by the Personnel unit chief that the Major demanded my immediate resignation or he would discharge me. It was not my work, truly I would be hard to replace, but he, the Major, was embarrassed by my presence in his office. I was the talk of the entire Field. Officers were inquiring about me. Soldiers were being conspicuous over me. I was no longer desireable [sic] at that post. The man's closing words were, "For God's sakes, either be a woman or be a man."

From somewhere I blindly gathered strength and resigned that day, packed and left. A chapter in my life had come to a bitter close!

At home I could but tell my mother the true reasons. She wept and I hated inflicting another pain upon her. The excuse to inquirers was my health. Again death seemed the only alternative, but it would not come.

In this time I began to type my book, planning to submit it to a publisher. If I could publish it, I could hold up my head again. My old friend Jeanne asked me to accompany her to Detroit on a lake excursion trip. I finally consented. My fears were borne out. I had dressed as manishly [sic] as I could, had not put a bit of face make-up on, really tried to be just a person. Hardly had the boat left the dock when it began again. I was asked if I intended to stay in Detroit ... "We could have fun in Detroit!" I hated Jeanne to see me trapped so, and for her to suffer the embarrassment she did. She has said she will never be able to forget how terrible it was.

I hardly leave the house now. I read and work on my book ... a study of myself. Lately I was 1-A again and this last Saturday was called to Army examinations.[8] I thought several other men watched me curiously, but I no longer had strength to fight their observations. This time when questioned I was not reluctant to telling them truthful answers to their questions. I knew the problem had to be faced squarely and honestly. However, they were in a hurry and asked me little. I was rejected for what they termed immaturity, just as I had been six months before. In another six months this process is to be repeated.

Perhaps I would not have minded the Army too much. My future as a civilian is just as uncertain! I've lost all confidence in seeing a prospective employer, of even entering life. But I cannot stay here at home.

So, Mr. Bellamann, this is my story. Forgive my writing to such length, but I knew not what to leave out. Perhaps I have overlooked a few facts, but in going over my life as I do so often, this is about what it adds up to.

Since reading "Kings Row" I have lost confidence in my own book. I know so little about writing. Your book is so eloquent and great that I feel I have fallen far short of being an author. I had dreams of playing women parts on the stage, but how to get started! Would people want that? To me it would mean that at 8:30 I become a woman and for a couple of hours I would be in another world. Knowing that Sarah Bernhardt played "L'Aiglon" and "Hamlet" has kept this alive in my mind.[9]

---

8. 1-A: Military classification meaning "Available; fit for general military service." Being drafted into military service is a continuing concern for Tedd throughout his correspondence with Henry.

9. Both male roles.

Perhaps now you can understand the gratitude filling me when you are kind enough to answer. I wanted to tell you these things, it is good to tell someone. I hope you shall reply in some way for it is as if I have known you for a very long time. If there is anything else you wish to know, do not hesitate to ask me. I shall be honest with you for I like honesty and you can be sure that here in Bellevue you have lighted a flame. For the first time in ever so long, I don't want to die.

Respectfully,
Tedd Burr

4

HENRY

Ansonia Hotel
New York City

September 30, 1943

My Dear Tedd Burr,

I was moved by your letter and I feel that perhaps I have a good deal to say to you. I am sure that much of it has to be said gradually as I know you better. As I told you I am not a psychiatrist. I know only such psychological matters as long reading in these subjects furnishes to anyone. I shan't pretend to understand everything about you although I may say that it does not seem strange to me.

Let's begin on a few assumptions. First off, please don't think of yourself as a "case." Let's try not to think of yourself as abnormal. So far as being different is concerned, we may say that each of us is unique. You are clearly different in one respect that somewhere in the deeps of your psychological (and maybe physical) makeup you are not wholly masculine. But since you aren't a woman you can't be wholly feminine. There's nothing reprehensible in being feminine. Most fine men have a deep strain of feminine sensitiveness and intuition. Being really "sissy" is something else. I don't know how completely frank you have been with me, or how frank you can be. Since you aren't a "practicing" homosexual, those problems are not in your constellation of difficulties. In fact a lot of your difficulty seems to be just repression. I doubt that the relationships you have mentioned were injurious. But repression isn't necessarily injurious either. It is probable that civilization has inched forward that way.

I do think you need a sympathetic hearing. I shall be glad if you wish to use me that way. I don't take the attitude that you are a pathological case, or that I stand in a doctor's place or even that you are a subject for "cure." You are merely unhappy and that unhappiness stands in the way of accomplishment and realization of your talents. I am sure that what you need above all else is a sense of accomplishment. Now, let's see if there isn't some commonsense way of going about that.

There is certainly in your nature many elements that make difficulties for you, and make your own way harder. For a moment be patient while I be a bit brutal. You wish you were a woman. Somewhere there are reasons for this for which you are not responsible. But you are not a woman. But you are insisting that the world (which is organized the way it is whether we like it or not) must permit you to dress as you like and to look as you prefer to look, and at the same time you are demanding that the world should not consider you conspicuous or even take notice. And yet you are not using make up and so forth for yourself alone. You are on this account and at this one point not very logical.

Now I'm going back for a moment to Jamie Wakefield. There was a real Jamie Wakefield. He was a friend of mine. "Jamie" has missed all boats, although he was talented. I said in Kings Row, Jamie was destined to the sterility of his kind. A hard word, Tedd, and it need not be so. All people have to be adaptable—all of us. But I think you don't wish to be that. I am a million miles away from suggesting that you should simply get up some fine morning and just decide to be altogether different, think differently, etc. You can't do that anymore than anyone else can. Let's accept certain deep down things—factors, characteristics in your nature simply as something which like the color of your eyes, you did not choose and cannot change. But in order, even, to preserve what you most wish to keep, wouldn't it be common sense to make some outward concessions to convention just to save yourself annoyance and trouble? You probably hate the word convention, but conventions are the protection of all individuals.

Not all people who do not fit neatly into the simple and distinct categories of masculine and feminine are necessarily intellectually sterile. Oscar Wilde, whom we can't admire for some dozen reasons, was yet a fine artist. Tschaikowsky was a great one. They had a pretty bad time, but Tschaikowsky's bad times were interior. Outwardly he was a fairly conforming person.[10]

(Incidentally, will you send me some snap shots of yourself— or photos.)

I am sure you are a very good looking boy. I can see much more clearly than you imagine why you use make up, etc. But I'm pretty sure that just as you are you are better looking without aids. And you only get yourself and others into trouble. I don't imagine that make up is one of the deep down necessities. This is just a suggestion. I see various boys about who wear makeup but I never felt that it really improved them, and it certainly leads to a lot of misunderstanding. Consider: suppose a girl dresses as an obvious prostitute and goes down to the New York water front. Do you think she should be offended or hurt when she is taken to be what she isn't? I suppose that certain kinds of men seeing you, would naturally decide that you were, let us say, available. They feel cheated when you don't want to play.

Later on, when I know you better, and you trust me fully, there are some questions I'd like to ask. Not now. They are not important.

I want to come at once to the primary purpose of this letter. You say you have tried to write a book. A book about yourself if it could be clear, well written, revealing and true might be an important book. You are, and don't let yourself dramatize too much your difficulties, but still you are in a somewhat tragic situation. But not hopeless. There are things for you to do and to live for and I suspect that you can be happy.

Once more I'm going to be a bit brutal. Your English isn't too good. But you sound rather talented. Now and then a sentence in your letter rings out. Maybe you could do an important book. If it

---

10. Oscar Wilde (1854–1900), Irish playwright and poet. In 1895 Wilde was convicted of "gross indecency" for a homosexual relationship and sentenced to hard labor. He was released in 1897, but the labor and imprisonment ruined his health, and he died in 1900. Pyotr Illych Tchaikovsky (1840–1893), Russian composer, suffered from depression most of his life. Henry seems to suggest here that the depression was caused by Tchaikovsky's homosexuality.

isn't <u>important</u> on a purely human basis, it will be no good. Any insincerity or pose or dramatization, over dramatization I should say, would destroy its chances.

Radclyffe Hall wrote a book about the dilemma of a girl who found she was not like other girls. That was called "The Well of Loneliness." It was a pretty good piece of work, simple and sincere and direct and unself-conscious. It presented the case for all such girls. It didn't win the popular sympathy that it should have. People smirked a little and spoke obliquely of it. I saw Radclyffe Hall later in Paris. I don't know if she was writing about herself or not, I rather suppose she was. She was a trim, beautifully groomed and rather elegant looking woman, severely dressed, and with beautiful manners. But she had made a place for herself in the world. I suspect that she was able to live more comfortably and inconspicuously in Paris than in England which like our own country is still uninformed on many subjects and consequently like the human race, is hypocritical at certain points.[11]

Back to your English again. I notice that you are often illogical. There are statements which are <u>non sequiturs</u>. And, your typewriter doesn't spell very well! These are minor matters capable of rectification. Do you want to send your book on to me? I am terribly occupied with work on a new book, but I will manage to read it—slowly—and make a report to you.

What you do so sorely need is achievement. If you could accomplish something, make some money out of it, win yourself back to your own genuine respect, most of your problems will be simplified. It may be that in time you shouldn't live there where you are. But won['.]t you have to win your way out of it?

For the present do you have to make a living for yourself? Don't answer these impolite questions unless you wish.

---

11. Radclyffe Hall's 1928 novel *The Well of Loneliness* becomes a regular topic of discussion between Henry and Tedd later in their correspondence, after Tedd reads the book. The protagonist, Stephen Gordon, is an upper-class woman who dresses as a man and engages in an ill-fated lesbian love affair with a married woman. While sympathetic to the protagonist, the novel refers to Gordon's sexuality as "inversion."

I think you'll have to keep your own counsel there. Will you forgive me if I say this, and try to understand my advice? I think you should try to think and plan and deal with your problems independently of your mother—no matter how much in sympathy you two are. I think I'd feel better if I knew that my frank talk was just for your eyes and no others. It is not possible to write for two separate temperaments.

If you think you need a friend and some friendly consideration I shall be happy to be what I can to your dilemma. Your appeal touched me and I should feel that I had failed someone if you think I can be of any comfort or assistance and I didn't do all I can.

About your book, now. Perhaps I can help you plan form and expression. I don't know. That depends on how good or how bad it is! There is much more I would like to say. We'll get around to much in time. (Better be glad you aren't an opera singer—they are, for the most part an awful lot.) Incidentally, I saw Bernhardt do L'Aiglon and Hamlet and they weren't very good.

Sincerely,
Henry Bellamann

5

TEDD

161 Sheffield St.
Bellevue, Ohio

October 1, 1943

Dear Mr. Bellamann,

I have read your letter for the third time and am so confused with conflicting emotions that I don't know how well I can collect my thoughts to answer you. I shall attempt to follow your own letter and present my reactions.

First, however, let me again thank you for your interest and kindness. I wait breathlessly for your letters since it seems an impossibility that you bother with me. It was that conversation between Drake and Jamie that made me turn to you. I felt it must come from some experience of your own. It was so true, like something from my life. I know a Drake and he has said some of the same things contained in those pages, but not so eloquently.

But on with this. I am glad that you're brutal. It hurts to know my English is not too good, but I hope such perfection will come gradually. I am primarily intent on giving you my story as you requested … "plain." As for the typewriter … it is the only model I could find to rent; it is an ancient Remington that prohibits the space bar from doing its job, and the question mark must be attacked with surprise.

Let me assure you that I am being as frank as I know how to be. I believe I would tell you anything you ask, for this is to be faced squarely and honestly. I am tired of beating around the bush with myself and others.

I am sending two snap shots of which I am not too proud, but they represent, I suppose, how I appear to most people. They were taken this spring. The photo was taken in the fall of 1941 just before I became ill. It served as my graduation picture. It was chosen from the proofs by the family and over my protests. I think it was chosen because it has little of the real me showing through. When

25

I thought I would be in the Army I had a picture taken that I hoped would represent this period in my life. In a week I shall have one of the finished photos to send you.

Your writing of makeup is so true. When I am in this house the world can't touch me, so with this false courage I instinctively use makeup. The moment I step into the outside I am gripped with fear. It is simply this—If I am not using makeup and am not noticed I am unhappy. If I do wear it and am noticed I am also unhappy. I know this is not logical but inside I have fought a logical conclusion. Makeup makes me feel worldly, a super something I'm not really. This is my only excuse.

Please do not hesitate in asking me questions, I feel devoted to you. Every time I go to the library I hunt up your picture, and although that picture frightens me, I can here let my soul pour to you freely.

I shall be eager and happy to send you my book. "Kings Row" has changed my attitude towards my book. As I said before, I feel uncapable [sic] of writing the kind of story I have attempted. I believe I would have waited but it seemed that the friendship of this Jeanne and others hinged on its completion. I am desperate for friends, so complied with their wishes. I fear I have overly dramatized it for I wanted it to turn somewhat from my own life. Much of the material exists only in my wildest imaginations. This would be the second half of the book. I have many additional characters that probably have no dimensions, but are thin creations of a young mind.

I started with these things in mind: I was writing of people, so background or settings were to be unimportant to the story. I wanted to write a simple story for everyone to read and understand, not just highly educated individuals. I wrote sensuously to get readers. I wanted to write differently, to be a treat. I do dislike conventions and have perhaps unwisely disregarded them in writing. I had a story to tell and I told it. I can't seem to build up a very good defense. I shall simply send you my book ... and wait. Oddly enough, this will be the hard thing to do. I hope you shan't like me less for my feeble attempts. I feel this way because "Kings Row" struck me as being a real, down-to-earth piece of literature.

I shall hurry to finish typing it for you and upon its completion dispatch it to you immediately.

No, I don't have to make a living for myself. My health has been regarded more important than working by my parents. But I can never be sure when my not working might be made unpleasant for me. I do dislike being so dependent.

Your letter is only for my eyes. My mother knows much less of me than you do. I have never "confessed" to her. Her knowledge comes from my obvious actions alone. When I had to explain the "Dayton Affair," I only told necessary facts. I want this correspondence also between us, and I hope mother understands my reluctance to give information.

I will be happy if you don't desert me until that time when I can send you my book. My world is grateful for your light.

Sincerely,
Tedd Burr

Photo of Tedd and younger brother Mark, included in Tedd's October 1, 1943 letter to Henry. Photocopy included in Tedd's transcription of the letters.

Portrait of Tedd Burr included in Tedd's October 1, 1943 letter to Henry. Photocopy included in Tedd's transcript of the letters.

Ansonia Hotel
New York City

October 5, 1943

My dear Tedd,

Thanks for the photographs. I feel that I know a lot more about you than I did. First off, let me say that you are a very fine looking human being. You have an intelligent look, an interesting look, and above all, a talented look. I think if you could realize what a good impression you must make just as you are you would know that you need only to be well groomed. You will never need extraneous aids for your appearance.

Tedd, I think you are a bewildered and a confused boy, but I feel sure that both in mind, character and talent you are worth doing your damnedest to realize what you should be. It is possible that what you should be is not exactly what you wish to be now. But that is a matter of growth, isn't it? If you never changed you'd be a case of arrested development.

Let us assume some of your difficulties as facts just to see what you need to do and to think that you may attain some kind of inner comfort and harmony. Evidently you have been sort of derailed in some sexual way. A few points you can clear up. I don't like the words fairy and pansy—etc. I doubt very much that you are really a true homosexual. You don't look it. (Though it does seem that you have been doing all you can to make people think so, and then you have resented their acting upon your own suggestion.)

You say you are not attracted to girls sexually. I wonder. If you aren't, are you definitely attracted to men? And I mean sexually. If so, how much, to what degree, and what do you feel inclined to do about it? Here is really the key. If you are so attracted to men and feel that realization lies that way, then you are homosexual, and your problem is a certain kind of problem. I am guessing that you are inhibited and blocked from doing anything very much because of your obvious refinement and general fastidiousness.

Now, you are sensitive. Any one of us worth a line of printer's ink is sensitive. In a boy scarcely out of adolescence this sensitiveness so easily becomes and is hyper-sensitiveness. And that makes life difficult for you. Refinement can reach too far and become a kind of squeamishness which is weakness. I don't know about you on these points. It's only that you will have to watch for balance so as to keep your best mental qualities in good functioning order.

I think there are certain consequences which threaten you that you have not realized. When you are young and good looking, it is not unnatural entirely to try to enhance your good looks. But if you do it the wrong way and try to look like what you are not, you increase your isolation. The very admiration you might like to have is perverted and you lose the admiration you wish and get the wrong kind. Deep down, of course, it looks as if you were trying to attract men sexually, and try to look like a girl in order to accomplish what you resent when you get it. Is that true? Please remember, Tedd, I am not blaming you for anything. I'm just thinking out loud. I'm only saying some of these things in order to point out the end of the road. I've seen various pretty boys, made up, and made up very well. I used to see them in Berlin in the twenties, so pretty they stirred one up a lot. But after all, they were not girls and one didn't wish to be stirred up unless something could be done about it, and any homo-sexual practice is unsatisfactory in the end.

The frightening thing is not these <u>young</u> boys well painted and sometimes wearing girls' clothes but what these same boys are like ten years later, twenty years later, thirty years later. There's nothing more terrible than an old fairy. There is one living in this house. He is something or other in the musical world, nothing important, but this ancient coquette is something you'd shudder at— you with your real gentleness.

I don't suggest that you do anything about all of this. Certainly not now. I do suggest, and I do even that much with the greatest reluctance, that you avoid make up and cut your hair shorter and be the very handsome boy that you are by nature. I think you cannot guess how everyone will like and admire that person you have hidden away. On the actual sexual question I don't suggest anything. I don't know what you want.

But here are my real suggestions. What your deepest psychic need is—that is what we must find out and that is what you must be able to do. You need accomplishment, I imagine. Suppose you could make yourself a fine writer, even a capable one, and could make money and make a place for your self with it, wouldn't that meet one of your demands? It doesn't matter how bad your book is at present. I suspect that it is bad. No matter. You write sentences that sound out like something. You communicate in your letters a fine personal warmth—without which no one writes successfully—and some of these things are your priceless equipment. Artificiality is always the pitfall of the young writer. But, you see, your letters are not artificial. There is the pulse of life in them. (Once when I was very young I began a novel laid in Spain—which I had never seen.) Or, self-dramatization, which the world isn't interested in.

I didn't mean your English was terribly bad. You slip on details. Very little things. Uncapable for incapable. When I said your typewriter didn't spell well, I meant that you slipped—as above. It's unimportant, but enrages editors. Now, I do hope that you have a sense of humor. Without a sense of humor you are indeed a lost soul!

Yes, I am not surprised that my picture frightened you. It frightens many people. But usually I myself do not. I think I have some photographs about here. I'll send some along to you. I wonder if what you found in the library was a biographical sketch done by—Oh, I've forgotten the company now. Anyway, I think it could have been what I am thinking about. It is incorrect and fictional done I think, by some enterprising young Jewish clerk in—it is Twentieth Century Authors, I believe, who disliked the German sound of my name. I used to use the full German form of my name because it was at that remote time useful in the musical world.[12] I was a pianist and a professional musician. I began to write only when I was what I am sure you think of as a very old man! But I remember youthful problems with vividness. Since I have always been associated with young people I keep an illusion of being in some sense contemporary.

Now, Tedd, wake up your sense of humor. I suspect you are going to be successful and important. If you want hard enough to be. I am equally sure it won't lie exactly in the road you think.

All morning I have been remembering one of the most talented men—Schuyler Ladd. He was,—I know a good deal about him—homosexual. He was handsome. He made up excessively, and was always in trouble. He played one successful role in the Yellow Jacket. It was made for him. He never played anything else well. For years he was in an insane asylum, having failed to make any kind of adjustment to the world and having sought surcease in drugs. Once he was brought out for a revival of The Yellow Jacket. He played it automatically almost, scarcely knowing what he did. He went back to the asylum, and I believe has died since. But, you see, he was an exhibitionist. He had to show off, and he faced a perpetual frustration, because the things he did to show off brought him disaster—ridicule mostly. This isn't an attempt to frighten you.[13]

As long as I can be useful to you, in sympathy or help, or in literary advice, I will stand by you. I don't know why I say this: I am a very busy person and not too well. I suppose it is that you could and did write with that communicating warmth that made me like you and feel that you could eventually write. Let's see. I am willing to help in so far as I can. If you are willing to slave with pencil and paper. It isn't easy. I rather think that very young novelists can

---

12. Heinrich Hauer Bellamann.

13. Schuyler Ladd (1884–1961), American actor. Ladd appeared as protagonist Daffodil in the original (1912) production of George C. Hazelton's *The Yellow Jacket*, which purported to be a Chinese drama. Ladd played the role in "yellowface."

write only autobiographically. They have not seen enough of life to write otherwise, but even that can be most important.

Sincerely,
HB

Henry's portrait from *Current Biography* (1942), p. 64.

7

TEDD

161 Sheffield St.
Bellevue, Ohio

October 8, 1943

Dear Mr. Bellamann,

I hesitated to answer your letter immediately for two reasons; first, because I am in a shaking state of excitement for hours after I receive a letter from you and fear I may not write you very intelligently; then, I wanted to think over the questions you asked me so that I could feel I was really giving you as accurate and honest answers of which I am capable. I have been thinking and deciding a great deal in the last days. I hope I can sum up these efforts clearly for you.

I shall be very eager to receive some photographs. The conversations I shall probably carry on with them! I have a feeble collection of about ten photographs from people I considered truly great. Now they consist of opera singers and actors, but I'm sure an author would look fine among them. My latest is from Katharine Cornell, whom I admire very much.[14] The first stage play I saw starred her, and I have been singing her praises ever since. Do you know her? Your references to the stage interest me. You must know many fascinating people. I have remained very curious over your remark that opera singers, generally, are an awful lot. I've wondered if you were just trying to cheer me up or whether you really meant it. My preferences in the opera world are Traubel, Thorborg, Bampton, Castagna, Moore, Huehn, and Pinza.[15] But

14. Katharine Cornell (1893–1974), American stage actress, theater owner, and producer.

15. Helen Traubel (1899–1972), American soprano; Kerstin Thorborg (1896–1970), Swedish contralto; Rose Bampton (1907–2007), American mezzo-soprano and soprano; Bruna Castagna (1905–1983), Italian mezzo-soprano; Grace Moore (1898–1947), American soprano; Julius Huehn (1904–1971), American bass-baritone; Ezio Pinza (1892–1957), Italian bass.

these are just a few for I find it difficult to pick favorites. Back to the stage for a moment, after having read two worshipful biographies on Sarah Bernhardt you come along and say her "Hamlet" wasn't very good. How can you do that to me? You must tell me more, please. Speaking of biographies, I want to tell you that all I know of Henry Bellamann is what I could find in the <u>Current Biography</u> and on the last page of "KINGS ROW."

I wonder if I could inquire about "KINGS ROW" for a moment? I haven't been able to forget that book. I keep remembering certain characters, namely Drake. Of course I read the book sometime after I had seen the movie and as I read the movie characters were always with me. I would say Warner Bros. cast it very well and adapted it very well. May I ask you if you were satisfied also? I'd like to go one further in asking if there was any particular reason why Jamie was not present in the film. In the movie, "The Ox-Bow Incident," there was a character that reminded me of Jamie.[16] These two parts I really believe I could have played well. As the author of "KINGS ROW" were you very closely associated with Warner Bros. as they produced the film? Our library doesn't have your other books, so it may be some time before I have an opportunity to read them.

You wrote of Berlin and from <u>Current Biography</u> I learned you studied in Europe. I am quite full of German blood and like it. As far as I can find out, my ancestors came from Bach, Germany. I hope to go to Germany some day and walk through the country. Who knows, somewhere I might meet Siegfried. You see, no composer can stir me up as Wagner can. I saw "<u>Die Walküre</u>" once, and when the third act opened I just cried. I don't know why but the tears just flowed and I was mad too, because I didn't want to miss anything and there I was, blind! "Lohengrin," "Tannhäuser," "Tristan," and "Walküre," I have seen and know, but it is the entire

---

16. Tedd mentions the 1943 Western film *The Ox-Bow Incident* several times in his correspondence with Henry. As he notes in a later letter, he would like to play the part of Gerald Tetley (played by William Eythe in the film), a pacifist who objects to lynching three suspected murderers.

"Ring" that I'm waiting for. Yes, I am truly at the altar of Wagner. Another man I hope to meet is the Wagnerian conductor, Erich Leinsdorf. Perhaps I shall be able to attend one of his appearances with the Cleveland orchestra. At 30 he has accomplished so much and since he conducted the Wagnerian operas I have seen to my complete satisfaction, I admire him very much.

But here I have been raving and you may be quite bored. Let's talk about me for awhile. I like that, discussing me. People say I'm either very happy on top of the world, or I'm sad and at its bottom. I never seem to strike a satisfactory medium. I guess they are right. Yesterday I wanted to kiss the world, today, well, I'm not unhappy. Just tired! I finished typing my book a short time ago, and will mail it to you first thing in the morning. How I wonder what you'll think of it. It has been an experience just trying to write a book. Now when I go into a library I don't see merely books and books. I see work, sweat, tears, and people. I have always been regarded as a conceited individual. I remember that everything I wrote in school I thought to be a masterpiece. But not with this book. If I'm writing on it I am very happy and energetic, but when I read it later, it makes me sick, discouraged, and I usually creep off to bed not caring much if I see the morrow or not.

Several days ago I decided something. I wanted to write you about it then, but waited until I would be positive of that decision. I'm not really positive about it, but I'm going to try damn hard. I'm going to put away my make-up. At first I thought of giving them to my sister (they're the best of cosmetics) but then, if ever I find a play role I like, I enjoy experimenting in how I would make up in that role, and so I wouldn't have the paint if I gave them to her. Nevertheless, I shall put them away. I won't lock them up or anything like that; I'll keep them where I can easily use them IF I drop my resolve. One thing I think my weakness has given me is the strength to stick out something. I do believe I can keep away from make-up.

I don't wear the "stuff" around the house, only when I go out. A few days ago I had an occasion to go to the high school to visit my former literature teacher. My, it felt good to go with a clean face. I felt free, really free. It was as if I were on the same level with everyone else. I didn't have to turn my face from people, could look them straight in the eye! If I thought anyone was looking at me, it was because I was self-conscious and they weren't staring at me anymore than I was at them. A person's eyes have to be on something. Oh, yes, a clean face for me from now on. And I had my hair cut. It looks much better. My clothes aren't unusual I know because I buy them in good, men's shops.

It was what you wrote about a nice girl dressing as a prostitute and going to the New York water fronts. That did it. I thought a lot about that simple statement. It was the key. Of course I can give in to convention that much. What a fool I was not to have realized it sooner. With things like my book and your letters to occupy my mind and time I don't care to bother with make-up. I guess I just want people to find me interesting and want to know me. If I'm successful at something people will want to know me, and I want to be without make-up when I shake their hands. Like make-up? Of course I do. It can do wonders for a person. But you've made me feel I don't have to have "wonders" on my face. If I had only realized something like this at Dayton. The trouble I would have avoided. I'm not angry with the Major that wanted to rid himself of me, it was natural. Now I want to make up for it all. Show them I'm not such a horrible creation after all.

I told you of my Dayton friend, Dorothy. She is coming here Sunday to spend her vacation with me. For several days we will be in Cleveland to see the ballet, Art Museum, and plays. I have sworn to myself that not a single thing goes on my face except soap and water while we're there. It will be such fun going freely among people. I'll try to make up to Dorothy for all she went through with me at Dayton.

Isn't it funny that this one item should mean so much? You will see that in my book I ask myself many questions about it. I have thought much of myself in ten, twenty, thirty years, and was afraid of exactly what you described would happen. That is why I want to work so hard to check it now. I want to be more fortunate than these others. I'd like to think I went through this just to be able to write this book, now throw off the garb and look for something new and different in the world.

Let this desire be locked away, surely most of us have desires locked away in us, and this one can be mine. Another, is any attraction I may have in my person for men. If in the years to come this thing does not leave, surely I can be attracted to someone and not show it. If I have something really big to occupy my mind, these attractions couldn't be very important and would soon die.

That brings us to this question of men. How do I feel about them? I just don't know. At such times as Army examinations I am completely repulsed by any sex thoughts. In the past when just any old person has approached me, I've always been scared silly and got away from them. I sometimes think when they say something to me I'd like to knock them into next week. That is if I'm not fool enough to be flattered by their attentions at the time. I wrote you that I thought I had fallen in love once. If that man should ever approach me with a suggestion, I'd hate him to my dying day. I don't want to have relationships like that with men. I want to be proud of myself and they would remind me of my weakness and a distasteful act. Mr. Bellamann, how can I say it? The bigger me doesn't want to have anything to do with men except to have the knowledge to decide if they are handsome or otherwise. If the little me starts with "wouldn't this be fun, or that be fun," I want the bigger me to laugh him right down. No, it wouldn't be fun.

I am not a woman. I think it would be nice being one, may always think that, but since I'm not, Tedd Burr isn't such a bad person either. You see, I'd like a house and buy nice things for it, to cook … oh, I love to … but then, doesn't Alfred Lunt go into the kitchen once in awhile … to have pretty things … but can't a tailor make a nice suit … perfumes … well, perhaps I could have a safe of them and look at them once in awhile … a family … why couldn't I be a swell fatherly-mother as well as a motherly-father … etc.[17] I guess my problems are not so bad. I just like to make myself suffer.

---

17. Alfred Lunt (1892–1977), American stage actor.

If I just tried to laugh half as much as I make myself cry I'd be the guy with the million dollar smile.

Now, about girls. I consider Dorothy and Jeanne very dear to my heart, but would not care to touch them sexually. I just don't want to, it simply isn't there. But, I would enjoy it if women were attracted to me and I could kindly smile 'no.' I'd like to think I'm something unattainable. This may sound terrible, but it's true. In Dayton where I worked most of the girls wanted my opinion on how they should wear their hair, or what accessories to wear with a certain costume. They always had me designing clothes for them, although my designs are strickly [*sic*] <u>Vogue</u>. I liked being a kind of authority. They weren't making fun of my opinions either because they usually did as I suggested.

I picked up your letter and read it again. I hope I've answered this man question. If I haven't, tell me and I'll try again. It's so hard to put into words. Perhaps because I don't know it all cut and dry myself, but I'm sure if as you say I accomplish something, I won't have time nor the desire to concern myself over them. If I were a WOMAN and could have everything that goes with womanhood, I'd want a man … maybe several of them. A man would be a very nice thing to have in bed … but TEDD BURR definitely wants to sleep alone and likes it. As I wrote, it wasn't a bit hard to turn down that man in Dayton when I had him as a bed partner … for one thing I wasn't sure what he wanted me to do, and I didn't want to embarrass myself by doing the wrong thing and thus show my inexperience. He proved to me that I wasn't what I thought I might be. But I could go on with this one way conversation forever so enough of it for now.

Oh, dear, I've looked at your letter again and I fear I may not have answered a question. You ask if I tried to attract men sexually. Well, I suppose that I must have. I suppose when there is an attraction between people the sex element is there in some way … either yes … or no. But I did resent their looking at me. I thought they were cheap if they did. I suppose I have the impression that men are pretty sexual … especially if they're young … so I chose that way to get noticed … but God knows I hated their stares. I had to learn my lesson. Now I think I know better than to be a fool running after something (womanhood) that just isn't going to be mine.

Mr. Bellamann, I do have a sense of humor. Believe me I enjoyed your comments about my English, etc. I was glad that was in your letter as much as anything. I feel that you're a regular person, that's why I let down my hair as I do. You're like some big brother, if you don't mind, that I've always looked for. And I don't think you're old. 60 isn't bad, it's getting there … oh, pardon me. But I read "KINGS ROW" before I saw your picture with the date 1882 beneath, and so you'll always be young to me. Your book was young. I marvel at your great understanding of young people. You must be very nice, and must know so many people, and so much of life.

If you would like to write me about your music and your tastes in that line, I'd enjoy it. I'm so eager tonight, forgive me. I had better close and silently steal away. I hope you're pleased with my progress, if I have made any. I myself feel free and like someone looking happily into the sea, ready to sail out.

Sincerely,
Tedd

8
HENRY

Ansonia Hotel
New York City

October 12, 1943

Dear Tedd,

This has to be a hurried note because any day is full of infringements.

There are many things about you that become clear as I read your letters. I think maybe your problems are simpler than they appear to be to you. Oh, how your great enemy is <u>artificiality</u>. You are too ready to carry into an adult world a sort of make believe. Now Tedd, everyone of us worth half a damn wishes to achieve: we want to do something fine: we want the acclaim and the recognition that follows. Perhaps without formulating it to ourselves we want to be important. But we should <u>not</u> wish to <u>seem</u> important, or wish to have people think us important before we really are.

I heard Ernest Boyd say sharply once to an aspiring girl writer: "You wish to seem important! For God's sake there is only one answer to that: <u>Be important</u>."[18]

I have an idea that, for a writer, the general run of people are the fascinating ones. They are his study, his material, and the means and purpose of his calling. I have known almost everybody in the musical world, here and in Europe. There are very few one would cross the hall to see. Rachmaninoff was a great man, but few people ever saw him or knew him in private life. My next-door neighbor in this hotel is Lauritz Melchior. He is very fat, very dull. On the other side is Bidu Sayão. I don't know her. I don't know Toscanini, but I have met him. I did not know Padewerski [*sic*], and never met him though he was once in the Curtis Institute. I came near to revering his playing. Most of the conductors I do know. Fritz Reiner is a great one, so is Koussevitzky, Bruno Walter and Mitropoulos. Leinsdorf is not, and was nearly put out of the

---

18. Ernest Augustus Boyd (1887–1946), Irish critic and writer.

Met. two years ago for incompetence—<u>alleged</u>. Stokowski is a good deal of a genius, but part-<u>poseur</u>.[19]

Flagstad I did not know though I saw her often here in the house. A superb singer, and probably a Nazi. There are disagreeable rumors rife in her wake.

I say they are a rather awful lot because they are vain, stupid, and shallow. Most of them are the product of many coaches and teachers. Rose Bampton was a pupil at Curtis while I was Dean. I thought her unmusical but she took Pelletier away from his wife, and so got herself a fine coach and a Met conductor all at once.[20] She is not a dramatic soprano as she imagines, but a low mezzo. She will probably ruin her voice soon.

No, Tedd, the great artists are too busy, work too hard, to be <u>social</u>. The near great are less interesting. The pseudo great are terrible. These men and women are not interesting in their work.

(In the current issue of the Musical Quarterly is an article on my old teacher Philipp which I wrote for his 80th birthday.)[21]

… You are going to have to work like a dog to be good at anything. If you do and have any talent you will be some kind of important person. When you <u>achieve</u> you will have all the recognition your heart can wish for, and if you are a genuine person you won't care anything about it, and will be intent in achieving the next goal.

---

19. Sergei Rachmaninoff (1873–1943), Russian composer; Lauritz Melchior (1890–1973), Danish tenor; Bidu Sayão (1902–1999), Brazilian soprano; Arturo Toscanini (1867–1857), Italian conductor; Ignacy Jan Paderewski (1860–1941), Polish pianist, composer, and prime minister; Fritz Reiner (1888–1963), Hungarian conductor; Sergei Alexandrovich Koussevitzky (1874–1951), Russian composer, conductor, and double-bassist; Bruno Walter (1876–1962), German composer, conductor, and pianist; Dimitri Mitropoulos (1896–1960), Greek composer, conductor, and pianist; Erich Leinsdorf (1912–1993), Austrian conductor; Leopold Stokowski (1882–1977), British conductor.

20. Wilfrid Pelletier (1896–1982), Canadian conductor, pianist, and composer.

21. Isador Philipp (1863–1958), French pianist and composer.

But with me you must <u>be</u> yourself. I shouldn't want you ever to say what you might think I'd approve or like. All I shall like is sincerity.

All of the sex questions can wait. Just don't feel that you are a sinner. A sense of guilt of any kind is deadly. Every past day is dead, the future is unborn. The present instant is your life.

I did not study in Germany. I detested Germany. It is very dull. Vienna was charming. I worked in Paris. The biographical stuff is incorrect. I never knew anything about Japanese art and did not write about it. Another biographical sketch says: "Mr. B. wrote erudite articles about Italian primitives—writing in Italian." I know nothing of Italian primitives and cannot write Italian. WHO'S WHO tells what I have actually done. I was and still am a good pianist, a better teacher (while I taught), and hope to be a better writer.

Yes, please—the one thing I do ask as a favor is the abandoning of make-up. You are fine as you are—and what you are inside your head is what counts.

One line in your letter was revealing: "I didn't know what he expected me to do." That's just it—the <u>what to do</u> does not seem pleasant. Forget about it. You have more interesting things to do. But I am troubled by a line like this: "Perhaps there I might find Siegfried." It is a homosexual line, no matter what you may think. You didn't say: "There I might meet Sieglinde."

But no matter. Don't take this too seriously.

There is somewhere a world of beauty for you to know and perhaps to express. But <u>not</u> a world of petty <u>prettiness</u>. Only great and serious beauty matters. Someone said once that the course of artistic effort in America was "the sweet, the pretty, and the cute."

I saw John Gould Fletcher yesterday—the poet. He seemed to me disillusioned and bitter. Was it because he pursued the <u>precious</u> instead of the legitimate material of poetry? I don't know but it's hard to read his "Symphony In Blue" today.

Good luck, sincerely,
Henry Bellamann

9

TEDD

161 Sheffield St.
Bellevue, Ohio

October 17, 1943

Dear Mr. Bellamann,

Here I am home again with many games of solitaire facing me in the coming week. I do miss not having the "Surf" to work on. I suddenly feel it difficult to read—it is always like that; either I read constantly or not at all.

What wonderful "hurried notes" you write. I believe it unusual for someone to give such honest and frank opinions to a stranger. How I dislike it when someone stutters and stammers and says nothing. I am referring to your discussion of musicians. I have met those who think every "performer" to be wonderful until you break them down and get their honest opinion that the "performer" wasn't quite so wonderful. I believe one has varying degrees of "performers" and should not hesitate in expressing one's self.

I was rather shaken a week ago by a story which sprang from this small town. There was a lovely girl from a prominant [sic] family here who married a politician and went away with him. In a few years she returned, not with her husband but with a daughter, Joan. This little girl was permitted no outside friendships, her mother walked her to school and met her after those sessions to take her home. Joan was a brilliant student and it is said she designed beautiful clothes. They lived in an uptown apartment.

Like everyone else I used to laugh at this mother and daughter. After graduating in 1936 Joan was constantly with her mother walking up-and-down through the town. They were both very tall and wore nothing but bright colored taffeta dresses which were pressed beautifully. They had little hats bedecked with flowers and dressed exactly alike. Their arms entwined, their faces stoney, eyes straight ahead, they walked in perfect step with each other. It was an art, but they amused Bellevue.

I often saw Joan at the library and since we both seemed enthusiastic over <u>Vogue</u> magazine, I wanted to talk to her, but I was so young and afraid of her.

I learned that a month ago the mother died. Joan walked alone now. She hid behind dark glasses and walked. My heart ached for her but still said nothing to her. Her mother had been cremated—and the daughter kept those remains in the apartment. At night she was heard crying out in her lonliness [*sic*].

Her father, the politician, suddenly turned up. He demanded her little money and Joan got her first job as a store clerk. But the other girls drew away and laughed at her black taffeta dresses trimmed in blue.

Last Saturday Joan wrapped herself in a sheet and with a rope around her neck—threw herself from her apartment window. They cut her down and rushed her to the hospital. There with, "They can't get me now," on her lips, she died.

When I heard what she had done that Sat. morning I was filled with mixed emotions. If I, or someone, had only had the courage to give her friendship, so I wrote her a letter. I wanted her to feel that she would be doing me a favor by permitting me to write her letters. I wrote of designing, music, books. Never did I mention her act or condition. But after I had written it I learned she had died. Since I have felt that we, all of us, failed in a responsibility; that girl was one of us, and we failed her!

Dorothy and I had a fine time in Cleveland. The days went quickly and I felt <u>good</u> until our last day there. I had grown sensitive about entering restaurants and decided that if I could go right into this coffee shop without anything happening I would be rid of my strange fear. There was a counter arrangement and I faced a line of business men. As I looked up there was a million eyes on me. I was stunned and a million crooked smiles were there! One fat old man called over a waitress and exchanged words with her. I wanted to run! The waitress came to me, leaned far over the counter to take my order, then back to the fat old man and shook her head, "I don't know!"

Oh, Mr. Bellamann, I tried. I did as I said—wore <u>no</u> makeup—tried to be like everyone else. Those men were finished eating but they sat there—smiling and nodding—and watching. After so long one can feel—doesn't have to see—what goes on! It was late and they left seconds before I did. That tore so much from me. What's the use!!—I've gotten lonely again—lonely for men—hysterical for them—I can hardly stay from my makeup and breaking my heart. I'm desperate for something—I don't know what.

Oh, I'll keep on the narrow path—I'll try to resolve again—but deep down are those fires; I'm grasping once more.

Tedd

10

TEDD

161 Sheffield St.
Bellevue, Ohio

October 18, 1943

Dear Mr. Bellamann,

You are probably in receipt of my recent letter. I might apologize for it but I shan't. It is the ending which has bothered me, but I mailed it nevertheless for you requested sincerity and that was a sincere outburst. I don't doubt for a moment but that it all was highly dramatized—but I live in such an atmosphere. Perhaps it all confirms what has been worrying you—that I am a homo-sexual—but I don't know exactly what you mean by that term.

I am one of dreams and of moods. I wrote you yesterday in one mood and in a few moments lay in another. Today I am trying to be rational, self-analytical, superior, and honest in dealing with myself.

Of dreams—a chance name or thought may send me into wild imaginative trances. I want to lie down and close my eyes—I am not Tedd Burr—I am a beautiful woman desired, loved, and cherished. I wrote you of Erich Leinsdorf. It was not really as a conductor I referred to him nor do I care if he is not a great conductor. I care that he is Leinsdorf, a man with burning eyes, and he is in my dreams. Would I care to meet him now?—oh—god—no. I want just to dream. How I delight in envying this Mrs. Leinsdorf for having him near and bearing his children. I wonder where Leinsdorf is at this moment—oh how he would laugh at this—at me!

These dreams are not practical, but you are practical, Mr. Bellamann. It is a battle—you and my dreams. This Leinsdorf shall pass—they all do—and then someone else shall be there. In this same unimportant way I have loved many. Yesterday I met one who for months ached within me, but yesterday there was not the faintest spark left—just a dark memory. I do not torture my body with passion for these. No, my body is a cruel reminder of my insurmountable short-comings. I love them as a woman—a mental longing and crying out is all I have. Dreams—dreams—dreams—they shall drive me mad.

I am lonely. Often last week I looked intently upon Dorothy. Nothing disgusts me more than her body or any woman's body. I want a constant companionship. In her I do not find it. Constantly I am plagued with shameful thoughts—her bad complexion, if only she would care for her hair, her dresses need cleaning, why doesn't she use perfume, etc—etc. Horrible. Always with women it is that way. With men? No! How many I put on altars! <u>Today</u>: I should adore Leinsdorf's hands, his thinning hair, his sweating body; tomorrow some other Tom, Dick, or Harry shall be there. I am as unpredictable as my style of handwriting. I despair to know my real person.

I don't know what I am writing—just writing—if only I do not lose you through this. You have become a part of me at these times—no longer are you a person to me. I am frightened of myself—my mind—its thoughts.

Moods—my moods are the results of my dreams. I am emotional—my mind never rests—always it churns about on something. Seldom do I act on the impulse of a moment—except in mailing foolish letters to you. Tell me of Oscar Wilde. The only book I have of him is pages of evasiveness. What mixed thoughts I have in trying to write you.

You shall hate me. Why does no one like me after a time? Because I think only of myself? Don't leave me now, Mr. Bellamann—I am dramatizing—I shall laugh in a moment. No, I don't want to laugh. Perhaps it is the suspense of waiting to hear from your thoughts on my "The Surf—."[22]

Perhaps what is with me most—shall I ever be loved? Loved in all shadings of love by many. Could I but lie in one man's heart as tragically as he lies in mine. Ach—what impossible and provoking sentiments. If I could but control myself. I swear—there is a big

---

22. "The Surf in Terror Fled" is the full title of the novel. Tedd discusses it in the film *Letters to Uranus* (2000).

me and a little me. The former is wise but weak. The latter is young and tantalizing!

A stalwart soul would count my blessings. I do—at times. But blessing makes one happy—I pray best when I am sad. In one past moment I was content but thinking on that word I grew cold in longing.

If you will, dismiss this letter as the one before. I have failed herein, yet this may be more worth to you than me.

Ever Respectfully,
Tedd

Portrait of Tedd Burr included in Tedd's October 18, 1943 letter to Henry Bellamann. Photograph provided by Amber and Adrienne Slane.

11
HENRY

Ansonia Hotel
New York City

October 18, 1943

My dear Tedd,

Thanks for the picture for it's very fine looking. I shall write you
later. I am not very well and it may be some days before I can get
to your book. Please be patient.

Sincerely,
Henry Bellamann

12

HENRY

Ansonia Hotel
New York City

October 19, 1943

My dear Tedd,

I fear this letter may be inadequate, because there is so much I would like to say to you and I have so little time to say it. First, thanks again for the photograph. It is, as you would agree, beautiful. I will disturb you by saying I liked the High School one better. The boy with glasses on is a troubled, lost-soul sort of person. The other is, I suggest, Sidney French.[23] But I do not think that Sidney French is what you believe him to be.

Let me go back again to some of the things I said to you in the beginning. I am not a physician, nor a psychiatrist, and I am not attempting to usurp their functions. It had occurred to me that you do not require either. I believed, as I still do, that you need a friendly interest and a sincere sort of advice. Today I am not so sure.

My suggestions to you, Tedd, have no flavor of moral advice. I am not much interested in such aspects of your problems. There are things you must settle for yourself. Besides, it is very difficult to know what is right or wrong for anyone else. I have made and will continue to make, if you wish me to, some suggestions that may contribute to making you happier. You see, anyone who is badly adjusted to his environment makes everyone about him equally ill adjusted to the situation thus created. I can find myself being very sympathetic to you, but equally sympathetic to those who have to live with you!

Listen, Tedd, I am an old man, relatively speaking. I have lived a lot and have seen many situations. I can only talk truth to you by hurting your feelings—worse than a surgeon could ever hurt you. If you can take it—if you are strong enough it may be

---

23. Sidney French, the central character in Tedd's novel.

good for you. If you think it is not the right comment for you, you are free to reject it and go your own way. You know of course that I have no axe to grind. I have nothing to gain or to lose in writing you what I believe to be disagreeable truths. So much in your letters has touched me. You see, I knew Jamie Wakefield. He was my good friend, and the later days of Jamie are not pretty.

So. Let me talk about Sidney French. I must say at the outset that you have not presented what I imagine was in your mind. (Technically,—oh, but you are a bad speller! Your English is rather shockingly bad. "His eyes were spiked with despise." That is not English.)

You said the Frenches were sort of top layer people. But you only said so. You know it is bad writing, for instance to say some one is witty. You have to make them witty. What, now, was your object in presenting the Frenches as a lower middle class family with the worst breeding and the most outrageous manners you could portray? You had said they were proud and socially prominent, etc. But that isn't what you put on paper. Nice ladies don't manicure their nails in the drawing room.

It appeared to me that Mamma French, sorely tried as she was by her freakish son, still behaved like an idiot. The only person in that book who got across in any degree was Mr. French. Now don't jump to the conclusion that I think so because of any moral implications. Not at all. He acted occasionally as a recognizable person. I shall shock you when I say I was ready to applaud when he slapped Sidney. That was the only regular reaction anyone in the book ever had.

Tedd, the boy you portrayed in this book is not just a fairy (and it is fairy not faery—which is something else) he is a fool. He demanded attention and approval, and then did everything to lose both. He hated the attention he did get.

The other day I saw a man come into this hotel to call on Doctor Potter. This man was dressed like Christ. Beard, sandals, a kind of robe, etc. And yet he was furious that people stared! He seemed to have forgotten that Christ dressed in the manner of the period. This substitution of externals for spiritual values or for internal attitudes is pretty foolish. (There is also a man here who is rumored to be the illegitimate son of Richard Wagner. He wears Wagnerian dress and looks pretty silly, while Friedlandia Wagner, (Richard Wagner's grand daughter, who lives up stairs somewhere,) really does look like her grandfather and doesn't have to advertise.[24]

Sidney French is a phony. He is not even a good homosexual. There, for instance, was Tschaikowsy, who was homosexual. But in a life that was almost conventional, in conventional clothes, and in the solid conventions of a good musician he made a great career and left a great heritage to the world. If we lived in a world where there were three sexes Sidney French might pass. But we don't happen to live in such a world. He was furious because people scoffed at his conventions. But don't you see how <u>he</u> scoffed at the conventions and ideas of others? He is egocentric to an insane degree. In fact, this book, Tedd, has one value. It is a pathological document. It is the frank exposition of a sick psyche. Even in the world of psychiatry which is not surprised at anything, this boy is a sick boy. All of his actions, everyone of them are the actions of hysteria.

Now, I understand <u>why</u> he is sick. I <u>do</u> understand that boy — only too well. But I also know that any harmony or happiness for him has to come from inside of him. Now, I am not talking about sexual problems or adjustments. For him they are probably not entirely possible. That is unimportant. Perhaps Sidney French has a right to whatever sexual outlet is necessary, but he has no right to purchase his expression at the expense of family, friends, or the world. After all he has to live in the world. If he had lived in the time of Alexander the Great he might have been one of Alec's attendant boys. Even that is not so pretty — even at this distance.

It seems to me that you are aesthetic. Sidney French is not. He is an exhibitionist. There is no difference between Sidney French flaunting an artificial prettiness in the face of an unwilling gallery than there is excuse for these tattered old men one sees in the park

---

24. Friedelind Wagner (1918–1991), German composer.

who exhibit their genitals to innocent little girls. It's a difference of category, but not a difference of base.

Among the things hardest to forgive this boy is his petulance. It is a girlish petulance and is presumed to be attractive because you say Sidney was attractive. But in ten years this petulance would be the petulance of an old maid—cattish, shrewd, snarly. (Just recently I had tea with two elderly fairies. One was a celebrated concert pianist—celebrated for a number of reasons not entirely musical—and to see these two silly elderly men quarrel at each other about water spilled on an antique lacquer table was really terrible.)

I find certain things in this musical set up incomprehensible. You said Sidney was a talented and discriminating musician. But he was considerably concerned with Debussy's "<u>Claire de Lune</u>." This piece which has a slight poetry is not representative Debussy, or even good Debussy. I met Debussy once in Paris and I had the <u>Suite Bergamasque</u> among my music. He dismissed the <u>Claire de Lune</u> as a sugar plum—<u>pas important</u>. Why couldn't Sidney have played the Pagodes, or the magical <u>Preludes</u>?

There are two places where I do not understand your object in setting up something and then knocking it down. The first instance is the supposed taste and breeding of the Frenches which you deny in the portrayal.

Then there are colloquialisms out of place in the body of writing. It is a vaudeville term to speak of a pianist as "a talent."

Can you write? Could you be a writer? I don't know. I recall one sentence that stands out of my morning's reading. (I have not yet finished the second half of the book.) "Each day he swore there was no God; each night he prayed." That is a fine sentence. It is dramatic and strong.

All of your people talk alike. All of them are high-flown. I can't imagine any really thoroughbred person putting on the purely snobbish talk of the Frenches. And fine people are never "haughty." Only false people and pretenders. Did you mean that after all they were under their disguise nothing but low grade people?

It is possible to write <u>out of the world</u> things—pure fantasy, and still be an artist. Oscar Wilde did that, though the plaster is falling from many of his literary skeletons with alarming rapidity. Is it possible that you have not been reading to critical purpose? On any block of any street of any town in America one can find the full gamut of human life, human comedy and human tragedy. But you have to write the truth.

The story of Sidney French, Tedd, is escapism. It is retaliation and it does sound dreadfully catty. I think you may have done yourself fine service in writing it. It is out of your system. You cannot wish to be like Sidney. You could not sanely wish such a life or such an attitude. I must say in all the honesty I can muster that it has no possible chance at publication, and that really from a literary point of view it is not good. From a psychological point of view it is a glimpse into the heart of a psychological inferno.

I suspect you won't feel very friendly toward this kind of ruthless, surgical criticism. But I rely a little on your honesty. I rely a little on your common sense. I hope there is sufficient integrity in you to rally. Put this book away and forget it. Don't try to write just yet. (Don't read William Faulkner with an idea of finding a model.) How about trying the new novel, "The Walsh Sisters" by Miss Janeway?[25] You will have to learn to write by writing, by backing up, by trying again, and profit by discouragement and failure. Maybe you aren't a writer. I don't mean to be facetious when I say maybe you are a designer of some kind. I remember the great French designers. Poiret was one of the world's great artists as surely as if he had worked with brush and color.[26]

Whatever. When you are well I should put on a conventional exterior. You are really misrepresenting yourself and inviting people who are not as good or as fine as I believe you to be. Try to take all of this well. You will not find many people in the world willing to help you to whatever realization of fulfillment you wish. You have already found this out to your discomfort. I think the

---

25. Elizabeth Janeway, *The Walsh Girls* (1943).
26. Paul Poiret (1879–1944), French fashion designer.

psychiatrists would only tangle you up. Forget the word abnormal. You must have had it flung at you. Whatever you are, you are by nature. It will change only as you need change, only that much and for that reason. But don't invite the world's calumny and distaste by being eccentric. It was always interesting to see Rachmaninoff passing through the halls of this hotel. If he hadn't been so extraordinarily ugly (that ugliness which approaches and passes distinction) no one would have noticed him. I see Toscanini on the street occasionally and no one recognizes him. He looks much like any prosperous Italian importer!

I don't know what else to say. As I said in the beginning if you wish friendliness from me, you have it. If I can be of any service to you, I shall be glad. You will have to decide that and write me what you think.

Thanks again for the picture. The sad thing about this beautiful photograph is whom and how it attracts. The real men of the world whom you like are attracted by the truly feminine. And here is a face that might have come from the planet Uranus—so foreign, and in the last analysis so unappealing. I like the boy with the glasses who looks out fearfully to a world that may be very hard on him if he isn't careful.

Sincerely,
Henry Bellamann

Whatever else you have in this world you can have in me a friend. I mean this. You wrote yourself out so well to me in the beginning. I should be grieved if I hurt you too much. I don't mean to. So— courage: courage is the supreme gift.

13

HENRY

Ansonia Hotel
New York City

October 20, 1943

Dear Tedd,

Here are your letters, and I want to say: Take it easy! A poor answer to your disarray of mind. Yes, I understood about Leinsdorf when I read your first sentence about him in an earlier letter. I perhaps have not realized how little you knew, technically speaking, of your own inclinations and obsessions. I am not sure that a reading of Sigmund Freud's Studies in Homosexuality would clear matters up for you. Homosexuality—I have to write as an amateur in these matters—is merely that departure from the norm where a man loves other men. When you say "love," you are referring to a mental state. Carried out to execution there are many forms of sexual abnormalities. They are as old as history. They are in the Old Testament and in Greek history. You see Tedd you do rather whoop up these states of mind and then there is nothing to do. You don't happen to be female and so there is no relationship, and then you grow hysterical through frustration. There is no escape from such frustration. You speak of being two people. That, too, is quite evident. You've read of <u>schizophrenia</u>—a word that means split personality, a word that defines what is not too well understood—names a condition rather than explaining it.

Schizophrenia is a condition where out of some profound dissatisfactions with life, a person begins to create an imaginary self or condition. It's a kind of make-believe. It is possible to go on and on in make-believe until the individual cannot distinguish between what is real and what is imaginary. The individual is then insane. It is [as] if the mind could not accept the conditions in one room and so goes into another room and closes the door. If he stays in the other room and does not return to a real and tangible life he is simply put into an asylum. To some extent such conditions may be under the patient's control. I don't know what doctors would say about the extent of this.

All of us are probably two people to some slight degree— ma[y]be we are several people. But let us take a case of a frustrated old maid who has had no attention and no emotional experience. Maybe to satisfy her own longing and to save face among her acquaintances she invents a lover who lives far away, or who went to war and was killed. Then she can lift her head among women and say: I had a lover but I mourn him loyally. She has saved face. But if she writes herself letters and begins to believe her own story you have two parallel existences before you which she is trying to live simultaneously. If she begins to live the unreal one more fully than the other she is definitely on the pathological side. Maybe a psychiatrist can pull her out of it—maybe not. Maybe she finds unreality tolerable, and reality intolerable. In that case maybe she remains insane.

A lot of the things which you think you like or don't like are really not the truth. You repeat this wish to be a woman. You tell me that you find the persons of women disgusting. Do you? Or, are you telling yourself that in order to justify something else? I don't know why you wish to be loved as a woman. You are a man physically with probably more than the usual sex drive. Are you saying you dislike women because you do not wish to use yourself as you would have to in order to have any relief from frustration? What can you do about it? The out and out homosexual does usually detest women. The story of Tschaikowsky's marriage demonstrates the horrible result of an attempt at what he apparently couldn't achieve. But are you sure? Was there some event or some unpleasant revelation sometime that makes you dislike the woman as such?

The unconscious mind plays curious tricks on us. We are convinced that we like or don't like many things when the mind is merely escaping some unpleasant association. That of course is where the real psychiatrist steps in. Sometimes he is able to find out what these tricks and subterfuges are and the patient goes on about his business free from painful compulsions. Perhaps you should read Freud. In the Modern Library series of publications is a volume called The Basic Writings of Sigmund Freud. On Page 553 the study of sexual inversions begins. Scattered through the volume are matters which might bear on your troubles. I hesitate to advise you. Look into the book and if you don't understand it very well or for any reason don't wish to read it, don't.

The phrase "a female brain in a male body" doesn't bear too close inspection since you can't prove what is or is not a female brain. Femininity is a constellation of psychic qualities which in your case could be imitative just as easily as they could be real. I don't know too much about such matters, Tedd. But common sense rather suggests that if you are ever to be happy and free from such tensions as you describe, you will have to live and act normally. I say normally, because there is no better word. You are a boy, physically. Let us take for instance your descriptions of your actual physical sensations of being a woman. That kind of thing could be hysteria—maybe. It's like this. It is possible to imagine a pain in your elbow and to keep on imagining it until your arm is useless. There may be not the slightest justification in the physical condition of the arm for the condition. Many of your sensations are a kind of wish fulfillment. Do you <u>have</u> to wish like that? When you describe women you invariably describe a repulsive one. Why can't you describe or think of an attractive one? On the aesthetic side a girl of your own age is certainly daintier, more agreeable to sight than the male. Notice, I didn't say more attractive. I'm talking about the aesthetic qualities which you deny to femininity.

I do suggest, just a common sense relief from the unwelcome attention you attract, that you at least <u>imitate</u> masculinity—for your own protection. The fact is you like to look like a girl. You really wish people to think what they do think. You imagine that in so doing you prove yourself superior to other people. That is not the case. You prove yourself inferior in being an imitation something instead of something real. <u>Better to imitate what you are actually</u>. That sounds paradoxical, I know,—but, Tedd, you are a boy. I think you are nicest as a boy. I think you like to appear to yourself and to others as a tragic figure. All of us are tragic figures. Life is largely tragic.

It shocks me more than a little that you do concern yourself so violently with a personal tragedy when the world is in the struggle of trying to save itself from destruction. I am told that such utterly repellent people as Goering and Hitler and many of that horrible gang are sexual inverts and perverts. Do you wish to be of that terrible company?

I have no way of knowing if your state of mind is due to psychic causes or to physical ones—I mean deeply hidden physical causes. I am not blaming you for what you may not be able to help. I am blaming you for what I know you can help. There have been men in the world who were sexual inverts who concerned themselves with important things. Tschaikowsky. I'm afraid I don't think a concern with Vogue or makeup or perfumes is important for anyone—male or female. It's dreadful to be concerned only with your self. It's also dreadful to be concerned only with trivial and unimportant things. Then you measure your stature by those things. A great pianist is great according to the measure of his humanity and his understanding of humanity—never through his disdain of humanity. Disdain or scorn of humanity is a sign of weakness. And that is why certain pianistic names fade so quickly. I know you feel that you have been despitefully [*sic*] used by the world. You've had some darned hard knocks—but nothing to what you will get if you can't find a way out of this. I want to say if <u>we</u> can't find a way out. I am willing to take time that is valuable to me to talk to you on paper and to recommend as best I can because I know you need a friend. And you must convince yourself that I am not unfriendly when I use hard words. I am concerned only with this: as a human being I would like to help you realize yourself. You called to me. As far as I can I have tried to answer.

I finished the book last night. The conclusion did not change my opinion. I know I am right because this is my profession. You can verify what I have said by the simple device of sending the book to publishers. Do you wish me to pencil some corrections through a part of it. Such places as where you say crumbled instead of crumpled. "He crumpled anciently ..." is bad English. It <u>is</u> too high flown and too arty. I can only believe that this is not really you at your best. It is <u>made up</u>. Good fiction is not really made up. It derives straight from life.

Oscar Wilde was convicted and sent to prison for sodomy. You will find that the dictionary defines sodomy as intercourse with animals. But he was really homosexual and it is probable that the term sodomy crept into the records as a figure of speech—I don't know. He was brilliant and talented and he defied society and society destroyed him. I am not classifying you with anybody or anything. Apparently you don't <u>do</u> anything, and you don't even know what you want to do. That is why I am trying hard to switch you to simple achievement—real work of some kind, until you find yourself.

How musical are you, I wonder? How talented? What pieces have you played? How easily and quickly do you learn? Of course your ideas about technic are just plain cuckoo—excuse it! The simple reasons for scales is getting command of the keyboard, smoothing out and polishing execution. Technic can be the most fascinating of mental adventures. Playing the piano well means you are a slave to the keyboard for years.

Did you mean to make Sidney French attractive? He isn't. He certainly has bad manners and never said a really humane or kind thing throughout the book. When he spoke would be kindlily [sic] to Isabel he was merely patronizing and insulting.

I would like to send your handwriting to my friend Dr. Teltscher. Teltscher is a psychographologist. This is not a handwriting expert but an analyst of the unconscious mind through study of handwriting. I think he is good. I won't do this without your permission. Your writing is that of several people. Sometimes like a small boy's.

Take everything easy. Try not to be hysterical and resentful and mad at the world. And please understand that all I say is just what seems to me to be the truth. I can be wrong about everything. I wish only to help if possible.

Sincerely,
Henry Bellamann

I know why you say you loathe the bodies of women. You want to be one and you are jealous of them and you try to convince yourself that you as an imitation woman are more attractive than they are. Isn't that it. When you describe their "loathsome" characteristics you describe characteristics common to all people. Everyone smells if he doesn't bathe. If we look too closely at the human animal we can easily become "nasty nice."

14

TEDD

161 Sheffield St.
Bellevue, Ohio

October 22, 1943

My dear Mr. Bellamann,

This is a very difficult letter to write probably because of the great confusion in my mind at the moment; yet I do not hesitate to write for I want you to have the immediate reactions from your letter just received.

Yes, you have today let my world crash around me. But in another sense I am not permitting it to crash until I hear further from you since my one disappointment was that you wrote on reading but one half of the book. I have always felt that looking at it as a whole was the only just thing to do in order to form conclusions—especially of the nature you wrote.

I do not like the first part of my book—I don't believe it gives the most interesting side of Sidney. And I also believe that when the story is finished the reader perhaps can feel that the author is looking in on characters and not splashing out with his own life. I wrote Sidney with knowledge of myself but also I thought coldly as the "world" might. I think a "Sidney" is doomed—so I killed him.

I do apologize for the two recent letters from me. Perhaps they gave something more of me to you—perhaps they were annoying. It was just that I had nothing to occupy my mind. I waited for your letter that did not come and in a mental turmoil I wrote them. After mailing them I feared you might be angry for being so bothered. You sound very busy in your letters now. And as I said before— <u>now</u> I don't want to lose you!

The picture. Remember I wrote that I had it taken for a remembrance of my life before the Army? The Army didn't take me.—You did. That picture is nice, but it doesn't mean much to me. I think I've changed—outwardly. Yes, I am conforming to convention. I have worn no makeup for weeks, my clothes never were

64

different from what others wore. I guess there is something about my walk—but I am told I walk just like my grandfather did! So, on that score—I am getting along.

That picture is Sidney French. I wrote this book—not because I like to write but because I wanted an opening for myself. <u>Then</u>—I thought—if the book had any "drama" possibilities I might—must—play Sidney. From there perhaps an unique career in the theatre could begin. These were my plans.

Well, I think those plans have grown up a little since you. I would still like to do Sidney in drama—but be an actor in so doing. After "Sidney" was over I would return to my own shell—if I could—etc.

When as today I think of the <u>by</u> me, which I have been referring to, I come to this conclusion: if I could be busy writing or acting and accomplish something—at the start—something to fall back on—I don't believe there would be need to worry about these sex questions. I honestly believe I could do without it. As I prepared my book for you all my sex energies went to my characters. Why couldn't this continue?

As I follow your letter I come to your technical paragraph. I am a bad speller but when I write it is swift and from the heart. Spelling can be the unpleasant task at the end—perhaps. I don't know what authors do about it. Also I had no time to check the book before sending it to you—I wanted it in New York as soon as possible. As for my English-convention again! You write of "spiked with despise." I like it—at least I see what I mean. If no one before has used "spiked" like that—why can't I be first? I hate the demanded use of nouns and verbs, etc. Why can't their uses be expanded into new forms? Also why shouldn't new words come into our language? All this I would have to talk over with you—and no doubt you would convince me how wrong I am. But in my English—I am stubborn.

I do believe I shall take Bridgeport from my book and put in a fictional city—perhaps a Barcroft, Conn. Bridgeport is too big—its society is too fine, I imagine for this story. I wrote of society as I see it here—a town of 7,000. Yes, society here is a mask—behind it a fairly low class of people. And I wanted my people to be people that a "low class" of readers might understand. My sister has done her nails in the parlor here and I do not object. And if my parents chose—we would be quite "society" here. Perhaps this manicure business displeases you, but would it occur so to ordinary people? I don't consider you ordinary. You are well educated, and just "well" everything. Not everyone is.—So—behind Windy Hill sit a family— not beautiful—just coming near to extinction and death. Perhaps once they were a beautiful family—but they have had their day.

When you get right down to it—in one sense—are people really pretty or fine? They can be fairly nasty I think—and I caught the French[e]s with their pants down.

I have seen people with two sets of manners. One for outsiders; the others tell their story. It is the revealing manners I want! What reader earning barely a living wants to have a book so above their understanding in reading? Don't think of these people as society (that was for convenience in the story) but as minds, and worlds thrown open. Probably my enviromental [sic] world and associates are very different from yours. But then I think of "Kings Row!"

What made Mina French an idiot to you? And I'm glad Mr. French was a little real. I put my dad into him somewhat. And I was glad he slapped Sidney too! I don't love Sidney. He's a character like the rest of them. It hurt me more to have Jayne die, than to have Sidney slapped.

Of course Sidney is a fool. I know that—I wrote it that way, knowing it. After so long Sidney realized his end. I wasn't trying to justify myself in writing this! I wrote of a person—I hope he was alive. Sidney means little more to me than Otto or George or the rest. I wrote Sidney as a part I could play in drama. Read it as if you don't know me—as many would not know me if it were published.

Yes, Sidney was a fool—but so was the "Christ" person with the sandals and the "Wagner" man. But such people exist and I wrote of one. Several people after reading my book remarked that they had never thought of such a thing. They knew it existed but never had occasion to think of it. Then why shouldn't they think of it now?

You say: "Your book <u>has one</u> value, as a pathological document!" Fine! That is all I want. Why can't it be accepted as thus?

Why drag me into it further than the author? I'm not asking any sympathy because of it. All I want to get is some money and a start. With what you have written—a colorless job as a typist must now face me. If that happens I shall be sterile.

If you understand this Sidney as you write you do—then it is enough, isn't it? Haven't I accomplished my end?

Sidney is bad—I have tried to make him real—so I made him unattractive. Your Dr. Gordon and my Sidney thought they were pretty wonderful.[27] Actually they weren't at all. I agree, in 10 years Sidney would be terrible. Thank God he died—but even before his death he wasn't nice to many people—for instance this Dale.

Now to something that has really concerned me. This "Clair de Lune" business. Why do you pick it apart? I love that music—I don't know why, but it makes no difference to me whether Debussy cared for it or not—I do—and so do many, many other people. People who don't know these other compositions you mentioned. If when I put "Clair de Lune" in my book the reader can hear it—it is so familiar—then that is enough. "Pagodes" or "Preludes" leaves me cold—I don't know what they are!

And so—Sidney wasn't interested in what Debussy thought. To him—as to me—Debussy meant "Clair de Lune"—"Reverie"—"Faune etc"—"Sunken Cathedral"—"La Mer." In "Clair de Lune" Sidney could dream. Besides Sidney was not a great pianist. He learned that concerto by the skin of his teeth. Sidney can just play well—that is all. If he had worked always with a goal as a pianist in mind what a brilliant life he might have had. But that is the sad part of the story—he was hopelessly sidetracked.

I don't understand this sentence: "It is a vaudeville term to speak of a pianist as 'a talent.'" You make me feel very ignorant. Now—this is natural—don't take this wrong. I have had only 12 yrs of school and your letters are from a learned and experienced brain. Forgive my bewilderment—and these letters are not something I can carry to my "lit" teacher for interpretation.

---

27. Dr. Henry Gordon, a character in Bellamann's novel *Kings Row*, unnecessarily amputates the legs of young Drake McHugh after an accident because he does not approve of Drake courting his daughter.

My people do all talk alike. I am not pleased with this—but I am just starting. Perhaps after some years at it that quality would come. As I wrote before: yes, back of Windy Hill's proud front—lived a horrible family. Not rich in spirit—but dying a terrible death. If this does not shine through as my meaning, I have failed in giving the story of the Frenches.

Then you say it can't be published. What is your literary point of view about it? Is every reader thinking the same as you as he reads? You know much more than most of us.

My first draft of "The Surf" was read by various people with many opinions resulting. Several said the book was so thrilling they couldn't lay it down until they had finished it. Some were shocked by it and scared to death after reading it. Most of them thought a great deal of the ending. One girl said it was like mysterious music, another, going down, down into one's soul. Someone said my vocabulary was too small. Another, that the ending was marvelous. Another, how could I know so much at my age? Several—who are not book readers generally—were quite spellbound—so they said. Many are sure it will be published and is a great book.

I liked hearing this—and I am glad I have you too. Your words mean much to me. Are you telling me to forget it because you think publication would hurt me? One man I know thinks this. So what if it isn't a <u>great</u> book? That is not what I'm after. I want a start—something to fall back on. Do you honestly feel that no publishing house would touch it and why? My book may not be good but look at the shelves of books which I think are pretty bad. Why not take a chance? Is there no publisher some place? Perhaps we don't see eye to eye on books. I like books such as "What Makes Sammy Run" by Budd Schulberg. I lose all interest and can't read past the first few pages of Hilton's "Random Harvest." I can't see that O. H. Prouty's "Now, Voyager" is a masterpiece. I liked Watkins' "On Borrowed Time." I shall never forget the greatness of "An American Tragedy" by Dreisler [*sic*]. I like a story—not a bunch of good words![28]

---

28. Tedd's list of books suggests he likes a good melodrama.

You say about this book—put it away, forget it. But can I? Have I ever done the "right" thing? Will I ever learn? I don't think so.

Ach—at a time like this all that Leinsdorf junk is just junk! It's getting in my two cents worth with men like you that is my life—it's the big me. Keep me busy and the "little me" doesn't exist. That is why I think it bad to forget this book—the "little me" would come out again! That's bad.

Hurt me—yes, you have in a slight way—but you make me want to fight. If there can be a new style of writing, etc, why shouldn't I be the one to bat my brains out doing it? The productions of many men weren't approved up at first.

Wagner had a hard time, as did many others. I don't like to think I'll be so unhappy—but I don't want to lie down yet.

Mr. Bellamann, aren't you expecting a lot from me as a beginner? I know, the world doesn't care if I'm a beginner or not! You say I need to accomplish! Yes, I do. This letter doesn't give me that. Oh, how glad I am that you are as you are, write as you do. That is why I can burn up in this letter to you. We are two fairly sensible people, aren't we? Then don't you think the best friendship is a completely honest one? Please understand when I say that your opinion is of one man. I respect it tremendously, but perhaps someone else must knock me down. Do you want me to read your letter and crawl into my shell—or be like this? In a short time I may feel badly for writing this but I had to get it out of my system.

Your friendship is the most beautiful thing in my life—believe that! I hope your illness does not last. I am selfish and don't want you so ill that you can't continue to aid me. I wait for your letters pityfully [*sic*]. I have been lost until this letter came.

If you have no further use for "The Surf" could you return the copy. At this moment I fear I feel that I must at least submit it to some publisher. If I didn't there might be that question of "maybe" always with me.

I shall wait breathlessly for your reply. I pray I do not lose you by this.

Gratefully,
Tedd

15
TEDD

161 Sheffield St.
Bellevue, Ohio

October 22, 1943

Dear Mr. Bellamann,

I was more than overwhelmed with happiness when I received your letter. It was more than I dared hope for. By this time you shall have gotten my answer to your discussion on "The Surf." I hope what was in that letter was what you expected to find to some degree. I had to blow off steam. Today I am fairly calmed down. I suppose I am ready now to look at the whole thing more rationally. I was quite tragic yesterday, but now I am prepared to dive into some of your recommended books: although our library is small and vastly inadequate.

Again you seem quite concerned about me. Yesterday I felt quite like an outcast. I knew it was foolish to build too many dreams of success for "The Surf"—but that is what happened.

Now as to this split personality business. I suppose it is evident at a time like this. Today I am superior—uninterested—in this "man" problem. I have so much more to accomplish—so many better things in the world. I have to laugh or at least smile at myself at times like these—I feel far removed from dreaming. I have too much time on my hands. When I am pursuing what I believe shall be my career—as in the past with music—there aren't enough hours in the day. Now there are too many.

This brings me to something which must be settled. Very well—my book wasn't what I hoped and others hoped it would be. My family and myself, who is tired of sitting around, are pressing this job question. The doctor warns about health—but I believe I am in best health when I work. Perhaps this doctor isn't thinking of the mental strain of inactivity. It would be a "clerk" job in an office for me no doubt. And so—would I become sterile? I have never thought of going on to school because I didn't know what I would care to study, feared college students, and probably would not have the finances. No, I have never cared to think of college. The Army waits for me sometime in March. If I could only have gone in September and gotten started. I fear the beginning, the adjustment.

My best—and only—friends are women—probably I do not find them at all disgusting when I am not in a mood. Truly, I could not understand why Jamie W. was so upset by them. They don't <u>usually</u> affect me that way. I like them and their company, I feel quite at home with them—fatherly! The sight of their upper leg or breast doesn't excite me, but embarrasses me. I turn away. "How awful if they would think I was staring" runs through my mind. I have not found in one yet—the complete companionship I would like to have. I wouldn't mind living with a woman—as a companion—but I don't believe I'd want anything else. I am at ease with a girl, not with another boy generally. The only event of any relationship that you inquire after is that little boy and girl episode I wrote of. I can remember nothing else at all. But may I say this, the one thing that angers me is when one advises me to stop loving men and love women. I prefer those who say—just stop loving men. I think I can accomplish that.

I have a habit of laughing at girls who set men on altars. These girls seem never to inquire after the "whys" of men. Perhaps that is right though.

No, I can't think of a girl with an ultimate sex merging in the end. But nothing would please me more than having a girl fall in love with me so that I could kindly turn her to another man and remain her dear friend. I am very vain and shallow (just like those opera singers!) and enjoy admiration of my physical appearance which this late photo has received from the nurses of St. Luke's Hospital where Jeanne has displayed it. The fact that these girls want to meet me, etc (not to really <u>stare</u> I'm sure) makes me want to be successful. Jeanne was so certain of this book—I can't let her down.

Mr. Bellamann—I am a boy, perhaps a man even. I like that. I don't believe I'm fooling myself in writing that. I should like being

an eligible bachelor. And when I recite "<u>Macbeth</u>" how passionate-
ly and yet how tenderly I clasp Lady Macbeth to my breast. I would
love to be a fine "Romeo" who hates to leave his Juliet as morning
comes. What could be more wonderful than being an actor with a
voice of dramatic and tender qualities and an artistic body? I don't
believe I could play any role—but Shakespeare—yes! How I have
longed for years to play Iago, but I do not understand the role now.
Will you be seeing "Othello?"

I am sure I am not a pianist. I could never memorize. I took
lessons for a couple of years—those teachers thought me fine.
Now I stumble through a simplified "Prelude—C# Minor" by
Rach[maninoff]—. "Clair de Lune." The first part of "Moonlight
Sonata." Things I like to try. I sing all the time. Love the role of
Fricka ("Die Walküre"—I have the score.) All operatic arias I
scream out. I think I could learn opera quickly. It is almost as if I
sing it by instinct.

Having run out of this kind of stationary I hope it won't seem
too awful to continue on other. I just can't leave with things unsaid. Oh, I talk all the time. Think and talk! What a life.

Please do send my handwriting to Dr. Teltscher. I shall be
both happy and grateful for your interest. Why—why do you do
this? Bother yourself so with one so unworthy? I am a horrible
sort of person, selfish, conceited, emotional, talkative to a tiresome
degree—and generally awful. But aren't we all—or most of us? I
hope there will come a day when I can help people. Adopt a couple of children or give to someone needing advice and encouragement. People have been kind to me—I am most grateful.

Dorothy back in Dayton has written that one of the office's
Lieutenants stopped her and said he had heard she had visited
with me on her vacation. She said that was true. He then told her
that he hoped the Major (who practically discharged me) would
not hear of this because the Major liked Dorothy but would not
have her associating with me. I think that is strange.

I had come to feel that the Major had done right in making
me resign. What else could he do? It was for my own good. But
how can he dislike me so? I admired the Major—yes—but only

because of his businesslike attitude—oh, he is an ambitious little man. He runs over everyone to get ahead. He is quite ruthless. Mr. Bellamann, honestly I can think of no time when I felt any attraction for him. He scared me to death—I always wanted to please him. Furthermore, his office was far from mine and we didn't meet for months. All my work went to him and never kicked back. When I had assistants working under me their work invariably came back. In fact I was told when I left—it certainly was not because of my work.

Nevertheless, I don't believe Major is being much of a man— at least I think he's being fairly ignorant. Lately I have wanted to apologize for my actions towards him—meaning all the trouble I gave him! But gee, maybe I shouldn't ever trod his path again.

So much written; so little said!

Back to "The Surf" if I may. Nothing could please me more than having you correct that copy. Do anything to it you wish. But I have a few questions. Could you give me a brief analysis on the other characters? Namely Isabel, Otto, and George. Also Henriette, Michael, and Jayne and Carl. Did Bradly or Abe interest you? They all mean as much to me as Sidney. <u>Just as much</u>! What about the plot threads of the story, the underlying currents—if you found any. The background. Paul Kearns. If you can think of Tedd Burr as the author or only as Sidney. I did not make Sidney attractive—and I'm not really Sidney. I don't carry on like that! Didn't I make him as hopeless as he makes himself? Why couldn't this be published? <u>Why</u>? I have counted on it so. Sidney <u>is detestable</u>. Wouldn't it sell? Books like "Equinox" are doing alright.[29]

I must stop, but remember, my heart is full of gratitude. I pray that some day I can return happiness for this happiness.

Sincerely,
Tedd

---

29. Allan Seager, *Equinox* (1943). The August 1, 1943 *Kirkus* review of *Equinox* begins, "Those who read King's Row for its lascivious and abnormal aspects will doubtless relish this unwholesome novel of New York literati. Personally, I thought King's Row vastly superior on every count."

16
HENRY

Ansonia Hotel
New York City

October 23, 1943

My dear Tedd,

Your letters came this morning. I am more encouraged about you than you can guess. I expect you to be hardheaded about a lot of things, because I know you will have to learn things the hard way. That is all right if indeed in time hard headedness can be combined with a capacity for learning. You ask why I bother. It isn't being a bother. I'm interested, and I'm not interested in you as a "case," because I don't think of you as one. I am interested in you as a person. I hope you have noticed that when I ventured upon advice I have never advised you on "moral" grounds. I didn't think you needed that. You don't seem to do anything to hurt anyone but yourself. My advices—such limited ones as I have made—are for and against such factors as may smooth your way, relieve your tensions and make things easier for you. I am very honest when I say I have no kind of reaction to your ideas on sex. They seem to me to be neither good nor bad, save as they concern your peace of mind. I have no judgements to make on anyone for anything. I do judge people on these grounds: what they do to others. The world divides into men of good will and men of bad will. The destructive people are bad. Personal habits, inclinations, etc.—these things are each person's business. I like you. I see you as a person terribly sensitive, and still taking attitudes which must inevitably increase your sensitiveness. You are like a person with one less skin than most persons. Things hit you harder and you react more violently. There are things in your make up which are hysterical. I think any psychologist (and I don't call myself one) would readily identify these qualities as such. People are likable or not regardless of personal idiosyncracies [*sic*]. The photograph of Sidney French as against the photograph of Tedd Burr gives the sympathy of my nature to the latter. Why? Because Sidney French considers himself superior and is saying plain as day that he doesn't need friends or affection and doesn't want them. And so the observer says: to hell with him. The other boy who looks his age and is all of the wistful appealing things that youth, bewildered and troubled youth can be, needs someone. I have been willing to be that someone if I can help.

All of my life has been spent with young people. I like them and I understand them better than I do my contemporaries. They have come to me for professional and personal advice by hundreds because usually I was in an official position to make that possible. Dean of the Curtis, of the Juilliard—etc., etc.

Now, a little about the book. I can assure you that your objections to my criticisms are not valid. Tedd, I can honestly assure you that the book is not good and that you won't find a publisher for it. That you will have to try for yourself in order to see. No—it isn't that my opinion is just one man's opinion. It is a professional opinion based upon professional training and experience. Just as I know bad piano playing when I hear it. It isn't just the subject matter, although that is against it somewhat. I imagine that a book based upon the inner struggle of a homosexual nature might succeed if tactfully done. Radclyffe Hall's "Well of Loneliness" did succeed. But it was censored in England, was published in France and smuggled into England, was first barred here and later released, and was generally misunderstood by the public who spoke of it obliquely, and leered obscenely at mention of it. <u>And</u> it was done in perfect taste. There were no <u>episodes</u>. She wrote on the assumption that the intelligent reader knew what Lesbianism really is. She wrote entirely of the psychological struggles, the inner stresses and strains. Her book was understood and liked by intelligent readers; it was read by all others in the hope of finding out something they didn't know or else in the hope of some kind of titillation to be derived.

I think your book only skims the surface. It doesn't cut deep. If you ask me to [be] more specific, I'd have to say I don't know how—I know only that this is true. You can't build an entire book on a lack of sympathy for the characters. There is hardly anyone there who commands sympathy. I think those whom you hoped to portray more fully are shadowy and unreal. The whole book is unreal—it is a kind of wish-fulfillment book. But, Tedd, it is a document, and as such will not find a publisher. For one thing the psychological literatures are filled with many such documents. It is not new.

A play was on here three or four years ago which dealt with homosexuality, and did it as tactfully as possible. Frances Starr played the role of the mother. The author made the severe mistake of placing the young boy and older man <u>both</u> on the stage at the same time. You could feel the wave of disgust sweep the audience. The play lasted only a few days.[30] On the other hand Helen Mencken played the role of a Lesbian in a French play here several years ago, and with great success. The "other woman" never appeared at all. She was called on the phone once. But all that one saw was the fateful struggle of the younger girl against a force more powerful than she was.[31]

You tell far too much in this writing. Sex situations cannot be as roughly handled as that. Yes, yes, I know "Studs Lonigan," Faulkner and the others. Faulkner falls short, too, because of his lack of literary skill. You can knock a reader down by saying less than all. Even in "For Whom the Bell Tolls" there are distasteful pages. One wishes to say: "Yes, yes, I know how it is done." You don't describe in technical detail a man going to the bathroom in the morning because all the world knows about it. It isn't necessary

---

30. Henry is referring here to Chester Erskin's *The Good*, which opened October 5, 1938 at the Windsor Theatre on Broadway and ran for only nine performances. In an October 6, 1938 review of the play in *The New York Times*, Brooks Atkinson pans the play, writing, "Mr. Erskin has written his play with the weariness of a man shocked by human depravity" (7). Atkinson calls the homosexual son an "unsavory character" and "abnormal son," but this is not the only part of the play Atkinson criticizes. The play also includes extramarital affairs and a suicide.

31. Édouard Bourdet's 1926 play *The Captive* ran successfully on Broadway for seventeen weeks but closed when the New York City police arrested the entire cast for immorality. The charges were later dropped, but the show never reopened.

and telling too much is a lack of literary skill and tact.[32] Now, you will quote "Kings Row" against this argument. But even there I didn't go too far. With Renee and Parris as children, pretty far, because there was an idyllic quality in their affection. But I had to rewrite that paragraph a dozen times to say all I wished without saying it. But you didn't <u>see</u> Dr. Tower have an affair with his daughter. Sometimes one writes for emotional shock or to create horror. It is very difficult to write out a disgust, very. And these efforts have largely been confined to a kind of distasteful "underdog literature" of little importance.

Now I will have to take sharp issue with you on the question of language. One may certainly expand the expressive powers of language <u>when the inherent resources are exhausted</u>. Of course that was done by James Joyce, who will nevertheless go down as a mistaken genius.[33] But you have not improved the expressive powers of the language with some of these oddities. You defeat your very purpose, because you arrest the reader when you do these things. You stop him dead in his tracks. You see you do not

---

32. James T. Farrell's Studs Lonigan trilogy—*Young Lonigan* (1932), *The Young Manhood of Studs Lonigan* (1934), and *Judgment Day* (1935)—are realist novels that depict the poverty and gritty reality of the Irish population in Chicago's South Side during the Great Depression. William Faulkner wrote many novels set in the fictional Yoknapatawpha County, Mississippi. His writing style is characterized as lyric (or excessively detailed). His 1929 novel *The Sound and the Fury* was written in an experimental stream of consciousness style. Some novels—such as *As I Lay Dying* (1930)—include explicit discussions of sex. His 1931 novel *Sanctuary* includes an infamous scene in which an impotent man rapes a young woman with a corncob. Faulkner won the Nobel Prize in Literature in 1949. Often contrasted with Faulkner in terms of literary style, Ernest Hemingway was known as a writer who wrote sparingly, just the "tip of the iceberg." This seems to be the advice Henry is giving to Tedd. Even so, Henry seems to take issue with a few sex scenes in Hemingway's 1940 novel *For Whom the Bell Tolls*. Hemingway won the Nobel Prize in Literature in 1954.

33. James Joyce experimented by writing fiction in a stream of consciousness in novels such as *A Portrait of the Artist as a Young Man* (1916) and *Ulysses* (1922).

present to the reader a new image, but only a new verbal combination which is either puzzling or annoying. Do that twenty times on three pages and the reader closes the book. Such innovations anyone might someday do when he is extremely expert. Language grows through necessities not through arbitrary determinations to make individual imprints on its structure. You can't force such changes. And, truly, I do smile a little at young users of the language improving it when they haven't learned to use what there is of it. The English language is incredibly rich. It is a vast language. Few people since Shakespeare have touched its limitations—perhaps not even those few. Anyway your concern as a writer is not with making an impression with language but with story and with ideas. Mr. Faulkner has distorted language too in his efforts to create effects, but his genius for a story carried him over such dangerous shallows and he has been read and liked <u>in spite of</u> these freakish innovations.

In the one sentence of yours I quoted it wasn't the word spiked I was quarreling with, though that is bad, too, because it gives the reader a mistaken image of what you meant, but using despise as a noun. What is the matter with "detestation"? Your shades of meaning are not helped by these things, nor, are they that important.

You will find that the book is not good because of its lack of reality. However much you may have drawn from real life you have not put it across. Most of these characters are paper thin, and their talk is fearfully artificial whether alone or in company. One thing I don't quite know how to explain to you. There are differences of opinion which are just differences of opinion, and other differences of opinion which are matters of fact. Just because you think a certain thing has a certain quality may be due to your limitation or lack of experience. Let me reduce this to lowest common denominator. You did try to represent Sidney as a genius, or he wouldn't have been acclaimed at an orchestral concert. But suppose you had said he sat in the twilight and played "Hearts and Flowers"? Wouldn't you say the writer slipped badly on portraying his genius? Listen, Tedd, not only Debussy himself, but any serious critic would say "Clair de Lune" is not good Debussy. This is now <u>consensus</u> of opinion. It is a sugary little piece, though still in Debussy's good taste. Don't fight back about trivial matters. I don't go off half cocked about matters of opinion. But matters of fact I state with assurance because they are not just my ideas or opinions.

If I could talk to you I could cover ground that I can't cover this way. I have to conserve strength because I am still recovering from a severe illness of two years ago. I have a tricky heart that doesn't permit me stairs or even picking up a suit case. So when I take time for this I am doing it out of a friendship that I hope can help you over some of the rough spots and save time for you, and save you hard knocks. I rarely see anyone. I have not seen even my publisher in a year. So please don't fight back unnecessarily. I have a certain amount of experience. I know certain things. I shall not offer you anything that is not genuine in the way of knowledge or suggestion. When I am in doubt I say so.

What one's friends or acquaintances say about one's work is worthless. Your friend Jeanne is clearly not a literary critic. So, if you wish, go through your manuscript carefully, correct spelling—you will recognize the spots—and try it on publishers. Beware of any publisher that asks any kind of payment for publication. They are the sharks of the publishing world and will do nothing for a book after it is published. So much is in promotion. My own publisher spent a year in prepublication promotion and must have spent a fortune in advertising. We got lucky breaks, though in general most of my books have had not too good, or else downright unfavorable critiques. I wish I could advise you to try writing something else, forgetting these highly colored and sensational effects. You know of course that it is axiomatic that one must write of the things he knows and understands. You didn't know Sidney French because you had no perspective on him. I didn't know Kings Row when I lived in a similar town. Experience and reflection on experience. I no more believe in an inexperienced actor doing Shakespeare than I believe in an inexperienced pianist with no technic being able to present Brahms' two concertos with the Philadelphia Orchestra. You are not down to earth. Not being down to earth is symptomatic of your age. If you were a first water genius you wouldn't need advice because you would have found your way. And I see that you must learn some things the hard way.

I will send along a grumpy photograph as a scolding presence—not quite, I don't scold. I'll get your manuscript off to you as soon as I can.

Your friend, sincerely,
Henry Bellamann

I must tell you that authors in general do not try to market their own books. They have literary agents. Sinclair Lewis, Hemingway—all of them. My own agent is the very Tiffany of agents but I don't recommend trying that office, just because I know in advance the verdict you would get. Perhaps you'd rather go direct to publishers. Many of them won't consider an unsolicited manuscript, and when it isn't brought to their attention by a reputable agent it may not get more than a cursory reading. There are bad agents who want fees for reading or for correction, or something of that kind. They are fakes. The reputable agent will handle only what he thinks can be sold. He charges no fee for handling. If he places the book he gets ten per cent of the royalties.

I cannot recommend an agent. If you wish you might write to the Authors League and ask Miss Sillcox to recommend an agent for a young writer with a first book. But I advise against it. I must. The address of the Authors League is 6 East 39th street, N.Y.C. I am a member of the League but I don't know the officials at all. I have never been to the offices.

When I say forget this particular book I am only trying to steer you clear of heart break.

17
HENRY

Ansonia Hotel
New York City

October 23, 1943

My dear Tedd,

Some things I forgot this afternoon. There is a story by Thomas Mann, rather a distinguished piece of work, called "Death in Venice." It is called a long story, but runs almost novel length, It is the story of an elderly German teacher on holiday in Venice and the lamentable result of a homosexual love for a small boy. I suggest you find it and read it. It is in a collection of Mann's stories. I suggest it because it is a great writer's effort to put one of these cases on paper. Now, you will say, there is such a story by a great man. But its success, if so, and its effect is due to superlative writing. You spoke of "Equinox." Did you read it? It also skirts the subject. It is intelligent, and it is well written. Even at that I understand it is not doing well. You can write about almost anything if you can write extremely well. I have been trying to say, without hurting your feelings, that you do not write well. My first disagreement with your book is that the story is not well conceived, not really very interesting, and not well done. Tedd, I'm being, as I told you I would be, utterly indifferent to how harsh my judgements are. But they are not personal opinions. They are literary judgements. After all I was a reviewer for many years and had a pretty good reputation as a critic. Anyway—

You know, if you wish me to stick around and try to see what we can work out for you, you must not be resentful, and above all you must not be catty. Remember I have never said you were homosexual, but one of the characteristics of real homosexuals is cattiness. They always have the worst of feminine traits.

To answer some of your retorts. Of course it makes a difference that you put some things down just because you happen to like them. You aren't writing for yourself. And there are artistic standards, literary standards, which are not simply someone's individual bias. They are based in a founded aesthetic. And one doesn't write just for uninformed readers, even if uninformed people read. You are going to have to meet standards of publishers.

I am not trying to crush you, or your ambitions. I am trying to tell you that you have much, much to learn and a long way to go. No, I don't really expect much of a boy. You are a boy, and an appealing one. I certainly don't want you to "crawl back into a hole." But I have said actual truth because I want you to be able to <u>take it</u>. If you can, you will escape having to take harsher judgements later when they matter more. All of us are likely to have to do disagreeable jobs. I've had terrible ones. All of us seem to have to waste so much valuable life just learning about life, and just making a living—the last being a noble enough cause, maybe.

Of course there are a lot of dull books, and a lot of books that fail and are a loss to publishers, and their future books aren't accepted, and they don't make money. I wrote four novels before Kings Row made a financial success. One good one, the first, two <u>very</u> bad ones, and a mystery story (a good one as mystery stories go) and then the success of Kings Row opened the way. Floods of Spring did less well, but the new book Victoria Grandolet has made a small fortune before publication—magazine, movie sale, and now a sale to the Literary Guild for their January book. I tell you this because there [were] <u>sixteen years</u> between the first book and the appearance of Kings Row. There were also two volumes of verse neither of which seemed to disturb the fame of Homer, Dante or Shakespeare! You see I had a long and successful career in music. I don't know that I pined to write but I read and thought and observed and experienced and felt my way toward a sense of form, etc. Even so, many critics referred to Kings Row as a chaotic book—which it is not. The form underneath it is as strict as that of a Bach fugue. The picture, which was an enormous success, was simply skinned alive by half of the New York critics, while the other half was enthusiastic. It has made millions for Warner Brothers.

I didn't begin to write until I was past forty, and for so many years after I had begun writing I had to continue making my living with teaching, lecturing, executive work, etc. I had no one to help even then, but I did seem to help others. Julia Peterkin, who was a Pulitzer Prize winner with her novel Scarlet Sister Mary was my piano pupil, and I did pretty much teach her to write also. She would say so, and has said so.[34] But no one thought I needed help. No one did help, and I, too, had to learn the hard way.

The actual technical use of language is difficult. To say what you mean, and not say something which you think is what you mean. Writing has to communicate. It does have to be very simple, very clear, very direct, and you have to build your story, your sentences and paragraphs as a carpenter builds, and as an architect plans. Here one often does have to have outside advice — a surgical literary friend with a blue pencil.

I have had no such friend, though sometimes sharp eyed editors in the publishers['] offices who say: "Do you really mean this paragraph?" You discover, seeing it with someone else's eyes that you don't mean it. It is a good plan to analyze some novel that you like very much and see just what the author did do. Tedd, it is the very fabric of your writing that I think is immature and far from ready for any kind of publication. I cannot be mistaken about this.

Suppose you do have to take a desk job. It will tire you out, it will break your back and maybe your heart, but it won't kill you, and you won[']t be sterile as a writer. Look at Dreiser! Look at DuBose Heyward, frail and sick, selling insurance, and writing Porgy![35]

This second letter is just to reassure you of my sympathetic concern for you.

Sincerely,
HB

---

34. Julia Peterkin (1880–1961), American novelist. She took a train from her plantation to Columbia, South Carolina (where Henry was teaching at the time) for piano lessons. She spent more time telling Henry chilling stories about the plantation than practicing the piano. Henry advised her to write her stories.

35. DuBose Heyward published the novel *Porgy* in 1925. He and his wife Dorothy worked with George Gershwin to create the opera *Porgy and Bess*, first performed in 1935.

18
TEDD

161 Sheffield St.
Bellevue, Ohio

October 25, 1943

Dear Mr. Bellamann,

Oh what joy when I receive your letters. You'll never know—I read them again and again—naturally keeping them all. I have been meaning to remind you of that promise of photographs, but I felt I must not be so impatient.

How aware of this autumn can you be in New York? There seems always to me to be so much excitement in a city that the changings of weather go past quite unnoticed. For a while the sun filtered through an atmosphere of pulverized leaves. Then suddenly it rains, the wind blows and moans, there is a roaring furnace fire and one watches for snow. The trees stand so bare! Today is very dark and foreboding.

This past weekend I have been reading "<u>Beloved Friend</u>" about Tchaikovsky.[36] Your frequent mentioning him got me terribly interested. I had always meant to read the book but ended in putting it off. I am glad, I feel more ready for it now. I cannot truly put my reaction into words. Merely—what a man. My heart aches for him. I am glad he is dead and has escaped; I try to read myself into his letters and miseries. I can't imagine a homosexual at 40 years. As to his wife—how strange, I mean their whole relationship. Occasionally I cannot understand why Madam Von Meck does not grow weary of him—and then thank God she did not! I was further thrilled that the N.Y. Philharmonic should include his 4th Sy. on their program yesterday. It fitted in so with my reading.

---

36. Barbara von Meck and Catherine Drinker Bowen, *"Beloved Friend": The Story of Tchaikowsky and Nadejda von Meck* (1937), which included excerpts of correspondence between Tchaikovsky and Meck.

The story of Tchaikovsky I place with that of Nijinsky.[37] They both mean much to me. I thought one of my ambitions was to someday in some medium portray Nijinsky. But I would not care to flaunt Tchaikovsky's life. He was too self conscious about "Thi."

I am quite calmed down now, Mr. Bellamann, in reference to "The Surf." How right you must be. I have been knowing that more and more as time goes. My horizon seems just as black as before, if not more so, but I'm not excited, awfully resigned, though, I fear. If I can find a job—O.K. Cleveland shall have many plays— etc—that I wish to see.

Briefly as to my morals—I believe my passion to be sleeping. I want to be too busy to think further of this.

I cannot get over the fact that I am so privileged in having your friendship. Before I left school I wanted much to go to either Ju[i]lliard or Curtis. Now, corresponding with the former Dean— how fortunate I am. And yet in writing you I can so be myself. Perhaps that isn't good; but I hate airs. That is why I should be afraid of meeting you—what a disappointment I might be. Someday I shall be in New York I am sure. I am forever turning my eyes to that Mecca of the east.

I will explain my moment of confusion. Now that "The Surf" is over I hesitate plunging into some other writing. Namely because all the stories I had in mind deal awfully with sex. I liked the fantasy of "On Borrowed Time" and sometime ago sketched the idea of time stopping—everyone stopping—except for one man. Perhaps if I think further on this something will come. Then too I have an idea which puts the story back in the other war. But not knowing that time I feel awfully handicapped before I begin.

Is my trouble over-dramatizing? If I could write plainly and simply—I may be no writer but enjoy experimenting.

---

37. Vaslav Nijinsky (1889–1950), Polish-Russian ballet dancer and choreographer. Nijinsky was hospitalized for much of his adult life with schizophrenia. In 1936, his wife, Romola Nijinsky, published edited excerpts from his diaries in a book titled *The Diary of Vaslav Nijinsky*.

About language—I laugh and request your forgivance [*sic*] and forgettance [*sic*]! It is natural for me not to want to bother with the very foundation of an art. This has always been a fault of mine. I am impatient—and so wreck my chances.

I know that you shall not mind my helplessness in worshiping "Clair de Lune." Believe me—I am helpless. But your talk with Debussy thrills me—and I know hardly a thing said. I have a habit of putting dead musicians in the ancient past. I cannot believe that Wagner—Tchaikovsky—Debussy lived so recently. I know nothing of Debussy—I can find no biography on him. A few rumors are all I have. I like that famous portrait of him. So dreamy!

The writer you refer to—I have never heard of! Miss Hall—this Faulkner—J. Joyce—our library has nothing! <u>Our Library</u>! With a few dollars they struggle along. They get best sellers—some other silly, unread books—and that is all. But I love the place.

I know only "Kings Row," glimpsed at "Floods of Spring." I do not own one of your works. Mother won't permit me to start a library—no room. That is true—with my music, clippings, and magazines, where for books. But I think I could smuggle some of Bellamann in someplace. God—your new book—how wonderful!

I am most sympathetic about your health—how sad that you should be so hindered. But you still have <u>such a mind</u>. A strange combination, this mental and physical. My "wordless" gratitude grows as I realize the effort for your letters. Perhaps soon I shall begin writing more worthwhile letters—serious—intelligent. Now I am terribly scatter-brained! I wish I might do something very, very nice for you. If there were but some task you wanted done— how I would try.

I hang my head—I have not read "Equinox"—only reviews. But I have been crying out for it and may soon get a chance at it.

Please—sir,—don't frighten me so. If you only knew how I want you "to stick around." I am not resentful—no, no! Not a bit. Just so thankful. I hope I am not catty—I hope I am not! People I think catty bother me. These amateur actors in Dayton that I was with were never concerned about a play—just fighting among themselves. I realize I have only too few moments of "being real."

I don't like insincere niceness turned on and off—but to be just one's self and well liked!

I keep writing and writing, thinking of much, saying little. I sigh with contentment—Mr. Bellamann, you are a light.

I always see your letters coming from way off. They're so impressive with gobs of stamps, Tedd Burr, Esq., and massive envelopes. From that moment my day has a turn for the better.

What shall we write of now? I could keep you busy just reading much as this—how annoying.

If I can get an income again I shall begin on the piano and perhaps the organ I am sure. Maybe this time I would know more as to what it is all about.

I must call on a friend and musician you know as Abe La Bonte. He has Tchaikovsky records and a kind interest in me. Until later,

Yours ever,
Tedd

19

HENRY

Ansonia Hotel
New York City

October 31, 1943

My dear Tedd,

I have not been well for several days, so I've not gotten off to you either photographs or your MS. I'll do so as soon as possible.

Thanks for your cheerful and gay letter. This I suspect is more like you.

Please feel free to write whenever you feel like it and as much as you like. My life is sometimes for periods crowded with un-avoidable intrusions beyond control so that I am too occupied to sit at my desk. I do have small (not serious) heart disturbances which annoy me and which keep me in search of an oxygen tank for convenience sake. But I'm not an invalid.

All good wishes,
Sincerely,
Henry Bellamann

161 Sheffield St.
Bellevue, Ohio

undated

My dear Mr. Bellamann,

I can stay quiet for just so long, and then I must write you something, hoping it is not too much of a bother for you to be on a constant receiving end. For the last few days I have been in a state of utter depression and the only remedy I seem to be able to find is rushing into the kitchen to mix something up, the results of which usually bring back my former state. That is a part of me that perhaps you have not as yet been informed about, but just let me get started on my abilities as a cook and I can discuss endlessly. I am happy and completely worn out after one of my super, super dinners. Let me see, in some book on horoscopes, etc., those coming along in July with Cancer overhead are to have futures as cooks, no less.

Last night, I began on your recommended "Basic Writings of Sigmund Freud," and I have enjoyed and have been impressed by all that I have as yet read. Freud does not care that I must refer to a hugitive [*sic*] dictionary every few moments, but in spite of this feature, the mere fact that I am looking into his book elates me. As in the past my ambition as to my career in life has turned to my latest interest. Now, if I could be a Doctor of Psychiatry, what could be more interesting? And so I am, in a few days it shall pass, and once again I shall be tearfully pulling at my heart. But thank you for Freud—I never should have found him—I can certainly read his observations, etc., as coldly as the next person, but perhaps with a little more understanding. It was and is all very interesting. I thought from your letter you were being slightly hesitant in having me read him. I certainly relished it and had no reaction of horror. I once struck on this … "A female mind in a male body." I thought this combination of thought and words originated with me, but in Freud there are exactly the same words. As I walked home through a night's blackness after dabbling in Freud I thought that much you have written me dates to the mentioned author. Am I right?

A few days ago, when I was so depressed, I began to write what I hoped might be my second novel. I started it twice, gave up. Perhaps what I had written wasn't so bad, but now I doubt everything. I don't know if what I put down has any worth or not. You see, I thought the "Surf—" came from the soul, and in its not ringing the bell, any effort since, which means much less to me, must surely be bad. What I started was a story of a mother and daughter … the mother's struggle for security through a loveless marriage, the reactions of the daughter as she realizes this … all seen through the eyes of a young boy just out of school, and seeing life for the first time really.

I have given you little here, but do you think from this there may be a story there? Unfortunately, I take much of it from my friend Jeanne's life. As you say, for me I must write almost entirely of myself or my close friends. And I don't want to hurt anyone, as I think I might in so writing.

In another autobiographical line lies the story of myself and the three girls that made up our Dayton quartette [sic]. In a year's time we have all been parted for some reason. We seemed so naive when we became friends and so much has happened since then. The very gay Bettye returned to her home because she was in love with a young man who did not return her spiritual love. His past and present were quite mysterious. He had a daughter, but whether he was married or not, we never knew. This man took to Bettye … quite physically … but that was not enough for her. We used to cry nightly over it. She packed up and went to Kentucky to forget him, swearing never to love again. In Kentucky she became her old self, and gradually broke with us. Her friends are of the moment and she goes on and on with silly, but unhappy, adventures. I shall always remember her for her unconquerable spirit that she would learn to smoke, no matter what.

Nancy was engaged to a Captain, who after some hotel-room-reservation episodes jilted her. A girl always wearing too much makeup and so typing herself, she became even worse and attracted many men. I was in some way jealous of her, but also felt her foolish to throw herself away on any man who chanced by. Naturally she couldn't understand me, or that there were such as me in the world. She went with many men, one a father of a small child. Gradually she and I became almost bitter enemies, and fought over the affections of Dorothy, the third member of the party. Nancy's appearance and actions were seriously criticized by the Major we worked for, but she, as I, went on her merry way. I have just learned that in the past few days, a soldier at the field held Nancy responsible for his contracting a social disease. The health officer, a good friend of ours, had to charge Nancy. Examinations found her diseased, she was immediately released, and I know no more except that she plans to go directly to Florida where I believe stays the one "nice" soldier she ever met. But before Nancy left, she saw to it that several other girls in the office were dragged through some dirt, and so lost their jobs.

I shall tell you of Dorothy too, knowing that you will hold this confidential. Dorothy is very near and dear to me. As a high school girl she was in love with a boy who believed in constant physical love. Dorothy would leave with him after church services and yield to him. Then after a comparatively long time, he broke with her and entered the Army. When I first met Dorothy she was almost mad. The fact that she had <u>sinned</u> directly after church and all those other times bore terribly on her mind. She believed she really loved this boy. Ever since I have known her she has not been able to stand the touch of a man. At first she wanted only to die, but since she and I began going to concerts, etc., she has more of a zest for life. Now that this has happened to Nancy, she seems utterly crushed again.

And then there was myself of whom you know quite everything, my struggle with myself and the world that "eyed" me.

Four of us, just out on our own for the first time. All this, these lives seem big to me. They are my start. I don't know why I write of them to you. If this is all just so much talk to you, throw it aside. But I believe in a friendship based on letters such as ours the smallest interests of one should be communicated to the other. You write of observing the gamut of life. Here is what I have seen, yet how can I write of it … yet. I am not sorry I have lived with the three I have mentioned … I know their lives and stories do exist. How unique seems the plan of each life … and we are just all beginning. What is to be the ending … ah, that is it … the ending. Perhaps I shall never know.

I like to write to you. I can be so honest … it is merely a writing of thoughts. I don't permit myself to ask … "Should I send him this or that." I rather act on the impulse. Perhaps in so doing this … I have a sort of fear of ever meeting you. I look at your picture in <u>Current Biography</u> every time I am there and read with renewed interest the sketch of your life. How I wish you would send me your picture. I wait impatiently for it. And so you are interested in Amy Lowell. "Patterns!"[38] A few years ago I sketched that poem with illustrations of a bad kind in an art class. I had the book bound, but it lies here unfinished. I never had an opportunity … or interest enough … to complete it. It is frightfully bad.

Now for something I have meant to write for some time. I know a conductor-musician who prior to the Army life he now leads, taught music of some nature at a college near here. He was short and fat with hands that waved through the air continually with his conversation. This man was satisfied I believe with not one of today's performing artists. He lived with the records of Gadski, Eammes [*sic*], and Nordica. If not with the records, with the memory, or of what he had heard from old timers. He spent his young manhood studying in Vienna and Germany. He was preparing the role of Lohengrin for his operatic debut when his father died here and the family's income stopped. He left his fellow artists, Fisher and Novotná, and returned here to teach.[39]

---

38. Amy Lowell, "Patterns," an Imagist poem originally published in 1915 in *The Little Review* and then in Lowell's 1916 book *Men, Women, and Ghosts*. The poem describes a woman walking through a garden after learning that her lover has been killed in battle. The poem focuses on the imagery of the woman's "stiff, brocaded gown" and the garden around her rather than narrate her emotions.

39. Johanna Gadski (1872–1932), German soprano; Emma Eames (1865–1952), American soprano; Lillian Nordica (1857–1914), American

I have never heard him sing or make notable reference to ever singing since Germany. He goes throughout the country attending concerts. He usually gets up and leaves after the first numbers. I remember he thinks Pons quite terrible, etc. etc. He also said that Bampton would sing no more soon. He said, "She's an ambitious Jewess, so she sings soprano. Someday, soon, her voice will go!" His name is Elmer Frank.[40]

I always felt a little sorry for him, because in my ignorance of artistry I could still enjoy music of today … he could not. Since then I have often wondered if learning music technically and critically did not spoil much. I fear I have put what I mean quite badly. For instance, Wagner is often spoiled for me because Melchoir [sic] almost always sings. I think his voice is tired, used, old, past its day of glory, and he won't give in. I hope the "Met" can this year give some Wagner to another tenor once in awhile. And he is your next door neighbor … I cannot imagine that. As you mention who lives in the hotel I can hardly realize so many names being gathered under one roof.

I enjoy so much your letters, that I want terribly to find other strangers to correspond with. Naturally I know that now my letters are written badly, but perhaps after some time I shall be able to write as did Tchaikovsky, Ellen Terry and Bernard Shaw.[41]

[no signature]

---

soprano; Sylvia Fisher (1910–1996), Australian soprano; Jarmila Novotná (1907–1994), Bohemian soprano and actress.

40. Lily Pons (1898–1976), French soprano and actress. According to an August 11, 2014 post on *Sandusky History*, a blog of the Sandusky [Ohio] Library, Elmer J. Frank (1904–1961) was born in Sandusky, Ohio to parents of German descent and studied piano and voice in Europe before the outbreak of WWII. After serving in the Army in the Panama Canal Zone for two years, he returned to Sandusky, where he taught music until his death in 1961.

41. Ellen Terry (1847–1928), English actress; George Bernard Shaw (1856–1950), Irish playwright and critic. Tchaikovsky, Terry, and Shaw were prolific letter writers, whose correspondence had been published. This suggests Tedd is already thinking about the potential publishing of his letters with Henry.

21

TEDD

161 Sheffield St.
Bellevue, Ohio

undated

Dear Mr. Bellamann,

A few days ago I wrote you but did not mail the letter for I felt it unimportant and of little value. Up to this time I have sent you my every thought and not sending these items to you did not cease in bothering me so you shall find the bulk of that letter enclosed.

I am grown accustomed to your occasional silences knowing that something is wrong. I am so glad then to hear from you but very sad over your state of health. I hope it doesn't give you too bad a time, but there is that time for so many when the physical gives out. Your invitation for letters as often as I care to write makes me most happy. How I have wanted you to write that and I have a particular reason. When I had a paper route while in school I acquired the awful habit of sometimes talking to myself on the route. In my lonliness [*sic*] whispering a conversation seemed to relieve me. And today, writing my thoughts—gay and disturbing both—makes me content.

How strange that I should have made you such an infinite part of me. You are like an almost silent partner within my life. I want to tell everything for it seems unnatural not to. I have a faith in your understanding or merely quiet listening. I don't believe I shall be revoked for my ideas and inner turmoils. If I could only really express all that I mean but my pen wanders away from my mind which today thrives fairly well, but in an utterly exhausted body.

Let us begin with my answering an advertisement by a Cleveland steel corporation for office clerks. They telephoned me and yesterday I was briefly interviewed and accepted for a very well paying and what I believe may be an interesting position. I should have been residing in Cleveland today but difficulties in

clearing me into that employment area necessitates correspondence with Dayton and all this requires time, so I am fearfully hoping my job shall be able to wait for me.

Living in Cleveland should make me very happy for there lie
my interests in art, dramatics, music, and literature. Also, people. I
must mention the fact that through this "job" ordeal I was entirely
at ease. My new appearance gave me confidence—thanks to you.
Without you none of this could be possible. I would have remained
utterly lost; but I do not care to think on "what might have been"
for I have too much faith in the actual design of my life. But nevertheless I am again expressing my gratitude.

While in Cleveland yesterday I ate in a fashionable restaurant
just to test myself—could I walk in there—would everything be
alright? It was. I saw the enjoyable movie "The Phantom of the
Opera"—how I enjoy the acting of Claude Raines (your Doctor
Tower).[42] In the evening I went to "Abie's Irish Rose." A sweet play,
but how it could have such records, I can't understand. Of course
by now the novelty of Abie and his friends is gone, and perhaps
that explains the tepid reception last night.[43]

Yesterday as I arrived home a neighbor who was discussing
the war with me informed me that one of the Rodgers boys has
been seriously wounded in Sicily. The name stuck in my throat—
Rodgers—the man I believe I loved as an eighth grade school kid
until now and beyond now. It was a fierce agony that stirred in me
until I learned it was not James, but his brother who had met this
injury. I cannot tell you of my relief. I had known nothing of Jim's
whereabouts for years. I further learned that this Jim is to arrive
home this week on a furlough after receiving his wings and com-
mission. I do not want to see him, rather I do not wish him to see
me. I fear that if I should glimpse him all the fires that cooled in the
past years shall break open.

---

42. Claude Rains played Dr. Tower in the 1942 film adaptation of
Bellamann's novel *Kings Row*.

43. *Abie's Irish Rose*, written by Anne Nichols, was a popular 1922
comedy about a Jewish man who marries an Irish Catholic girl.

Do I love him—and how strange to bring this deepness of me before you. Try to understand me, I need it on a point such as this. James is in a way my Michael—M. Rodgers—J. Rodgers.[44] Sidney's meeting Michael was much as I experienced myself, but what followed was as you said—a wish fulfillment. I don't know why I have any feelings for this young man, he never hardly saw me. It is a torture left from about five or six years ago. Whatever "love"—and it seems so strange to write "love" in that sense after Freud got down to facts, etc.—existed in me was a purely mental state. James is the one person I am content—as nearly as I can be— to stay in the background for and "love" in a quiet way not even in sight but in prayer for his safety and happiness. I want nothing of him or from him as I am, but would give my life if in the next ten days I could be the woman he learns to love spiritually as well as physically.

There, I've said it. Woman. That's in me, I have conformed externally, Mr. Bellamann, but I'm bitter and dream still. It's hard for me to express this "woman" desire of mine, but it's there. Does it make a difference to you? Oh, don't hate me—I love so helplessly. And hopelessly.

Now that this has been said I feel relief and in better spirits.

How did Tchaikovsky love—mentally or always physically? That biography through letters is fine, but it cuts such a wide part from him. Such are strange people.

I have received an invitation to come to Trenton to visit a flier friend of mine stationed there. I hardly believe I shall go—this young [man] was my model for the character of Hank Gladston, and probably he writes in the belief that this Tedd Burr is the old Tedd—you know him—the pretty boy. You see, that episode in "The Surf—" with Hank and the other three was not very fictious. Anyhow, a few days ago I had most of my hair cut off and I look absolutely skinned. That is a drawback of Cleveland, its stores have so many lovely things that a wanting to possess them grows in me. All my old wishful thinking returns.

---

44. Sidney's love interest in "The Surf."

I have renewed my correspondence with "Pat Prisor"—remember him? I'm sure as a sailor with no home—he's an orphan—he will welcome my frequent mail. To end quickly this forced finis let me tell you not to rush the manuscript back—take your time with it, and keep well.

Sincerely,
Tedd

22
HENRY

Ansonia Hotel
New York City

November 6, 1943

Dear Tedd,

Thanks for your cheerful, warming letter. If I have helped, or can, in any way, I am and shall be very happy about it. I do wish you to remember that I have not attempted any diagnosis beyond what you yourself have indicated. I think you see yourself pretty clearly.

The most I could wish for you is that you will be able to acquire a technique of living <u>with</u> the world instead of living <u>against</u> it. Inside of yourself you are whatever you are, <u>maybe</u>—maybe not. Whatever it is you must have no sense of guilt. A sense of guilt is the very devil of a destructive agency—much more than an inferiority complex. So, I do not suggest that you try to make yourself over until you know what you are making. But we <u>conform</u> in this world. You wear clothes because other people do. You adopt the standard use of a knife and fork in conformity. There are a lot of other things you must do in order to achieve the dignity of an aristocratic privacy—to go along unnoticed for any particularity.

There is a notable inconsistency in one of your points of view. You have imagined (I suppose) that you are not attracted by the feminine personality—<u>and</u> person. And yet you have tried to make yourself feminine because you <u>do</u> think it is attractive (as it is!). You see you <u>have</u> made a switch there somewhere.

I'm glad you are reading the Freud studies. Yes, they are difficult and many words are not in the dictionary. (I don't believe there is such a word as hugitive—even if there should be.)

I should like to see you living happily, adjusted somehow to your surroundings. One of the first and best steps you have taken already. I am certain that your own simple boyish self is the most attractive version of you you can make. Like your High School picture.

I don't suggest that you write yet. A technic of writing you must get somehow—either in spending yourself in straight letters to me, or in a journal, or whatever. But you haven't done your literary five finger exercises! Nobody yet has escaped that necessity.

I know a man in N.Y. who is I suppose a homosexual. But he appears as anyone else. What his private life is I don't know. I have no curiosity about it, but he is never conspicuous; he doesn't advertise, and he holds one of the highly paid jobs in his field. But he is a profound student, a serious scholar, a sincere research worker. There is no substitute for intelligence, and certainly none for a <u>trained</u> intelligence.

You see I have never accepted the idea that there is anything <u>wrong</u> with you that you can't adjust and live with. It is a question of adjusting and being happy <u>within</u> your own self-prescribed pattern of life. I am not a good enough psychologist to give technical advice: I can make only common sense recommendations and be very sincerely friendly.

I enclose a sheet from a current magazine: a note in writing by Maugham.[45]

Faithfully,
HB

Was your name originally Theodore?

---

45. *Enclosure:* W. Somerset Maugham, "Write about What You Know: A Word of Advice to Young People Who Want to Be Authors," from the November 1943 issue of *Good Housekeeping.*

Write about what you know

By

W. SOMERSET MAUGHAM

A word of advice to young people who want to be authors

Instead of writing this article I should be writing a letter; but I hate writing letters, and the prospect of writing this one is peculiarly odious to me because I have written it a hundred times already.

I have just been reading some short stories that a young man, twenty years of age, persuaded me to let him send me. He tells me that he wants a candid criticism; but I know, as he in his heart knows, too, that what he really wants is praise. And that is what I cannot give him. The stories are not badly written; he has at least taken the trouble to learn the elements of grammar, a precaution that young writers, both male and female, too seldom take; and his characters, though shopworn, are sufficiently individualized for the purposes of a short story; but he has chosen to write of subjects which, it is only too evident, he knows absolutely nothing about. That is precisely the error that so many young writers make, and it is because I can do nothing but point it out that I have been obliged to write the same letter over and over and over again.

It is at first sight strange that they should do so, since one thinks it much easier to write about what you know than about what you don't. The explanation, I suppose, is that they find the familiar commonplace and think that romance must be sought in the exceptional. That is why they are so fond of writing about painters, actors, singers, and fiddlers.

In one of the stories I have just been reading, a middle-aged farmer's wife, who, we are told, is a gifted pianist, suddenly writes a remarkable sonata and gets a distinguished conductor to orchestrate it. It doesn't require much knowledge of music to know that even a heaven-sent genius couldn't write a good sonata unless he had studied harmony and composition and if it is a good sonata what would a conductor be doing in transforming it into a symphony? Another story deals with painters in Paris. I would bet a considerable sum that the author has never been to Paris or even stepped inside a painter's studio. I know the paintings he describes as great masterpieces. They were painted half a century ago and now hang in the deserted rooms of provincial museums. Old ladies still think them good.

The fact is that when you write about things you don't know you fall into ludicrous errors. Of course a writer cannot have a firsthand knowledge of everything, but his only safety is to find out everything he can about the subject he proposes to treat. Sometimes he thinks himself obliged to fake things; but to do that with plausibility needs skill and experience, and it isn't really worth doing, for it is seldom completely convincing; and if the writer cannot convince his readers successfully, then he is done.

Now, the only way I have ever discovered he can do that is to tell the truth, as he sees it, about what he knows; and the point of this statement lies in the words *as he sees it.* There are no new subjects (and incidentally there is none so stale as the great singer, the great painter, or the great violinist); but if a writer has personality he will see the old subjects in a personal way, and that will give them an interest. He may try his best to be objective, but his temperament, his attitude toward life, are his own and color his view of things.

Let me give an example. James Farrell in *Studs Lonigan,* aiming at complete objectivity, has drawn a picture of lower-middle-class life in Chicago that gives an impression of complete verisimilitude. It is photographic, and they say the camera cannot lie. I suggest that another writer with a different personality could take the same environment, and even the same characters, and produce a picture that would be almost completely different.

My point is simple: the value of a piece of fiction depends in the final analysis on the personality of the author. If it is interesting, he will interest. It is true that the young writer cannot expect to have a personality that is either complex or profound; personality grows with the experiences of life; but he has some counterbalancing advantages. He sees things, the environment in which he has grown up, with the freshness and the energy of his youth; he knows the persons of his own family and the persons with whom his daily life since childhood has brought him in contact with an intimacy he can seldom hope to have with people he comes to know in later years. Here is material ready to his hand. If his personality is so commonplace that he can see this environment and these people only in a commonplace way, then he is not made to be a writer and he is only wasting his time in trying.

It is far from my meaning that he should not exercise his imagination. His imagination will work upon the facts and shape them into a pattern of significance or beauty. His imagination will enable him to deduce new facts from the facts he has observed. A writer need not devour a whole sheep in order to know what mutton tastes like, but he must at least eat a chop. Unless he gets his facts right, his imagination will lead him into all kinds of nonsense, and the facts he is most likely to get right are the facts of his own experience.

But now I must write that confounded letter, and the chances are that this boy will think I'm just an old fool who doesn't know what he's talking about.

47

Front page of Somerset Maugham's "Write about What You Know," *Good Housekeeping* (November 1943).

23

TEDD

161 Sheffield St.
Bellevue, Ohio

undated

My dear Mr. Bellamann,

This is my fifth attempt to write to you. For some reason I am finding it very difficult to gather my thoughts. There are any number of subjects weighing on me and to work them in properly is a task. Last night in my mind a lovely, poetic letter was composed. Alas, now it has flown. Bear with me, please, as I jump around.

An article in yesterday's paper has me a little confused and in a "Disappointed with life" mood. As you probably know "Outrageous Fortune" opened in the 48th St. theatre in New York recently.[46] I have learned that one of its themes deals with a homo-sexual. Of course I was interested. Naturally since reading Freud and your letters I have become homo-sexual conscious. If

---

46. Rose Franken, author of "Claudia" and "Another Language," opened her latest play, *Outrageous Fortune*, at New York's 48th St. Theatre November 4, 1943 with a stellar cast headed by Elsie Ferguson, who was returning to the stage after more than a dozen years, Maria Ouspenskaya, Margalo Gillmore, Margaret Hamilton, Eduard Franz, Frederic Tozere, Brent Sargent and Dean Norton. The play, dealing with tolerance of race, anti-Semitism, and homosexuality received mixed reviews. Critic Howard Barnes of the *New York Herald Tribune* wrote, "It is rather awful to think of being stranded with the people of Outrageous Fortune. Neurotic and defensive, they are explosive and rather disagreeable." Critic Wilella Waldorf of the *New York Post* wrote, "Outrageous Fortune may be more of a clinical study than a play, but it has an enlightened and tolerant viewpoint on some old problems, and it dares to talk out loud in a sensible manner on subjects that are usually mentioned only in a whisper, or never mentioned at all. See it." Franken describes the character Barry Hamilton as "tall, slender and good to look at. If he were a woman, he would exude a kind of inherent fragrance. In a male it must be marked against him as an extreme fastidiousness, and a sensitivity easily mistaken for a lack of virility." (Tedd's note)

a homo-sexual is one attracted to one of his own sex, physically, spiritually, and mentally, I am such a person. But if only attracted physically, and working towards physical possession, that is something else. I don't know what this "Outrageous Fortune" person is, but it sounds like a natural. Wouldn't I have a deep understanding of such a character? An intelligent understanding? But here I am, completely left out and undiscovered, lost in this massive world.

For as long as I can remember I have wanted to be an actor. There is much on the stage that attracts me; the costumes and makeup, the task of creating a character and mood, etc. What could be better, than to learn stage presence in such a role as in "O.F."? Even as an understudy. You see, what holds me back it seems is the knowledge that I am not one to play every type of role ... especially the masculine man type. In the past ... lately in Abie's Irish Rose ... I have seen young men play handsome, romantic parts that they were poor at. In time I suppose they would learn, but at the present they are disgustingly amusing for they act awkwardly ... their arms and hands too much in the way. I am summarizing what I mean very badly, but hope you know what I mean.

While in the Dayton group of actors I came near to the part of Blake in "Skylark."[47] I refused to be even considered for such a role, I refuse to be knowingly miscast as a romantic, handsome guy. It would only end with my being horribly conspicuous and foolish looking. So I can't bring myself to go into a group that would naturally expect the members to accept any type of role. In a role of a homo-sexual I would think there would be a chance for me to get my feet planted. Oh, how silly this all sounds. In the letters just thrown away, when I got to this point I gave up. But here I go a little further.

When I read a book or play I usually play each part as I read. A character appeals to me through its possibilities, not through its sex. So I came to find myself wanting to play many female parts ... found hope in the accomplishments of Bernhardt ... I wish you would write more of her ... such roles as Hedda Gabler, St.

----

47. Samson Raphaelson, *Skylark* (1939), a comedic play.

Joan, Opharre of "Wingless Victory," Regina of "Little Foxes," and "Rain"'s Sadie Thompson. I think I really have a model for this one. These are but a few. On the other hand I like "Macbeth," "Hamlet," and "Romeo" and "Shylock." Also Danny of "Night Must Fall," Gerald of "Ox-Bow Incident," Clay or Aubrey in "Penhallow" (the novel) etc.[48] I choose Shakespeare because of the poetry in movement as well as verse. But such parts are few and far, far between. Then along comes "Outrageous Fortune."

In the "Ox-Bow Incident" there was a part of a young boy who was awfully feminine. The actor playing the role was not feminine in appearance, merely not outstanding. It struck me that someone had explained the part to him and he did his best to carry out instructions. In one scene one of the prisoners ... wonderfully played by Dana Andrews ... smiles on him, obviously this Gerald is attracted to the man. Mr. Andrews seemed to understand the situation clearly, but the Gerald was lost. I almost rose protestingly from my seat. I have never forgotten it. It is enough to make me cry that I wasn't up there doing Gerald with all of my soul.

And so I think, who is playing in "Outrageous Fortune"? Is he doing justice to the part? Again I've missed an opportunity.

I had better shove off on something else. I write myself right into a hole.

Have you read "Penhallow" by G. Heyer? I feel in that novel an ally against you. If you thought my French[e]s a bad lot, you should meet the Penhallows! It took me a long time to get going in the book, but was I helpless once I got started. It is a murder mystery. I don't read many such books ... expecting something like "Rebecca" that gets into the best seller group.[49]

You see, with all this stage business, "The Surf" comes back to me and again I become reluctant to accept its end. Forgive me. You see, I've fallen into a state. This Cleveland job affords me security

---

48. Danny, see note 6; Gerald, see note 16; Georgette Heyer's *Penhallow* (1943) is a murder-mystery in which the cruel patriarch of the family is poisoned one day when the whole family is gathered at the country house, and every member of the family is a suspect.

49. Daphne du Maurier's gothic novel *Rebecca* (1938).

and how I hate it. I'll go see all the plays, etc. but always be the audience. I might try to write another book, but I just won't let myself rise to it. I'm a horrible sort. Why don't I throw security to the winds and dig into drama if I want that. But then I think, young actors have love even if they don't have security and success, and I have only myself. How sick I am of myself, too. I want to share someone's life, have them share mine. Am I always to be alone? Marriage, oh, how careful I would be to make such a step. As never before I realize what it involves.

I wish you'd slap me down, write what you actually think of me. It's only then that I fight back. I'm not a pretty kind of person. Tell me so. Beat me to the ground. I'm weak. Miserable.

Last night I still lay awake as the clock struck midnight. I thought of Jim. The street lamp nearby sent a rainbow of colors playing on the window glass. In the last days Jim's brother's death has been widely discussed. They talk and say "Rodgers" and I start and hold myself. I want to scream that Rodgers is a part of me, but I don't. I just sit and say nothing. He comes to me often now, and it's [so] beautiful that I want to cry, then suddenly you're there, snatching him away, and throwing reality at me.

Mr. Bellamann, expecting no answer I ask, why is it like this? How I would accept his love, give him hope as he flies in the war areas, take him when he returns, his children if he wishes, poverty wouldn't matter, and kindness, companionship, and devotion in old age. Of course I'm dramatizing. He's twenty-four now, unmarried I guess. Why? Surely I have no bearing on his life.

Somewhere in this town he is … now … last night. And here am I. Very strange. Very hopeless. I wonder what you really think of me, of this confession. You must loathe me. I wish I didn't mail things like this, but I have already destroyed myself before you.

And I don't really mean what I just wrote. I'm terribly mixed up. I wanted to write you, have tried so often without success. I'm just in a low mood, and yet I'm quite happy.

What else did I want to write? I don't know now. Three things were bothering me. I wanted to be in "Outrageous Fortune."

"Penhallow" was much like "The Surf" in some respects. HE is someplace here now. Three dreams remaining dreams.

I'll mail this silly thing, and write you really soon. At the moment how I would like to reach across the miles and take your hand. It is almost as if you are here now. With your firm countenance. But I am so underneath that look, even Henry Bellamann seems unreal. You aren't a person to me now. You're a spirit.

And now I must close for a million words are in my mind that I forgot to put down.

You have been such a help to me, such a part of me, may I say that I love you very, very much.

Sincerely,
Tedd

24

TEDD

161 Sheffield St.
Bellevue, Ohio

undated

Dear Mr. Bellamann,

Since my morning letter to you is sealed, I'll just sketch this note in appreciation of the letter just received. It all makes my previous efforts awfully silly but as I knew—once I wrote I would feel better. And your letter is like a cool hand on a feverish brow. For some reason I feel absolutely jubilant.

That article by Maugham did me worlds of good—thank you. How right he is and it was certainly well written and fun to read; but I wonder what author he was referring to. Did you think like my family here that I was writing of things I knew nothing?

I wanted to write this immediately after reading the "Tedd Burr, Esq." thing (how I love that) but was requested to stir up a Geo. Washington pie for lunch. Now I forget all my efforts.

For some reason I was expecting this Theodore business. People usually inquire. My father insisted on christening me Ted so I wouldn't go through life with a "nick-name."

So I was made Ted—just Ted. Now dad calls me Theodore. A teacher started doing it Tedd—I liked it and adopted the spelling. Oh, I've often wanted to change my name. Once I tried Buzza Cardoza. Then for sometime I was Teddira French-Burr. I even insisted while I was in school giving my name there as such.

Something in your letter made me happy: "I think you see yourself pretty clearly." I think so. I'm glad if I do. I like to think I'm looking in on it very coldly.

And I am glad you are not putting on your spectacles and diagnosing me all the time. I don't believe that I need it—golly I'm just another person.

I could start in with more disturbing discussions but I'll be different here. I get tired of being morose. I like to just go on and on saying and thinking nothing.

You sounded quite chipper in your letter. Feeling better I hope. I'm awfully proud at knowing you.

Respectfully,
Tedd

25
HENRY

Ansonia Hotel
New York City

November 10, 1943

Dear Tedd,

Off to you today are some photographs. Not too much like me—
the one definitely flattering. I shall answer you at length later. I just
wondered about the Theodore. I like Tedd; it's a good name.

You are right: you are not a "case." Let's forget clinical words.
You are just a person—and my friend.

Sincerely,
HB

Portrait of Henry Bellamann, included in Henry's November 10, 1943 letter to Tedd. Photocopy included in Tedd's transcription of the letters.

26
HENRY

Ansonia Hotel
New York City

November 10, 1943

Dear Tedd,

Do you mind pencil and copy paper? I <u>am</u> busy, but I am always concerned about you. I am glad that you write anything and everything that you wish to <u>say</u>. You are assured of a sympathetic and cordial reader. I recommend that you forget about the word homosexual; There are so many variations in human types that labels are difficult and misleading. And labeling yourself is like discovering symptoms of hay fever—presently you have it!

I don't know what you are, except being a very nice boy—and it doesn't matter beyond whether you are happy or not. I am never diagnosing. I can only make practical suggestions that may aid you in adapting yourself, discovering yourself, and unifying yourself.

You have a danger signal which has nothing to do with sex—directly. That is your extreme dejection followed by extreme exaltation. Part of that is just being young. But I'd try to avoid the extremes. I don't know if you know the name of Dick Morgan—he was a foreign correspondent, lived all over, all countries, wrote for smart magazines (wrote badly, too), did some terribly bad novels (and probably paid for their publication), he haunted the great and near great and lived in a state of picturesque hysteria—on top of the world and then down under it. He developed a persecution complex. He is now in an insane asylum. He is my nephew. A grain of common sense, a tiny bit of self-control and a few attainable (instead of impossible) goals might have prevented the catastrophe.

Don't let yourself run to emotional extremes. <u>Check</u> them. It's like rocking a boat, further and further until the momentum of the oscillation upsets the boat.

You <u>are</u> somewhat hysterical. Perhaps I should use the milder term of <u>unstable</u>. You react too violently. These are red flags. Calm down. You are also as a person (I should guess) three times as attractive when you are on an even keel.

Tedd, I have to be brutal about your book to save you heartache. It is immature. It is hysterical, quite unreal, and technically bad—bad writing. I don't say you can't write. Who can at eighteen? It isn't your subject. It's the complete nightmarish unreality of all that happens except in a few instances.

I shall send you "Equinox" in a few days. My publishers sent in a copy yesterday. Some of it is bad as bad can be. Some of it is fine. There are irrelevant paragraphs that shock for no reason. They don't get on with the story. The incest theme is discreetly done. There is a shadowy portrait of the girl that is touching. The portrait of the villain, an amateur psychiatrist—a mischief maker, that is really masterly. But about most of the writing is a reality that is rare.

One of your troubles so far is that you <u>cannot see</u>. You look at the world but you are seeing something that isn't there so that when you write what you think you see the result is false.

… All the agonies of spirit, whatever they may be or about whom, may turn out to be growth of yourself. I am determined that if you are going to be my young friend that you <u>must</u> amount to something good. I dislike the shabby people of the theater— <u>most</u> of them are, but if it turns out to be the theater, all right. No matter what so that you develop a <u>real</u> talent, and that your work is honest and fine, and not a <u>retaliation</u>. You still want to hit back at a world which you think doesn't appreciate, to hurt them, <u>to show them</u>. Tedd, my dear friend, no matter what you show the world they, or it, doesn't care a damn. You will have to work to satisfy an inner urge and demand.

Everybody wishes to beat his hometown and family into the dust of humble admiration. Why should anyone appreciate us for what we have <u>not yet</u> accomplished? When you do achieve you will have left them so far behind you won't care <u>what</u> they think.

… You cannot allow yourself to have a sense of guilt for anything you think or feel, no matter how much of a luxury it is. I was your age once and I remember awfully well what a distraught Hamlet I was! I recognize your stages of feeling. You must believe that I do understand them well, sympathize but I don't over dramatize them because you are going to come out of all of that one day—<u>triumphantly</u>.

Yours affectionately,
HB

Nov 10 1943

Dear Tedd

Do you mind pencil and copy paper? I <u>am</u> busy, but I am always concerned about you. I am glad that you write anything and everything that you wish to say. You are assured of a sympathetic and cordial reader. I recommend that you forget about the word homosexual: There are so many variations in human types that labels are difficult and misleading. And labeling yourself is like discovering symptoms of hayfever—presently you have it!

I don't know what you are, except being a very nice boy—and it doesn't matter beyond whether you are happy or not. I am never diagnosing. I can only make practical suggestions that may aid you in adapting yourself, discovering yourself, and unifying yourself.

You have a danger signal which has nothing to do with sex-directly. That is your extreme dejection followed by extreme exaltation. Part of that is just being young. But I'd try to avoid the extremes. I don't know if you know the name of Dick Morgn (?) — he was a foreign correspondent, lived all over, all countries, wrote for smart magazines (wrote badly, too), did some terribly bad novels (and probably paid for their publication), he haunted the great and near great and lived in a state of picturesque hysteria — on top of the world and then down under it. He developed a persecution complex. He is now in an insane asylum. He is my nephew. A grain of common

First page of Henry's November 10, 1943 letter to Tedd.

27

TEDD

161 Sheffield St.
Bellevue, Ohio

undated

Dear Mr. Bellamann,

I have decided to answer promptly, perhaps unwisely so before I have collected my thoughts, but you are such a tonic of energy for me and already you have become a necessary habit to my system. You can't know how impatiently I wait for those photos: a few days ago in the library I accidently [*sic*] came upon your photo and was quite startled by its familiarity.

And I had given "Equinox" up. I believe our librarian awfully shy: indeed our shelves are full of naive, lovely volumes, and practically anything hinting at shocking is forever barred. Oh, no, I am being unkind and foolish! Our library has little money for books: thus, the careful buying.

My dear sir, in thirteen letters think what you have done for me and with me! You have built me to the skies and you have dashed me kindly to the rocks of, hopeful, despair. You got me back on the track, outwardly. You've straightened me on a number of things. I can't help but feel that a great deal you write I have known for a long time, within myself, but had to have it spoken through another.

Mr. Bellamann, in the past weeks I've written to practically all my acquaintances and have received frightfully small answers. Of course, as I am now I have so much time, and they are busy.

I can sympathize there … but I hope these people like me. I thought they did. I have to get words out of my system, so I write letters, heaps of them. I do love the walks at night to the post office to mail them … That is compensation enough for my efforts. I like to write to soldier friends. I know quite how that is.

I try to write just as they know me or to fit their individual personalities and interests. Oh, but I should not let this little matter affect me.

But I hate this lonliness [*sic*]! I feel it so lately. Everyone is pairing off … I fit in on the sidelines with everyone. I suppose this is the position one enters before love or marriage, or is it youth? Oh, I know I'm close to you and all that but you are older and wise … I think we need friendships on a more common level of age and intelligence too. Now, with Dorothy nothing need remain to be unsaid.

In further reference to Dayton: it seems I'm awfully tied there. The government really froze us to our jobs. So far I cannot be released to work in Cleveland. This calls for all that Dayton business to be distastefully raked over the coals.

Whether I can leave after that or not still is in question. I cannot work in my old place for the obvious reason—and I can never go back there. My pride and all that! So I hang uneasily in the balance.

How really morbid I am but not really, merely bored. Tolstoy's "Anna Karenina" is just started and lies yonder waiting. But any novel of such length discourages me awfully. It took much bravery to plow through "Kings Row."

You do not write like a musician, definitely not, yet I have but an intuition as to how a musician would write.

And when I get to this point I am gay and smiling. "So," I think, "I'm going to write him something sensible tomorrow." But by tomorrow I'm still not grown up.

Faithfully,
Tedd

28
HENRY

Ansonia Hotel
New York City

November 15, 1943

Dear Tedd,

Now what kind of tact is it to tell me you had to "plow" through Kings Row? Is that a small scratch?

I'll send Equinox as soon as I can lay hands on paper and string. It's a very bad book and when I send it I'll tell you why and what to look for.

As a technician I'd say it has just about everything the matter with it. And the author is a professor of English! But English professors are notably bad writers.

I'm sorry about the Cleveland job. I think you need a job. You've too much time to think about yourself.

I'm probably not quite as ancient as you think of me. You don't grow old in New York. One dies, I suppose, in the effort to stay young. I must say I don't try and I would suspect arrested development if I stayed too young. I wouldn't be really young again for the universe. Do you recall that Shaw said youth was really wonderful and that it was a great pity it was wasted on young people.

Sincerely,
H.B.

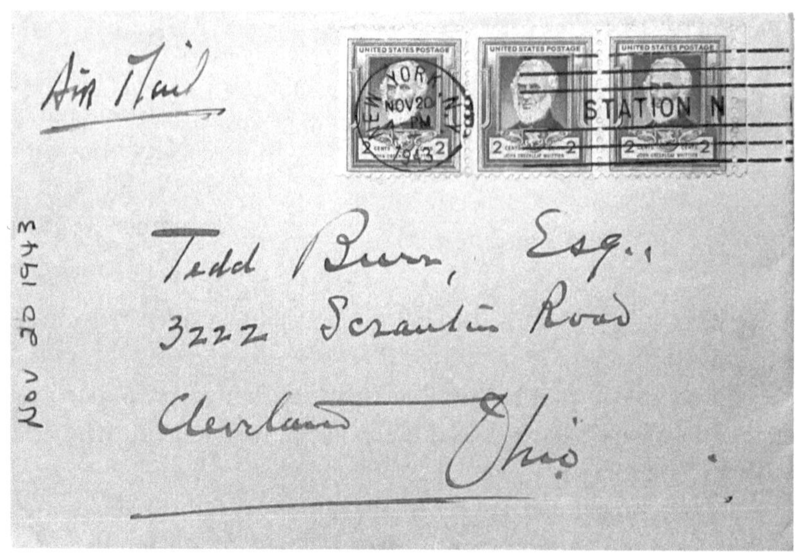

Envelope from Henry's November 20, 1943 letter to Tedd, with Tedd's new address in Cleveland.

Ansonia Hotel
New York City

November 20, 1943

Dear Tedd,

I am delighted. All of this sounds like a way out—and I think it will be and is a very fine world for you.

I've not been well—colds and the usual pestiferous small ailments of changing seasons. I have looming ahead many engagements <u>plus</u> Supreme Court jury duty—a terrific bore.

I have a few suggestions. You'll know which ones to take, which ones to ignore.

Make yourself as inconspicuous as possible. <u>Don't talk too much to anyone</u>; it's the magnificent curse of the artistic temperament. Very few people know what you're talking about anyway. It's better to be a bit lonely—until you see your way around.

I hope you'll write as much as you wish. And will you excuse short notes for awhile? I shall be terribly occupied trying to get a serial novel in shape. I shall think of you and be interested in what happens. <u>Nothing must happen</u>. You are probably on your way to whatever you want.

Faithfully,
H Bellamann

---

50. There seems here to be a missing letter from Tedd to Henry. Tedd must have gotten the go ahead from the Dayton military base, for it seems that Tedd was able to start his job at J & L Steel and make a move to Cleveland.

3222 Scranton Rd.
Cleveland, Ohio

November 28, 1943

Dear Mr. Bellamann,

One of the quickest ways to dissolve a long distance friendship is through silence, so I shall increase these efforts to you. I hope you are well and your novel progressing: which makes me wish you'd tell me more about it. How awful for every one to know of it except me.

I am off soon for the concert of the Cleveland Orchestra. But I am not too enthusiastic about going. Last night I saw the Russian Ballet and they are superb! I believe there is no comparison with the inferior Ballet[s] Russe[s]. Truly I was inspired with the new works "Dim Lustre" and "Helen of Troy."[51] I believe ballet should be modern—but the modern music for symphony orchestras generally make[s] me shudder. It is so radical and desperate.

I seem to be getting on at work with Mr. Hack taking time to teach me every angle of the "set-up" which he has not done with any other employee. I do hope I shall prove satisfactory and valuable.

I have spoken briefly before of this strange boy, Emil, in the office. He is by profession an Adagio dancer. He has quite a male following. He denies any practice, but I think it is all quite obvious and that most of these friendships cannot be purely platonic. Two sailor friends were coming here from Pittsburgh for this week-end and he wanted me for the foursome. But my youth would not permit me to bars so I went to the ballet. There are no

---

51. *Dim Lustre* (1943), choreography by Antony Tudor and music by Richard Strauss; *Helen of Troy* (1942), choreography by David Lichine and music by Jacques Offenbach.

women where I work so there is no restraint among the men. It is very repulsive.

I suppose every week will bring developments—some I fear.

Faithfully,
Tedd

31
HENRY

Ansonia Hotel
New York City

November 29, 1943

Dear Tedd,

I have lost your address and am sending this home [to parents]. I have thought of you but have been very occupied.

Let me know again where you are.

Faithfully,
Henry Bellamann

Ansonia Hotel
New York City

December 3, 1943

Dear Tedd,

Here is a second letter from you which doesn't sound happy—
and I don't know how to reach you! I don't know how I lost your
Cleveland address. You gave it to me only once.

Let me hear from you.

Faithfully,
H Bellamann

3222 Scranton Rd.
Cleveland, Ohio

December 3, 1943

My dear Mr. Bellamann,

Up there is my address and I am so happy you have been thinking of me. I remember vaguely what I last wrote you … it must have made no sense. I was just feeling strangely and melo-dramatic.

If I could but talk to you: it is so difficult to relate here the things I have lately learned. But I shall try to sum them up. But first, how are you and your books? I must get "Floods of Spring"— it is rather awful that you are just a very kind person to me and not a pompous author of best sellers. For some reason I cannot read these days.

I shall go home for this weekend and how good it will be to see everyone. But I do love <u>this</u> city—it seems to offer much and is a little frightening.

It is being drawn into surroundings and adventures, and I feel helpless. That is, something in me drives me on into unwiseness [*sic*]! I do not stop—I know to go on is disasterous [*sic*].

Cleveland has a club for homosexuals and I am being drawn in, but because of my age I shall perhaps never be able to go. There are 2 "queers" in our office and they plague me. My past life makes me ill!!—but is it <u>just</u> for knowledge and curiosity that I listen to them? Through them I met a h.s.—he was middle aged, wore cheap perfume, chalky powder, and hides his face self-consciously. Seeing and hearing him made me shudder, and I could pray when finally alone. Should I learn all I can of this or ignore it all?

It is difficult to escape these 2 men when working with them all day—and then, my face does make one wonder. I have been shocked by the tales from these of the actors and ballet dancers who visit the "club" and have affairs. It makes me search for why — why — why!! Is this what you meant in your frank opinion of such celeberities [*sic*]? Oh, my world has been rocked.

Can you advise me about this? I may very well not accept it, yet <u>I believe in you and your wise, wise words</u>. Remember that.

How I hate discussing just this. If it only were not so important ... unescapable [*sic*]. It cannot be shoved back — or can it? It all makes me very weary.

I wonder if I should try another book.

But I am getting on at the corporation, I really believe that. My work has grown to proportions that I now have two desks. I hope I go on and on here and accomplish. Restore myself.

Sincerely,
Tedd

34
HENRY

Ansonia Hotel
New York City

December 6, 1943

Dear Tedd,

I am glad to be in touch with you again. There are so many things I want to say to you, and I have so little time. I am not well and may have to go to Arizona next week for the winter. I hope not.

First: I'd like to clear myself on one point. I don't approve or disapprove of anything except on grounds of good taste and fastidiousness. You will have to do whatever you <u>have</u> to do: I only hope <u>for your sake</u> not for mine that you won't be ashamed of whatever it is. I understand that you must be under tension and pressures.

The situation of the real h.s., which I think you are not, is that of a man beset by thirst who is surrounded by sea water. H.S. practices increase the tensions: they are not a real release in relaxation—the tension grows and one abnormality follows another.

I think of you as a sort of original personality: I like to think of you as being—well, I guess <u>sweet</u> is the word—clear complexioned, etc. It happens that you are very good looking and appealing. It would be a pity for you to be spent and squandered and spoiled like an old and jaded prostitute.

There's something better in the world for you.

When you are young and artistic and superior you feel that you have to prove it by being different. Does a man six feet six inches tall have to stretch to prove he is a tall man? When you are superior you don't have to do anything about it. The world will find it out. A HS Club is a whorehouse!

It isn't that I make this recommendation on moral grounds—not at all—but on aesthetic grounds. I think you are too nice for sordid surroundings.

Again, Tedd, you'll find out sometime what from your inner nature you <u>must</u> do. Whatever that turns out to be, let that be your own genuine experience and not something <u>sought</u> out, or looked for. You're too fine grained for just <u>any</u> thing.

I am very fond of you. I can say this without seeing you.

I count on you being inconspicuous, dignified, self-contained. You will have to have the attributes of an aristocrat.

Will you try being these things—just to see how it works? I wouldn't for the world give you a bad lead.

If you were my son (or my daughter) I'd still give you the same advice. It is all a question of taste, of elegance, refinement.

Your outlet—your self-expression, artistic and sexual, will find their way.

My real affection—
Sincerely,
HB

35
HENRY

Ansonia Hotel
New York City

December 9, 1943

Dear Tedd,

You are a bit given to melodramatics. Nothing but death is as important as you make these matters sound.

You don't have to do anything you don't want to. But when one wishes tremendously to try out things the likelihood is that you will. So what? Don't take anything too seriously.

I can't see you in that kind of sticky world, but I don't know. I am your friend, Tedd, as long as you need me. I think pretty highly of what you can be. Being a little "crazy in the pants" maybe won't ruin you. But keep a sense of humor and don't take yourself too seriously.

Faithfully,
HB

Ansonia Hotel
New York City

December 9, 1943

Dear Tedd,

I suspect that I am the least fatherly person you have ever known. You are more likely to find me contemporaneous as our acquaintance progresses. I don't want to write a thousand <u>Don'ts</u>. That would be very tiresome for both of us and finally futile.

It is rather that I know pretty well a great many of your mental and emotional states and sympathize in some instances, in other instances I don't. You are under obligation to be intelligent.

The besetting sin of people who feel themselves exceptional is a kind of fidgeting with life, bringing about such piffling results. I hope to see you grow in stature: not that I'm finding fault with you really in any way. I remember your age and experience and I don't think you've done badly.

I wonder if you heard Rubinstein play the Brahms' B Flat concerto last Sunday?[52] I thought of you as I heard it on the radio. A really magnificent performance.

Tedd, you can't be and do all things at once. But if you wish to be something notable you very probably can become that. I'd like you to keep your dignity, your intellectual and emotional integrity. It is easy to rationalize yourself into thinking this or that is necessary.

So—<u>take it easy</u>. Live on a lower key. You're keyed too high for comfort.

Sincerely,
HB

---

52. Arthur Rubenstein (1887–1982), Polish pianist.

TEDD

3222 Scranton Rd.
Cleveland, Ohio

December 13, 1943

Dear Mr. Bellamann,

The first of your letters amused me: the second made me ponder: but only slightly for I feel gay despite the fact that a gentleman on the bus just bawled me out for being in such a hurry to get off at my stop. These happenings really used to bother me but I take embarrassment rather well these days.

Oh, there is so much to tell you so I'm writing even though my stationary is practically nil. If I could but tell it verbally with my hands running through the air or even a typewriter would help. But here it is.

Saturday evening I was invited to this club I discussed before. I accepted on the impulse and was scared to death. I went with these two other men from the office: one, 23, a professional dancer the other, 40, and tiresome. We were met at the door by the proprietress who lifted the rule once to let in a minor: So you see, probably I shall not go again, at least for a year or more. There are two bars, a small dance floor and tables. It is quite dim.

And so, throughout the evening I observed. I lost my nervousness and did enjoy it. But one thing, the dykes or lesbians took me for a woman and were too staringly [sic] attentive until they learned better. My 40 yrs. old friend, Al, pointed at one "slapp 'em down" girl and said, "That is Stephanie from 'The Well of Lonliness [sic].' Just like her."[53] I did not know having not yet read the book. One woman, wearing pants, smoked a monstrous cigar. Don't think from this that I was laughing at them really; it all seemed quite natural, but these women do puzzle me.

---

53. The character's name is Stephen. See note 11.

Then the "queers," the gay boys. They ranged from all ages. One very distinguished elderly man seemed to have a passion for the younger boys. These boys mostly were well dressed and like everyone else—in the conventional world. Oh, there was a blonde that was too, too, and looked down on me, a minor. These men danced affectionately together. I danced too, the first time in my life. I was forced into it, and I'm not sorry. Then came a "drag" queen, a boy dressed as a woman. There was not the slightest stir over this. He was not very attractive but still perfectly at home in this role.

These people let go, they lived as they desired to all day long. I don't know whether this club is right or wrong, but it is a haven for many.

On this particular night there were not many looking for "queers," that is, straight men wanting adventure. Most of these people were having affairs. It was not unusual to hear break offs and tears. These people have some kind of ceremony and get married: but when it is over it is over, I guess. They talk about their husbands a great deal. And one refers to these male "queens" as "she this or that."

There was a young man attracted to me and asked to kiss me. I saw this "necking" going on about me, but I could not. I simply did not want to. I tried refusing kindly and did.

That started me thinking and for a while it all became a little repulsive. Truly these people are over-sexed. I cannot stand that sex element in it all. If they loved it would be spiritually too, but I don't think many are capable of that. Everyone kissed everyone else. I could not do that. So commercial and cheap. I have told you before of the young man I thought I fell in love with when in the 8th grade. (How strange to write that) Whether I do love him or not (and I have doubts) it could never be sexually. Any such suggestion would sicken me. Now as I think of him I see myself only as a <u>wife</u> and <u>mother</u> in a dream world!

I think I want to be kissed; I believe that is what I am searching for, and yet when the opportunity was there, I declined. I suppose I have a dream kiss and reality is too vulgar.

By the end of the evening the sex element was high and it amused me in wonder and some disgust. These people, I think, how desperate they are. They have affairs, men of all ages, and then lose their men. They live together and all that but it does not last. Oh, I have a store of observations, questions and thinking matter from this.

In my book, having Michael kiss Sidney was difficult because I thought it could never happen; but now I am sure it can.

By the way, the law dropped in. My friend hurried over, sat down and leaned in front of me. I was stricken with fear: being found in such a place: my family, if I should ever hurt them with my foolishness! But it passed quickly and I was alright but for a good scare.

You spoke of this club as a whorehouse. Well I suppose that takes interpretation. I don't believe, I'm sure, rooms are not let out and all that, but it is a meeting place, etc.

Mr. B., I'm not sorry I went—it was an amazing experience and I think I learned a great deal. It was certainly instructive. It also gives a picture of a side of the world a lot of people don't consider. In a way it is all fairly pathetic.

I hope you haven't minded going through this with me: perhaps you know all this very well. I think it may be a stroke of god that I'm too young for admittance to the place: I might go there too often and be swayed into an existence I'm not at all sure I want at all!

And now I want to apologize for bearing so on this one subject, h.s., in all my letters. You must get very tired of it: but I am young and desire much information about all sides of it. But, dear me, on to other things.

You know, I am not very well informed about you although I feel very close to you. I hope you won't mind if I ask questions to find new ground occasionally.

How are you and Arizona? I rather hate to think of you're going so far away. But I want you well too: I mean that. Your health is of much concern to me—don't mind please. I like to be so near you as to have a right to be concerned.

Are you teaching now: and did you have interesting students? I suppose you have a wide correspondence: I'm jealous a little, forgive me. Did anyone write to you from a clear blue sky, like I did? Do you get fan mail and requests for photos? And by the way, before I went to this club I looked at your picture and the eyes looked deep into me. I don't know what they said, but I felt as if they were wondering and advising and saying. "I'll be here when you get back. I'll be here."

I was home when Rubenstein played here and I am very unfamiliar with Brahms—except for his song about the lover standing out in the cold night. If it had been Tchaikovsky's 2<u>nd</u> I would not have missed it. Shall you be going to the opera? And does Melchior shout enough to give you free concerts? Lately I have seen the plays "Blithe Spirit" and "Angel Street."[54] The latter a Cleveland Playhouse production.

I have always wanted to be of the Playhouse: but now I fear actors: I found my Dayton stage friends so catty and small.

Golly, how long have I been writing: It is dark out and I have a million things to do. You can see from this that I am an endless talker. I'm in a mellow mood tonight and I pray it lasts. I am quite settled at work and tomorrow plan to have my gobs of hair sheared. You know, Cleveland is wise, they read you like a book. I'd like to change my cover.

Respectfully,
Tedd

---

54. Noël Coward, *Blithe Spirit* (1941), a comedy about a spiritual medium; *Angel Street* is the American title for Patrick Hamilton's 1938 play *Gas Light*, in which a man tries to drive his wife insane.

Ansonia Hotel
New York City

December 14, 1943

Dear Tedd,

Well, now, let's see. I must answer some of your questions.

I don't have an extensive correspondence. I rarely write letters. I see very few people. I am known as a quasi-recluse. Probably see my publishers only once or twice a year. I used to have to move much in musical circles while I was in official positions. I like very few people. Humanity, yes.

Individuals are hard to take sometimes. My new friends in the world have been men. But I like women—girls—whatever, and have a well-stocked memory.

Yes, I had thousands of letters about Kings Row—a few from lonely souled boys who sensed a sympathetic hearer after having read about Jamie. They passed out of my acquaintance after one letter or so. I seldom go to the opera because I've seen too much opera. Besides, I don't like opera much. I only nod to my neighbor Mr. Melchoir [sic]—I dislike him extremely for a hundred reasons. I have some few friends in the music world. But I'm not a misanthrope. I am merely a rather reclusive person. I'm excessively particular about who crosses my threshold—either the real one or the mental one. That should not sound snobbish, because I am not.

I suspect I have an extraordinary sympathy with the poor and lowly of the world. I like them better, and think they are kind and good more than they are something else.

I was born in moderate circumstances. The first part of Kings Row is a portrait of my grandmother, and myself. I call myself very democratic in theory, and my old friend, a banker, says I am in practice a dammed [sic] aristocrat. We fight and have fought over this for nearly forty years.

It is said I seem much younger than my age, I don't know, or care. My nearest friends are young people, and many of them young girls. I like everything about them, and we get along very well.

I have a wife—who wrote once a particularly amusing book called "My Husband's Friends"—a book that nearly ruined my reputation. It was a story of a scientist husband and his love affairs. It was purely fiction.[55]

My domineering mother died last year. I have the complete responsibility of a brother and sister who live in the West, both much younger than I. I scarcely know them.

Does that answer you?

I'm uneasy about the club, because you could end up in the hoose-gow with a fearful attendant scandal.

Now, Tedd, I have never warned you about anything on moral grounds because I'm not sure of my advice there. But I am most practical. The whole business sounds a bit icky. It doesn't seem good enough for you.

My concern with you is that you should not mix with things that are common or degrading, and that you should learn to live with dignity—self contained, really proud and master of yourself. Within that pattern you will someday find a means of complete self-expression.

Let us come back to the question of h.s. affairs. If you are so, born so, or made so, you will have great difficulties. The world's contempt you will get and have to meet and suffer—justly or not. The world is not advanced enough to know what all of this is about. Maybe I don't either. But I know awfully well how you feel, what you will do, and what will happen. That is why I urge you not to run with this crowd. You'll find yourself shut out of too much that you will want. You will have to be inconspicuous, and play safe. It sounds like poor advice to a fine spirit, but if you don't do this you'll lose jobs and find it hard to get on in the world.

----

55. Katherine Bellamann's novel *My Husband's Friends* was published by the Century Company in 1931. See "Postscript: In the Name of Jamie Wakefield" (303).

I don't know why the real h.s. feels that he must defy the world and demand public approbation. Suffice that I decide that I must have a mistress—one in a dozen—do you think I should advertise?

One of the only ways in the world to get on anywhere is to keep your private life completely private.

I really think these clubs are a bit "hick." <u>They try</u> to ape similar institutions abroad which were run for yokels only!

Homosexuality has a long history. Most prostitution in Greece was boy prostitution. I can only say from what I know of psychology that nature did not intend this to happen. You are constructed physically for heterosexuality. There is nothing you can do that ever satisfies you. Think over the various forms of h.s. practice. Don't they rather repel you?

Of course I don't know why relations with a girl <u>could</u> repel you. If they do, then they do. You wrote a bit nastily about it in The Surf but all natural offices even to brushing one's teeth, are not pretty practices.

But many of them—such as eating—are very good and very satisfying and do set the soul free.

You describe your reactions well: they are the reactions of a virginal mind—whether you are so or not.

It would be pretty wonderful if you could keep out of such a messy business as that club until some <u>great</u> experience came along.

These jaded perverts will of course like your freshness and good looks.

But—Tedd; you can't be a wife or mother since you happen to be a boy! Not even in your fancy. Let's try to get down to Earth—hard as the Earth is! … I'm not a stern or a severe person, Tedd. I am a tolerant and laughing and good humored person. I'm not being a judge or a <u>don'ter</u>. I'm trying to save you for something better than you see for yourself.

… I shall send you to that address a copy of <u>Victoria Grandolet</u>: since advance copies have come in.

Sincerely,
HB

Ansonia Hotel
New York City

December 17, 1943

Dear Tedd,

I am having to do a rush piece of work between now and January first. I am certain that I shall not have time to write at all, but after that I shall be free again for a while. I am not going to Arizona. Am feeling better.

This is just to wish you a very happy time, and to hope every good thing for you in the New Year.

I am sending a copy of Victoria to you tomorrow.

All good luck <u>to you,</u>

Affectionately,
HB

40[56]

HENRY

Ansonia Hotel
New York City

December 27, 1943

Tedd,

If you write me another one of those letters on the bias, I'll disown you! They give me a crick in the neck.

I hope you had a nice Christmas. I didn't. Worked. The story comes along all right, but I'm at the stage of being sick of it.

I've thought of you a lot, even if I was busy.

Take best possible care of yourself. I'm sure if you <u>think</u> a bit more as you go you're all right. So—for a better and happier New Year.

Sincerely,
HB

---

56. A letter from Tedd seems to be missing in this sequence.

41
HENRY

Ansonia Hotel
New York City

January 4, 1944

Dear Tedd,

I don't know why a letter should have been returned to you.

Will you please send that envelope along to me. We have new mail clerks I imagine in the hotel.

Disowning you was a jest, of course.

I am still being very busy and am rather tired.

Take care of yourself through all of this bad weather, and write as much as you wish.

Always,
HB

42

TEDD

3222 Scranton Rd.
Cleveland, Ohio

January 5, 1944

My dear Mr. Bellamann,

Your letter made me so abundantly happy that I actually laughed to have all that tension of where you might have gone suddenly non-existant [*sic*] and, what a fool I am, but your subtle remarks are wasted on me and leave me quite up-set. And lately your picture has looked so sternly out at me: ah, ha, there one learns that I have a guilty conscious [*sic*]. At least I have been letting myself think too freely and act probably unwisely.

So far I have come along quite all right through sickness around me. I hope you have too. I drank lots of water and for an uncomfortable throat took medicated drops. But this evening it rains, slowly but heavily with big drops and I got wet feet.

I am happy and a little afraid. I am being promoted into a very difficult position. It has been a joy knowing you, or your talents, are wanted. I have been here but a month and a half and already a raise in salary. This work has such responsibilities that I do hesitate. I cannot help but take things that I do seriously.

I have learned so much while here: not only of steel and the business world, but of life and people and the need of decisions.

Mr. Bellamann, I may be living very unwisely but I'm being carried by a current. I tell myself it's a desire to learn that has me: yet being in the company of 'gay' boys such as I have met not only fascinates me but presents me an opportunity to relax and be that which bubbles inside.

You see, I'm an outcast of one world—and again of the other. In the latter I believe in utter honor, and it is so lacking.

Sometimes I think I should like going to school after the war and work at physicology [*sic*]. I should like to work with this problem, take up from Freud and Ellis and find the h.s. his badly needed niche in society. His explanation.

I have swallowed hard, shook my head at a new suit and banked my first installment towards this new desire. Could this be my torch, could I help and accomplish. Oh, how, how can these people go on living in the underground? Can't the world accept them, their right to happiness. Save them from the inevitable.

Or am I being very foolish—and again overly dramatic?

As to drama, if you could but be here to see "The Old Ladies" at the Playhouse.[57] There is genius. This group is a gem—artistry blooms and swells.

Did Donald Dickson study at Juilliard while you were there? He is the noted baritone, you know. I work with his brother Bob who says Don is home now. And of Patrice Munsel—is she another Marian Talley—so quickly to go?[58]

The "Well of Lonliness [sic]" still occupies me—I live each page—each word. Stephen—Stephen.

Did that doctor friend ever analyze my writing—that intrigued me—I did not forget.

Do get well soon.

As ever—
Tedd

---

57. Rodney Auckland's atmospheric thriller *The Old Ladies* (1935) was based on Hugh Walpole's 1924 novel of the same name. The story focuses on three women in their seventies who live in a run-down rooming house.

58. Patrice Munsel (1925–2016), a coloratura soprano who made her debut with the Metropolitan Opera at age 17 on December 4, 1943 in Ambroise Thomas's opera *Mignon*; Marian Tally (1906–1983), also a coloratura soprano, made her debut with the Met in 1926, at age 19, in Giuseppe Verdi's *Rigoletto*. Tally's singing career was fairly short, her last professional engagement occurring in 1938.

First page of Tedd's January 5, 1944 letter to Henry, white ink on dark stationery.

43

TEDD

3222 Scranton Rd.
Cleveland, Ohio

undated, between December 27, 1943 and January 4, 1944

Dear HB,

Oh I have not meant to neglect you, no I didn't—but life has carried me on at such a pace—often with my reluctance—that only now I grasp out to you.

And are you again well—shall you be moving—I have thought so of you.

I am quite surprised that I am not yet in the Army—the day must be very soon. Perhaps I told you of my feelings of illness and all that. I saw my doctor and learned I have heart trouble and probable blood anemia—or something. It is this that makes me so exhausted and continually tired. How I suddenly dislike this handicap!

The other night my room-mate forced his attentions on me—I was so repulsed—he slapped me several times. It was shocking and awfully dramatic—it surely will appear in my next novel. Remember the scene with Paul in my "Surf"? Almost a prediction really.

The whole thing upset me at first until I decided not to be morbid but regard it as an experience. It was a splendid opportunity observing the human animal, his views—we get on quite well since this understanding of mutual dislike.

I may move—have had two invitations—one a man at work who is a h.s. wants to share an apartment where he can bring up what he picks up. I should not be able to stand this. It is as if he exists to spread filth through the world. He takes such nice, clean men—husbands—and degrades them to his low level—it isn't love, it's insanity.

The other, a young man—he is kept by his lover—but sparcely [sic]. He doesn't like to work, is restless and confused. He said he liked me as a friend—perhaps because I fed him two days and listened to him. He is very puzzling.

I do believe he has contempt for anyone. One night he took me to the colored district to a boot-legging apartment. These negroes adore him—and he expresses near love for them and their problems. As I sat marking in my memory the exciting details, he talked with them of mutual understandings. When the door closed on us he turned on me and expressed his loathing of them. I almost cried. And so I suspect where I stand—a convenient sucker. You called me selfish—but for one time I really felt unselfish—a desire to help this young man.

Someday he shall not be young or loved—he must learn to work. Self respect would return, the respect for others, and his fears could go. The unemployed find it difficult.

On one condition I'd live with him—if he'd get a job. I'd try so to keep him on the job, instill ideals in his wrecked mind—you see, I don't believe he's h.s., merely finding it convenient. If this could be taken from him—restore him to normality. Even if I should lose in the end—money—or heartache—I do want to help him.

I am sending you the letter that was returned. In it you shall find an adventure. I am sensitive about it: not because you are reading it: but because it, itself, seems some degrading. Yet I'm so glad I had the experience, the thoughts, the pitched emotions.

You no doubt know we are losing Conductor Erich Leinsdorf to the Army. Cleveland is quite upset; he was very popular and really took the reins. I saw him conduct several weeks ago: he is fascinating, quite the exhibitionist: not in any offensive way at all: he simply gives all he has. Dorothy Maynor sang and never have I heard such ovations as paid her.[59] It was breath-takingly inspirational.

Tomorrow night Leinsdorf gives a Tchaikovsky program and I plan to attend.

Oh, how happy I am to have your letter. So much seems erased from my mind now.

---

59. Dorothy Maynor (1910–1996), a black American soprano.

My parents are having a wedding anniversary (24th) and I am glad I have arrived at an appreciation of them. Never before have I been so grateful to them for my home, security, good life, their kindness and love.

I feel quite as if I haven't seen you for ages and am having a good old chat which I must end before you drop with exhaustion.

"<u>Victoria Grandolet</u>" is not forgotten. I must collect my thoughts and opinions if I am to write of this book to you. Victoria her<u>self</u> has not concerned me as much as you.

Thank you for your invitation to write: I shall, often.

Respectfully,
Tedd

Hotel Ansonia
New York City

January 7, 1944

Dear Tedd,

Your returned letter went by mistake to the Hotel Alamac and was either stupidly misread as to address and so sent it back to you.

Better address me

Hotel Ansonia
73rd & Broadway

I'll write you at length when I have really enough time. Altho there isn't much to say. This is apparently the usual run of such affairs. If you don't like being mis-handled, you don't, and I sympathize with you. I have no suggestions because I think you don't know what you want to do. And I can assure you that probably none of the what to do's can be very satisfying, physically or aesthetically.

Aren't you even attracted to girls? I just wonder. You lashed out so at regulation sex in The Surf (which I still have)—but the irregular aspects of sex are no prettier.

Just try to be calm about all things. None of these things spell the end of the world.

I think you go into great despair about them and yourself because you are sexually unsatisfied. I have no advice to make. Try to be assured that I don't disapprove of you.

Faithfully,
HB

3222 Scranton Rd.
Cleveland, Ohio

January 11, 1944
1 a.m.

Mr. Bellamann,

If I say just a few things before bed I think I'll feel better; so just regard this as a letting you know I'm still here.

I re-read your late letter and thought of it. I do think of you a great deal, compose huge letters in my mind, and then scribble something like this.

You are right: I don't know what I want: but it can't be left at that. I must and will choose a road and the choice I regard seriously.

From many angles: my dream of a success of some nature, big or small, in this world: my family, name: my conscience: the years ahead. I can't take this lightly.

I believe I'm completely normal in all respects: but compared to so many many people—I'm sexless. Truly, a girl does not appeal to me: except as a friend (ex. Dorothy) but I envy them so! It is uncomfortable, envying.

I have never regarded homo-sexuality as down-to-earth and "nasty" as it must be!

I thought only of beauty, loving only in beauty: not blood and guts stuff!

Tonight I had an opportunity of joining a man. I didn't and couldn't and now am glad <u>I went my silent way</u>!!

It is this Emil. He weaves a sort of spell that I don't ward off. But later when alone, common sense pricks me. I would give him up—he's no prize as a person—(and I don't mean to be catty here)—but I'm lonely—terribly.

That is where my trouble springs I believe.

Then too, for years being a woman, having such a lovely body, wearing lovely gowns, etc., to me was heaven. Simply because as a kid I was shoved from boys to the girls, and practically became one. So since a child I have had that gnawing at me! I was not equal to them. "Didn't I have the right to that?"

Now, as a young man this wild notion is still here and won't leave.

These "queens" I've met are just body crazy and it becomes disgusting. I think men should love only women.

Because in my eyes, I am more woman than man.

Well, I have said little I started out with, but this is a fragment. Is it wrong to concentrate on myself so much? I feel I must straighten things out soon.

It is my philosophy that much thought is good for the soul—and growing up.

Please do write me as you can: I am so happy at receiving your letters, you are very kind. I cannot tell my heart to others: Thank you for listening.

Faithfully,
Tedd

Hotel Ansonia
73rd St. & Broadway
New York City

January 13, 1944

Dear Tedd,

Sometime I should like to write you some of the pleasant things I think about you, but you yourself ask questions that call for clear criticism. I fear I give you a lot of it. But there is something about the final result of "licking a cub into shape" that justifies the cub's discomfort.

Yes: you are too self centered. You think too much of each small effect you make and you do overdramatize things. A lot of things in the world are so unimportant.

Just now a lot of people are dying, Tedd, and dying most unpleasantly. They are really going out that a world may survive in which you can live comfortably. You <u>must not</u> live trivially. It would be ungrateful, undignified.

There are many things you may do or not do which are of no importance—some of them not even to you. But whether you are a dignified human being deserving the incalculable gift of existence depends on you.

I'd try to keep out of range of some of this doubtful company you speak of. They sound so dammed trashy.

There are a great many boys with fine bodies—bodies they treasured and cared for who are hacked to pieces in the South Pacific, or blown to bits in Italy. "Compare some of these people with the individuals you mention." And for the good of your soul, once a day, compare yourself. When you learn real humility you will be somebody.

I heard someone say the other day: "I wish to live charmingly, aesthetically. I feel that I have a right to the best of everything because I do so appreciate them." I had to say, "<u>Why</u>?" A boy in a basket in some out of the way hospital so people won't have to see him—a boy with no legs, no arms, and blind. <u>He</u> earned the right for a nincompoop to "enjoy the best"!

I want you to think of better and bigger things. It won't hurt you to be lonely. And don't imagine that you can live the life of the great world in a provincial city and feel that you are worldly, sophisticated and quite a devil of a fellow. <u>Be lonely</u>. It won't hurt you. You'd better get close to some great books, some great music. Measure yourself, and <u>deserve to live</u>.

I'd rather see you shredded by German machine guns than to grow on into one of those too, too precious persons who can go ga-ga over chartreuse silk or something equally trivial. We are truly living in one of the great periods of the world. It's staggering to human vanity to clearly measure one's self against the plain heroism of common people. They are being so much bigger than most of us.

Here ends the sermon. I'm very fond of you or I wouldn't yell at you.

Henry Bellamann

47
HENRY

Hotel Ansonia
73rd St. & Broadway
New York City

January 24, 1944

Dear Tedd,

I have been very ill. Not having heard from you I wonder if I have lost some of your letters. Or horrid suspicion!—are you sulking about something?

Anyway I've missed hearing from you.

Sincerely,
HB

48[60]

HENRY

Hotel Ansonia
73rd St. & Broadway
New York City

January 25, 1944

Dear Tedd,

I am sitting up but not well enough to be at work though my agent is sniffing at my heels.

About VG [Victoria Grandolet]: There is no confusion of time. Horse and buggy means at least before 1905. But Niles says clearly "A new Century has begun." Time was of no importance in this story, hence, it was ignored. VG has had mostly good reviews, one catty one written by an elderly novelist, and a curt dismissal by the New Yorker—also a review written by an unsuccessful novelist. Some people honestly disliked it. You were supposed to dislike Victoria, though her perversities are within the periphery of the normal. Victoria is a best seller. The Literary Guild bought 120,000 copies, the regular edition has sold over 50,000 in these two weeks. The picture is being made. Joan Fontaine is playing it—so I read in the N.Y. Times. I have already made more money out of VG than out of Kings Row though KR sold half a million and continues a best seller.

What I am saying is this: I am writing for one purpose only—money. Remember what Dr. Johnson said about writing for money.[61]

---

60. There seems to be a missing letter here. It would be one in which Tedd critiques Henry's latest novel, <u>Victoria Grandolet</u>. I find it curious that this letter is missing, meaning that Henry either misplaced it or did not keep it with the rest of the letters he had saved. Tedd relayed the story in the film *Letters to Uranus: The Hidden Life of Tedd Burr* (2000) that he told Henry that he "didn't like it very much." Tedd said that he didn't think Henry was very happy about his critique, stating with an impish smile, "getting criticism from little ol' me."

61. "No man but a blockhead ever wrote except for money." Quoted in James Boswell's *Life of Johnson* (1791).

Anyway if a book turns out good or bad is another matter. Some books are for some readers only. How many people read Mary Webb's <u>Precious Bane</u>, one of the finest novels in English?[62]

No author knows if his books are good or bad. He may have the best intentions and fail to put it on paper. I seldom read reviews except the New York ones. They do not affect sales.

I hope when the present serial is off hands (not planned for book publication) I shall feel like getting at the second part of KR. There are two more volumes planned.

<u>White Cloud</u> is the house I nearly bought two or three years ago. I still think wistfully of it, altho its 59 rooms present an appalling problem nowadays.

… I think you have a lot of reading and listening to do because you <u>are</u> immature. There is much in life that must puzzle you until your experience is widened. You know, Tedd, most of our world experience <u>has</u> to come from books because we can't do it all ourselves.

Take care of yourself and try
to think hard about the biggest
things you're learning.

Sincerely,
HB

---

62. Mary Webb's *Precious Bane* (1924) was a historical romance novel set in England during the Napoleonic Wars. One of the novel's main themes is the corrupting influence of the love of money. The French translation, *Sarn,* won the 1936 Prix Femina Vie Herueuse, a French prize for literature by women.

HENRY

Hotel Ansonia
73rd St. & Broadway
New York City

February 22, 1944

Dear Tedd,

I've gotten so used to writing to you that I miss doing so: but I have been busy at work on this serial which is at last finished, tho editors always have a last word to say.

I've not been too well, though nothing beyond the usual winter's tale of colds, etc.

I am going to move from the Ansonia late in April to a place on Fifth Avenue, high above the park with the reservoir under my windows. It will be like having the country outside my windows. I always like the country better than glass anyway.

I have not been about much, nor seen anyone much, and I feel moss growing on my mind.

I hope you are having a good time and are happy. Write when you can.

Affectionately,
Henry B.

3222 Scranton Rd.
Cleveland, Ohio

undated, likely February 22–24, 1944

Dear HB,

I'm in a dreadful mood today—catty and irritable—and in all moods I write letters to you—mentally—mental letters I compose a dozen times a day—real letters that you never receive. You are truly always by me—I measure my actions with you in view— your frowning picture that has been a comfort and guide—more than my own father who gave me a good home and fine food but left me flapping about in life's water.

I am so ill today—many days—ill of life—this Emil and Al I work with—these h.s.'s who revel in the squalor of their cheap lives. I have grown so sick of this undercover world—I detest it all. I feel utterly foreign to it, except for the ties my hair and aches make to it. I want to run my fist through it all as if it were a sheet of glass and smash it to bits. Yet I want often to help—to study and learn and spread information to both worlds. Here I think of post-war college. A long life.

Then again, it is hopeless! I become discouraged and want to stop my dreaming. They don't want help. In a discussion with Al yesterday I became heated and asked: "Do you expect medical science to make a drug—an injection to free you?"

"Yes!"

"Yes,—that would be the easy way—for you! But why should science take on your burden if you won't help yourself through yourself, your efforts and pains."

He flushed and made fun of me. My age. Telling him, a man of 40. Yes, a man of 40; true, a man with 2 children he lets trail far behind—a woman's life—divorced—upset, probably frustrated and now, cruel. On and on he goes, blazing a trail, hurting people, giving pleasure?—I say, receiving contempt!

I'm young, young with hope, some courage, ideals, religion, honor,—things he has lost. He goes from day to day and his chart of awfulness grows. The young should be heard! They come forward with freshness and strength to accept their allotted time with the world. The old often grow incompetent, tired, and must, must cede their place. Didn't Oscar Wilde, who did catch much in his lines, say: "Youth! There is nothing like it. It's absurd to talk of the ignorance of youth. Life has revealed to them her latest wonder."

I go to lunch with these two h.s.'s because I lack facilities for packing a dinner. I endure, observe, but feel detached and ill and ashamed of them. Not they as people—but as stupid individuals.

I have come to believe in some kind of insanity about them. They eat but do not taste their food—their eyes are on bodies, wanting them, looking for impressions beneath the trousers, flirting, advancing to young school kids, grabbing soldiers and sailors, sighing and yearning—animal—bodies—bodies—contempt!! Oh, I don't blame the world for not accepting this; it is more vile than the worst whore.

What is a definition of a h.s.? Or is there a third gender. A definition to include the honorable—the desperate—the idealistic? Or is it just that society puts on fashion rules—yesterday a powdered wig, satin breeches, snuff—today it is gone. Is there a simple solution?

I want to help—I want to help clean a bad house. I believe society does and will accept h.s. If two men live together, love, share their interests, their hopes, their age; society would accept! But street walkers, rouged and powdered, signs dangling across their twisted faces and souls—no, not this, never this—it would eat the foundation of civilization.

Please do look beneath my dramatic caperings for what is real and what I truly feel. These are my colors—and they grow stronger.

Mr. Bellamann, please help me, continue to advise me: let me bring you my tears, for others as well as myself. Don't let me torture myself by barking up the wrong tree. I'm desperate for achievement, knowledge, and engulfing work and interest.

It's very strange how each day brings me closer to these men I work with. Even last night they said: "Tedd, you're just like one of the mill men now." And it's not all act—this swagger I have—for the first time I like and admire real men—men with homes and families—weakness and dogged determination.

One of them—how it filled me—so different from the Dayton experience. One said, "Anything I have is yours"—another, "If anyone ever does anything to you, let me know, I'll take care of them." To me they extend their honest friendship—men with open distaste for Emil—Al. Perhaps it's the struggle they see so often in my face and understand. They are so good and helpful—their words something to cling to.

And so I'm getting on here at work—a raise—but more important—acceptance. Even my hair is overlooked—they attempt valiantly to forget it is there.

Mr. B., I'm happy—happy so much of the time—happy though tears come now and then. I want to be strong. Be weak, too, for that is being human.

Let me walk to lunch with Al and Emil—but all the way I shall be fighting them and their kind.

Maybe I'm laughing at myself for all my talk; but I hope I never stop talking.

The other night my new roommate, Chickie, told me he was leaving, his mother was ill with blood poisoning. I was shocked and felt suddenly lonely. I remember pacing the floor dramatically and nervously smoking. Through my mind went: "Everything happens for the best ..." I have come to believe that. Now I would turn from irregular hours to serious study, books, music.

Chickie, so unsettled, said last night, "I'm not going!" I was struck with sudden keen disappointment. I hated the feeling, but it was there.

Remember my resolutions when I moved into this room? Oh, they're still there, but confused. Naturally I had to learn of this person, the horrible past he has lived in the few years of his life. He is a deadly liar—often in earnest, other times in stagey moods.

I have tried desperately to keep him working and he has until his brother—(twin in mind and deed)—is persuading him to his old life. If this happens I shall leave for I refuse to support either one or see them in such despicable circumstances—kept people!

It hurts not a little that this boy should sink lower and lower. I am learning that it may spring from the family—in this case one not termed Typical American! And yet I cannot but believe that a boy with inborn good character could rise above circumstances: at least realize that being a kept person is not admirable.

So I don't know—what shall happen—It shall be experience one way or the other. I've liked living with Chickie; always thinking I was helping him; then this set back. I realize that he asked my mate-ship so that he could wear my clothes, etc., but I hoped that would pass and he would grow up. You see, he has a love hold on a nice young man who works hard, dreams, and has good ideas. I should not like to see Chickie choke him more than he does now. It is an odd relationship from the sidelines. Naturally I have the impulse to wish the young lover could see all dimensions of Chickie, but that is impossible—love is strange and accepting. So it must go on or come to an end—perhaps bitter—but I refuse to destroy Chickie before one's eyes—especially his lover's. If it comes, it must from its own beginning.

Perhaps from this you can see how confused it all is: though I enjoy its opportunities for analysis and voyage into lives, I wish I might see other lives too: lives not connected with h.s. If I want to write it must be of life and not one subject. I wonder about "The Surf"—its being re-written entirely—a new book, true and informed. Would it be wise to put down one's life? I cannot think of a fictitious plot; I can only realize what I have learned.

Monday I heard the pre-opera concert here—glorious voices— beautiful music. It was so grand it hurt me inside—it seems so inaccessible—as if merely listening is not enough—that I must interpret it in some medium myself. But facts accepted, I move on.

Tonight is a world premiere of a new Greek drama at the Playhouse—house of great genius.

Through the hours I have stretched this letter I have grown from being disturbed to expectancy for tonight's drama, Chickie's decision, and further reading of "Well of Lonliness [*sic*]."

I do hope you shall find time for an occasional letter to me—they are truly treasured.

Faithfully,
Tedd

p.s., Emil has lost his job and prepares to crash [the] New York stage. I have not seen Chickie for two days. He has succumbed and I am ill for him. Yet happy, for I can write all this to you.

Hotel Ansonia
73rd St. & Broadway
New York City

February 25, 1944

Dear Tedd,

My letter probably crossed yours, so you will have heard from me. I have supposed you must go through all this—I hope you'll find it a phase and will come out of it, because happiness cannot be that way. There is only a kind of frustration and physical as well as mental <u>unease</u> that accompanies the whole business. You see it is already so! And then you try to turn it against someone else to try to torment someone else by being <u>unobtainable</u>. What is there to obtain? This is vanity.

Then I think you try to relieve a sense of guilt by being sentimental about home and mother!

<u>Don't have a sense of guilt</u>. This is paralyzing. All these adventures are nothing much. It would be too bad if this were to be your <u>real goal</u> because you condemn yourself to everlasting lack of fulfillment. So it seems to me. I may be wrong. In any case, don't feel bad about anything. Try to be gay and happy.

I am in a hurry, so no more now.

Affectionately,
HB

Hotel Ansonia
73rd St. & Broadway
New York City

March 19, 1944

Dear Tedd,

I have been, and am, ill with a first class case of flu with all trimmings and aftermaths. You could write!

Affectionately,
HB

Card sent from Henry to Tedd, March 19, 1944.

53

HENRY

Hotel Ansonia
73rd St. & Broadway
New York City

April 4, 1944

Dear Tedd,

I am sending you today an article on Homosexuality from the Journal of Criminal Psychopathology. It hasn't much information in it, but some.

I am always afraid of your getting involved with somebody and getting a bad break. Because I am afraid you don't know there are heavy legal penalties for certain h.s. practices. That's what Oscar Wilde was in jail for. Courts are very unsympathetic to such affairs. There is a certain prominent <u>fine</u> musician who is out again, I see, after serving a prison sentence in San Quentin.[63]

Take care of yourself, my friend. Stick to your music, your thinking, your writing as much as you can.

Sincerely,
HB

---

63. Henry Cowell (1897–1965), a prominent pianist and composer, was imprisoned in San Quentin State Prison from 1936 to 1940 after pleading guilty to "oral copulation." See Joel Sach, *Henry Cowell: A Man Made of Music* (2012).

HOMOSEXUALITY

Eugene W. Green, M. D.
Surgeon, U. S. Public Health Service

and

L. G. Johnson, M. D.*
Assistant Surgeon (R), U. S. Public Health Service
Medical Center for Federal Prisoners, Springfield, Missouri

A review of some of the vast literature dealing with homosexuality has been carried out in order to show in what ways, perhaps, psychiatry can help in solving this difficult problem.

Historical

Down through the ages, man has been intimately concerned with homosexuality. Some of the most ancient historical documents, dating back several thousand years before Christ, make definite statements in regard to homsexuality, indicating that this form of sexual expression has long been known. In ancient Egyptian papyri, the gods Horus and Set are described as homosexual deities and worshiped as such. A well-known extract from Plato describes his seduction of Socrates. Homosexuality was socially acceptable in the Golden Age of Greece. It is said that the derivation of the word "pedagogue" is from the Greek word signifying the slave-attendant of wealthy Greek youths whose duty it was to guard their charges from the seductive efforts of Athenian noblemen. With the advent of Christianity, homosexuality and other forms of sex offenses were severely penalized. "If a man also lieth down with mankind as he lieth with a woman, both of them have committed an abomination. They shall surely be put to death. Their blood shall be upon them." The "sexual abomination" of Sodom and Gomorrah is biblically punished by fire from heaven and this myth creeps into our language with the word "sodomy." In later Roman times, homosexuality was often believed to enhance virility and soldiers were at times discouraged from female cohabitation. In the middle ages, homo-

---

* Now Captain, Medical Corps, U. S. Army.

First page of Eugene W. Green and L.G. Johnson, "Homosexuality," *Journal of Criminal Psychopathology* (January 1944), included in Henry's April 4, 1944 letter to Tedd.

Hotel Ansonia
73rd St. & Broadway
New York City

April 22, 1944

Dear Tedd,

I am in the throes of moving, hence no note paper is unpacked. But I must take time to scribble a letter to you. You know, Tedd, I told you at the beginning that I would never disapprove of you on moral grounds because I'm not a preacher and perhaps don't fully understand all that goes on in your funny organism,—Also that I would never think of you as a 'case,' which would be beyond my technical knowledge. Any advice I have ever offered is merely a suggestion from the way it looks to me from here, and from my larger experience of people.

But I have ventured to advise and "yell at you" on <u>practical</u> grounds and very much on aesthetic grounds. I still stand in the same friendly place.

I think you are mixed up with some very messy people who aren't good enough for you. They seem to be pretty freakish, pretty poor members of <u>any</u> society, beside being grafters, chiselers and parasites.

Don't you see that these people (and you, too, much of the time) live in a perpetual state of hysteria, and self induced crisis. All of this emotional "carrying on" is pretty silly, and is devised to catch sympathy and be "interesting" because of an imaginary "suffering so."

Stop it! Be yourself—which I think is a superior self.

Live by yourself. Stop going out to lunch and dinner with the wrong people. A lot of them are being tolerated in business now because the army draft has left them, and nothing else.

You are not in a position to <u>help</u> anyone yet, because you can't help yourself. That is a blind you are working on yourself. You wouldn't put up with such people as "Chickie"—my God—what a name!—if you didn't like him more than you admit.

Tedd—I can't go into all of this in a letter, I haven't time. Nature devised all living organisms with two powerful twin drives—self-preservation and the continuation of the species. The whole physical engine is geared to just that—I say "that" because the former is contained in the latter. Physically that's what we are. Nature makes many trials, and makes many mistakes. The born homosexual is one of them. These mistakes perish quickly—or nature would perish without leaving a trace.

Leaving out the question of procreation, homo-sexuality is doomed in itself to all final dissatisfactions. Having set up a resistance (often psychological) to normal sex relations it <u>cannot</u> find satisfaction in any other experience.

Don't you see that's why all of these hs' are so nervous, irritable, and <u>old-maidish</u>. They are for themselves, and for others a pain in the neck.

I'm rough with you—brutal, because I'd like to see you be happy, and adjusted to the world.

I know very little about homosexuality beyond what is in an extensive and technical literature, and all of that imposing mass of print boils down to a very little. I'm not sure that I know what goes on inside of you. [But I do know the patterns of behavior and I do know what will become of you.]

Many of us have to make painful adjustments to life—adjustments that are not to our liking, but we do have to save ourselves from disaster.

Most of what you <u>do</u>, what you <u>feel</u>, and incline toward, spells disaster, but you can save yourself from it, and the saving may be painful, too.

You ask society's "acceptance." Society isn't going to do it, and society is right—instinctively right.

Do you know penguins? Their marking? Their black sides and snowy feathered fronts—looking much like evening dress? If one is born with black feathers mixed with the white of his "shirt front" the others will have nothing to do with him. He has to walk alone. Cruel? Yes. But look—if he mates, he will beget other penguins with mottled markings. Why is that important? Because of safety. The original marking is camouflage—if that marking is lost the camouflage is lost and with it the safety of the whole flock. Nature destroys him.

No: society will not accept. Sophisticated society tolerates, but barely—and the law brands the whole business as <u>criminal</u>. You can see why. The corruptions of those who are <u>not</u> homos by those who are is a crime against the individual, and society is represented in posterity. You can't go against the great directional force of nature. So, be sure that society isn't going to be good to you. A few people (scientific minded) with pity, from the others—contempt—there's the penguin that walks alone.

<u>What to do</u>? Here is the most difficult thing yet. You have a possible great refuge of the spirit. I mean in the acquisition of a great and deep culture. That is a life work, a life satisfaction, and a shelter. The world will accept a <u>mind</u>.

Do you recall saying French conversations in a book annoyed you? Why? Only because you don't know French well enough. If you did you'd be proud of not being stumped by a few lines of idiomatic French.

The homo-sexual mind is often extremely superficial. You are very young. Live alone and like it. Work alone toward a far off but certainly satisfactory goal. Learn French—but really. Instead of contributing to the support of a parasitic bum, put your half dollars into private French lessons.

Learn about music—but really. Find some literary, or artistic hobby and work at it for the rest of your life.

I don't know if you have this kind of 'intestinal fortitude' or not. I don't know if the fiber of your mind is tough enough to work like hell, or not. If not it won't matter whether you're safe or not. But you can acquire great qualities by working hard enough to <u>have</u> them. The reward is in the thing.

Neither society, nor nature cares if you die tomorrow, or if you starve, or not. But we <u>are</u> something beyond the physical organism. The concepts of beauty, goodness, truth, hope, faith, charity—etc do not belong to the animal world, or even to the 'natural' world. They belong to the realm of the soul. Where are you going to live?

Button your pants up tight, Tedd, and open your mind!

Calm down. Nothing was ever done in froth and lather of hysteria.

And believe me to be

Affectionately yours,
HB

Keep your hair cut short—what are you advertising otherwise? You are a handsome boy—but not a pretty girl.

My address is 2 East 88th.

3222 Scranton Rd.
Cleveland, Ohio

undated

Dear HB,

Please forgive me for intruding again but I need you again this moment and am very torn. There are times when I resolve so strongly, times when all resolutions are torn down to tears, and times when things creep out of me and shock because I didn't know they were there and seem not to be able to stop them.

I have just finished "Well of Loneliness" and so am upset. I've been reading it for weeks on trips to work and home. Tonight I walked and walked home with it open, reading, gulping the last pages. Read the end, after pg. 400 and on. And then can you say what you do. Yes, you are brutal and I think I know why, to save me, yes <u>save</u> me. Thank you—thank you. I love you for it. And I become brave because of it, but also shallow and mean and no longer understanding. Isn't it too big merely to say "messy people." Oh, my God, even though many are trash, what of the Stephens and the arguments she put forth. I felt for her and like her every page of the way, reliving so much, feeling what I always thought probably lay ahead. Can I too close my ears and eyes and mind? Truly, have you closed yours? Be honest, completely honest with me as to what you feel. Your recommendations after days confuse me: perhaps an honest and thorough understanding with my own personality forgotten would accomplish more in the end.[64]

But I feel your wiseness as I write this and remember this letter is but an outburst.

---

64. At the end of *The Well of Loneliness*, Stephen (the protagonist) and her partner Mary are together but shunned by society. As an act of charity, Stephen pushes Mary into the arms of a man so that Mary can live a more conventional life.

I wrote this "Chickie" that I wanted to be alone, but he answers with assurance of his quick return. I look around my room, my books, culture; can it always be a refuge? My God, there shall be times, as now, when it melts for it has not warm, strong arms of flesh and returned affection. They are cold, these pages, meant for not my eyes, but the world's.

My second letter was an announcement from my supervisor of Dayton about the birth of her daughter. How glorious. This woman of heartbreak and tears has all this today. How happy I am—and not bitter. I remember eating with her once, observing her discomfort as the meal proceeded, her fierce and humiliated eyes. Then I learned it was because every eye, both female and male, had been turned on me and remained so. She could never dine with me again. And I think of Stephen. Oh, I don't blame this girl: but the terrible memory. Then, she read my book, came to me to discuss it, but could only weep, miserably. I was at a loss.

The third letter—from Mother, my refuge—but she knows little of it—I cannot bring it to her; I cannot add more grief to what she feels already.

I turn to you for something—new courage—resolutions—at the moment I don't know.

I can only say that in hurrahing Stephen's final sacrifice, her words burned more deeply into my heart.

Faithfully,
Tedd

56

TEDD

3222 Scranton Rd.
Cleveland, Ohio

undated

Dear HB,

I do so appreciate your letter of today: it is a fine letter.

If you recall my last mailed you remember it as I do as a mixed-up affair. I had no sooner sent it than I felt like writing you again to tell you I was alright—it was just that book and my exhaustion from work that made me so.

I try to control myself and succeed usually: at work I'm on an even keel which was not so before. It is not pleasant seeing this Al in all phases of what is probably this frustration you write of. I don't want to be like him: most of the men, naturally, are not.

I am tired generally because I have much to do on my job and work hard. Perhaps this is my cause for being upset at times. I know I resolve too much and feel too often like a Jekell [*sic*], Hyde.

That is what I don't like: my mind weighing decisions, but my body seemingly having other ideas. It is like a war.

I am reading "Floods of Spring" and wonder at it so much. I put you only in a world of knowledge and music: When did you learn the odors of soil, walking through a woods with its musty warmth and then cold, the little bug, all the actual impressions? I know them because I lived in a small town within a short walk of a woods, a ditch, and all you write of. And is it you or Peter who thinks so of books? What bothers me most about you is religion. It figures in your books so much: and forgive me for prying.

I liked very much "Betend dass Gott dich erhallte, so rein und schön [und] hold" for I remember singing its setting in music by Schumann at a contest.[65] I was ruled out because of no decision as

---

65. Translation: Praying that God preserve you, so pure and fair and sweet.

168

to whether I was a tenor or soprano. But I had wonderful praise that I would make an artist of German Leider [*sic*].[66] Someplace I still have that notation.

I took my mother to "Le Nozze di Figaro" and we had a fine time. Bidu Sayão sang but why, how could you not meet her. She is lovely.[67]

I always come here too soon: but first, do you like your new home, does it overlook the park?

Sincerely,
Tedd

---

66. *German Lieder* = German songs.

67. *The Marriage of Figaro* (1786), Italian opera by Wolfgang Amadeus Mozart; Bidu Sayão (1902–1999), a Brazilian soprano who sang with the Metropolitan Opera from 1937 to 1952.

57
HENRY

2 East 88th St.
New York City

May 3, 1944

Dear Tedd,

Letters are unsatisfactory, aren't they? So much remains unsaid, that would temper and modify statements. I have meant to be hard on you at times, but I have never been really unsympathetic. I have always pushed in the direction of working you toward happiness.

I have been so sure that some moves of yours did not lead that way.

One must have companionship and affection. But for one's own soul one must also retain fastidiousness, reserve, reticence and such qualities. I have usually disliked the sloppiness of most h.s. relations I have seen, even though at some distance. I told you you would have to work out many necessities for yourself.

I remain fairly well. I have to do some work yet on the magazine version of this new story—Red Shoes Run Faster, which Metro is making into a picture.

Then, if I feel well enough, I hope to start right off on the second volume of Kings Row which I anticipate will prove a difficult job.

Write when you can, and when you feel like it.

Affectionately,
Henry B

3222 Scranton Rd.
Cleveland, Ohio

May 1944

Dear Mr. Bellamann,

I've written so much tonight that I'm just wrote out … but for three days I have been wanting to sing praises of "Floods of Spring" to you. Gee, I consider it a masterpiece. Here is your second volume of "Kings Row." Oh, how could you ever conceive this—I am wordless! I lost my appetite for supper as Peter began breaking in Saracen! As I read of Robby's death I cried all the way home on the street car. I probably looked silly, but I just didn't care.

If the public overlooked this book, they missed a whole world for all these people step out before you, in perspective, in flesh and blood.

There is something of Shakespeare's life of seven acts. This is a drama. How fortunate are those permitted to play your characters. I loved <u>Robby</u>, and David, but Peter is a creation!

Could you tell me of your new story—"R. Shoes—"? And where it is to be published? Tonight I cease to be your close friend—tonight I write fan mail for I am at your alter [sic] as back in September.

Did I tell you that Cleveland College has accepted me for a course in psychology this summer?

This "Chic" is back—I don't know what shall become of it! I feel cold and strange towards him and hate being so. It's not nice. Well, just when things are settling, things pop!

I am embarked on "Of Human Bondage" now.[68] I won't waste time on car rides! And tomorrow "Floods" go to the office to begin the rounds, so full of wide-eyed talk I have been.

Sincerely,
Tedd

---

68. W. Somerset Maugham, *Of Human Bondage* (1915).

2 East 88th St.
New York City

May 26, 1944

Dear Tedd,

You do warm my heart by liking <u>Floods of Spring</u> which I like much among my books. Particularly that you liked Robby. "Floods" was a Literary Guild book so that it did sell around 175,000 copies, but the popular reaction was not so ready as in K.R.

Floods of Spring has just been bought by Sweden when Kings Row was a success under the title <u>RURGAR PO VALLUET</u>—Circles in the Water.

Victoria Grandolet has been sold in Switzerland for translation into German and French, and to South America for Spanish and Portuguese.

Tedd, so often my intentions are good but I forget to follow them. Did I send you a copy of <u>Victoria Grandolet</u>? I meant to, and don't want you to buy any books. I shall be glad if you read 'sem and like 'sem.

<u>Red Shoes Run Faster</u> is too much story to tell in a letter. A sadly condensed version will be published in The American Magazine. If I can find an extra typed copy of the original story I'll try to send it on to you if you'll send it back. I understand Metro is already at work on it. Robert Nathan, the novelist, is doing the picture script, in which I am most fortunate. He is a sensitive and fine artist.

Write when you can. I am gradually getting settled in my new apartment.

I hope all goes well with you.

Sincerely,
HB

2 East 88th St.
New York City

May 27, 1944

Dear Tedd,

Did you receive the manuscript of <u>The Surf?</u>

Best,
H Bellamann

61

TEDD

1954 East 71st
Cleveland, Ohio

undated, likely May–June 1944

Dear HB,

A proper way to finish this Sunday is in conversing a little with you. It is warm on this 4th floor and from my new windows I see many flat, black roofs and open windows displaying others' kitchen tables. Some kind of swift concerto is flashing from my tiny radio, the eyes of your picture scowl just over the top of my clock—it was McDowell's 2nd Concerto.

This is an apartment of a widow who "lived like a millionaire" for three years after the "Mister's" death. Then one day she said, "Mother, it's all gone; I'll have to go to work." So for twelve years she has "and in this business—well, I could write a book." One instinctively wants to call her "Mom."

There are to be females in the front rooms, a still unrented one, me, and her own small quarters. The stairs are fierce to this near seventh heaven.

My room has new flowered wallpaper of light green, white woodwork, hard-wood floors with two small throw rugs (not even Savina's rag ones), a chair, the usual dresser and mirror, high bed, and a table where rest my line of newly acquired books. The drapes are thin and flowered and swell with a breeze! The closet wanders far back in the walls, curving and turning.

It is here where I hope to rearrange my life, study, and be regular in habit and thought.

My 'steel' work may yet be increased and with much responsibility.

Since Saturday my hair has been much, much shorter. I can't wait to see if the men really see my haircut this time. It is so hot there with the ingots rolling down past our door that my shirt is almost off, my trousers rolled to the knee. Fortunately my chest isn't hairy so I am not embarrassed. My legs are quite large and I remember when I liked so to high-jump during track season. We had a jump in a back field. One felt good being sweaty and warm, patched pants and old sweater, a bicycle out to the Grade—our mud hole—for a swim and ghost stories under a "bugged" street light. There was always a bat threatening our hair.

I thought of home today.

I wonder if I shall <u>ever</u> find one: not of my making if I shall be alone, no exchange of words. I don't want to live for myself.

The widow said I was too young to sit around last night so I was pushed to a midnight show and slept late today. The awful heat one wakens to, a stiff neck; even a tub won't do the trick. A lunch and off I was to the Museum of Art. I spent my time in the theatre arts gallery with a display of the history of the stage, it- self. Then an organ recital by Walter Blodgett.[69] With 6:00 o'clock I began walking through the park. Beauty! All the green, the near wilderness in the heart of this city of heat and smoke. People at their ease, and I was lonely. I thought of you—perhaps that is why I write this—there was a Shakespearean Memorial Garden—it was a fountain, no more—a group of idle chauffeurs; a garden party further on, the men with white gloves and so dignified—previous- ly I had seen 3 Negro zoot-suiters with white gloves—I pretended I was a witch or a waif I wanted so to go to that party—then found I did envy them—but I should be so awkward and speechless, in such a life.

I walked for miles and hours. I had heard h.s.'s came here and I was embarrassed for I was alone and didn't want anyone to mistake me. I diverted my attention from everyone and this was the one point that spoiled the beauty. As evening threatened I hur- riedly left.

Those 2 at the mill: Al does not speak to me—one day I grew tired of hearing of his horrible pleasures and after he had made me

---

69. Walter Blodgett (1908–1975), curator of musical arts at the Cleveland Museum of Art from 1943 to 1974.

the object of conversation with a gate guard, I grew bitter. Actually I said little and he is not angry with me, but the world. He has said this for months; he gets on with no one, home life is afire, he takes all from associates, returns nothing. So I am always the same, and he is furious for lack of pampering. I flatly told him I had no more fears as to eating alone and being strictly on my own around the place.—Emil is back from New York—unsuccessful—but for a disgusting line of affairs which is actually his only ambition. He does not bother to call me.

I'm sorry to relate this, but down comes just what my mind is turning over.

It is almost unreal, this change. It was easy, very easy, yet difficult when wanting a pat on the back. I lay it at your feet—but still have a huge sense of self accomplishment. I'm so proud and holding to it all.

The day after Chic had returned I was troubled at work. It was one of the old days—black and funny feeling. I was so tired, I fell to sleep when I got home—Chic was to be working. But shortly he burst in with—well, his sort of lover. I was very agitated and could not make conversation. His first words were, "You didn't mind if I wore your shirt, and shoes, and socks!" Such a familiar sentence. I discovered my possessive attitude then, my will to control him. So he hadn't worked—that was his business. But inside I flared— jealousy for his day in the country; and because he hadn't trod the road I had planned out!

Finally I could not bear their company: I grew nervous and sick and hurried out for the papers. Located a room ad, showered, and rushed here. For 2 hours I thought, then took it and moved by hand until 2 o'clock. Chic wasn't too surprised, I had made no secret of my reading those ads. But he didn't know what he would do. I did. Make love to the ugly, but sweet, landlord's daughter and so earn his oats. He had already. I could not stand by and see her get hurt. Before he had left, Chic had made love to an old, old woman who in return had done his laundry and fed him. How I shuddered when I learned this from him.

Gee, I didn't mean to go on so—but you are like my diary. And for some reason I just go up hill with every line. Goodnight, and do write me soon.

Affectionately,
Tedd

2 East 88th St.
New York City

June 11, 1944

Dear Tedd,

Somewhere in this wide house and its many closets is your novel, but I can't find it. I spent some dusty time looking. I know I wrapped it (it was in a yellow box) and intended expressing it to you, but evidently didn't. So it is here somewhere. I hope, in any case, you have another copy. Have you?

I did lose a MS once of a complete novel ready for publication and the poor author had to write it all over. I didn't ask to see his manuscript so I felt less responsibility.

Anyway, your MS is here, but I don't know where, just as I don't know where anything of my own is, either.

I haven't had time to reply properly to your letter, but when I don't write you know I am busy.

Does the photo 'scowl' at you? I suspect that I am the most patient and best wishing friend you have. I use patient only to assure you I am not <u>im</u>patient. I think I understand pretty well much of what you go through. I do think you re-act much too violently to things. Sounds hysterical. You'd be more comfortable if you took everything easier.

You have a natural desire at your age to "see life." [Some of what you say and do isn't life: it has to do with a crazy fringe. The substance of life, the real business, is grim survival, tragic and hard and violent but one has to brace one's self and try to take it standing.

Loneliness is bad — one of the hardest things to know, but in the stretches of loneliness you can do these lifetimes of work. Just being gregarious isn't so much. The best things <u>are</u> born in solitude.][70]

---

70. This section was missing from Tedd's transcription.

You dramatize. That's all well enough. A talent for dramatizing and make believe may stand you in good stead. You may make important use of it someday.

Take care of yourself, Tedd. Being a little over fastidious also is all on the good side.

And be assured of my affectionate friendship.

Truly,
Henry B.

63

TEDD

2066 E. 77th St., Apt I
Cleveland, Ohio

undated

My dear Mr. Bellamann,

Last night in bed I composed a swell letter to you, energetic and fine flowing; now, in a few spare moments on Mr. Jones and Laughlin, I'm flapping about like mad to say all the things bubbling in me since I got your letter which came at a most opportune time. By this time you will have gotten my address … I'm sorry that every time you get it situated, I unsituate it again … but this time of dire necessity. About the opportune time a few lines back … you see, I met Chic on the street and we became involved in a furious discussion, all the things that comprise a conversation between two "different people" … namely getting settled in life … and with Chic … his Walter … so tiresome was it I could have screamed. But it did one thing … confirmed my wiseness in moving. For some reason this person upsets me very much … his ways, conversation, and attitude in life. When finally he was gone I re-read your letter half dozen times, and was soon feeling good and writing back on the ceiling above my bed.

Lest this opening paragraph tires [*sic*] you let me shove right off. It has struck me, especially with this letter, that perhaps now you and I can deal in things other than myself … your writing … my wanting to … a dash of art … (a course in historic costume at college is bothering me) … music … and my telling you how wonderful is Cleveland's <u>Playhouse</u>. I saw one of its leading men strolling down the avenue, with, probably, his wife, the other evening and I could not have been more thrilled had it been Raymond Massey. Also a character actress with a bad complexion but a kind smile. These people are splendid artists and I am all out in admiration for them. I dislike being a <u>fan</u> because it's wild and thoughtless and lacks individualism, but I suppose I am just that. I rather think of it as just giving to these people the praise they deserve as one does to Beethoven or Rembrandt or Goethe. The actors' medium is even stilted for he can leave little more than a reputation behind him.

Yes, how I like <u>Floods of Spring</u> … I think of it, remember it all day long, consider it a masterpiece of American literature. It has made a profound impression on me that shall last. <u>Kings Row</u> had a lot happening and made one quite breathless but with Peter one slowly grew and wondered and realized over a period of a slow and methodical lifetime. One lived … lived with each character … saw the huge dimensions of life and human relationships … it reminded me of the priest of <u>Kings Row</u> … though I never quite grasped this character. Above all it <u>FL of SP</u> lacked affectation! Perhaps it is just because it's so English, but Maugham's "Human Bondage" tale is always out of reach. Though Philip grows from boyhood to the obvious romantic youth before one, the feeling of time and maturity in a logical sense are lacking … his mind is tiresome … and in the author's style there are such casual sideline characters […] strewn along which naturally influence him but are so abstract and often unreal. I have covered but the first 300 pages so must retire from further and unjust criticism. After meeting Mildred I'll probably be all out for Maugham. Besides his <u>Rain</u> and his badly written, in my eyes, "<u>Moon and Sixpence</u>," I like his recent <u>Christmas Holiday</u> … found I wanted somehow to buy the drama rights to it … save it for sometime … I was deeply affected by the story and now I find that Hollywood has it … a good Robert in Gene Kelly … but the girl, Deanna Durbin … it just makes me sick. The character is so strong, the acting so demanding … and Miss Durbin! A fine singer but with a toooo pretty face, perfectly plucked eyebrows, bowed mouth, and such a correctness of her every look, stiffness, seemingly limited abilities, and tears, always too artificial. Margaret Sullivan would have been ideal. Then they put some newcomer into the relaters part when they have Van Johnson there, a superb actor who can display every emotion with a shadow like crossing on his face. Well, so it is. They have changed the story into a typical cook-up instead of presenting it as a tragic episode of life.

Mr. Bellamann, this letter has been stretched over almost a week so forgive, please, its incoherence.

Back for a moment, I hope they leave your books alone, Hollywood I mean. I thought <u>Kings Row</u> fared quite well with them. When I saw <u>Jane Eyre</u> the other evening I decided Joan Fontaine would make a good Victoria. She can say so little, but one has a feeling of turmoil behind her shifting eyes. She is small and will look the weakness of Victoria.

Yes, you did send me a copy of <u>Victoria</u>. It came just before Christmas and besides this, I had it before the book stores and was so proud. I have my own copy of <u>Floods</u> and have lent it enthusiastically as it is always received so. One man here at work seemed so grateful that I had him read it for he could not lay it down even though he had an examination in accounting at night college the next day. If you should be able to send me your novelette to read, I would be pleased. You can understand the thrill in reading something so personally from an author. Generally I dislike the usual run of magazine stories since they are naturally limited and was surprised you're writing for American. One story carried in the <u>Esquire</u> by that favorite of mine, Budd Schulberg, called something like the <u>Smashing of Innocence,</u> struck me as being a gem among a lot of poor writings.[71] Then too, I am limited in the subjects that interest me and miss much no doubt.

Your card mentions <u>The Surf</u>. No, I have not received the manuscript back.

Today when I got up I heard immediately from my radio of the invasion. A kind of sob ran through me. I rushed out expecting a sort of city reaction but every face on the streetcars were [*sic*] expressionless and sleepy. At work talk was little since one man's son is a paratrooper over there. So I dwelled on it within myself. I felt suddenly conspicuous and uncomfortable and wished I were over there, though I knew I thanked God for being so fortunate as not to have to be killing people. I hate the feeling of living on

---

71. "The Downfall of Innocence" appeared in the July 1, 1943 issue of *Esquire*.

the security, freedom, won by others. I have worked hard on my "war" jobs, but not because of the war; because I have inherited a dogged perseverance from my Dad. A perseverance for 8 hours of work I hate … and with no energy or total lack of perseverance for those things I love, I gain nothing.

So today I built up excuses for my being where I am. They all were thin and fell apart before me. I knew for a fact that I have been available as much as anyone. But perhaps the Board realized my own war had worn me out; my war to adjust myself to the freedom I found did not exist. The freedom from society. I don't know if I'm better off as I am now. Better off with society, yes … but, what of myself. This is the first time I have boldly questioned myself.

You have said nothing of my going to college to study a bit of psychology. My Dayton poet says, "I know why you are going to study this, but do <u>You</u>. Is it an excuse to associate further with the people you have been trying to escape from?"[72] I never thought of this and it has made me wonder. I say no, but Freud makes me feel if we aren't always "we." There is almost an uncontrollable part or spirit in us … a mystery to ourselves. Can this girl be right … am I defeating myself? I don't feel that I am so in writing this I am very cool and not excited as you might expect.

I'll end this on paper now, but go on thinking of all the unwritten paragraphs that will take form with me. Perhaps by my next mail, which will be soon (how well you know) … I'll tell you of my plans of study, of the thing that has bothered me since a kid one day in church. But I do sound like a serial, don't I? Write when you can … it means so much to me … makes loneliness fly.

Sincerely yours,
Tedd

---

72. Dayton poet = Tedd's friend Dorothy.

64

TEDD

2066 E. 77th St., Apt I
Cleveland, Ohio

July 3, 1944

Dear HB,

They tell me we worry most about the things we don't do, rather than those accomplished. This letter proves its truth. For such a long time I have been "meaning to." I did tear up one sad attempt, and then, too, I was waiting for a special reason.

I worked late tonight through an unexpected pile of business. Tomorrow's "4th" means more of the same also. But, now, after a bath and shampoo, cool pajamas, I feel relaxed and ready for you. But "Information Please" is blaring out at me, so you may not be able to comprehend all this.[73]

I am quite the same: I cry occasionally: just live: get all lonely: like cool summer nights: and think awfully of you.

But to the special stuff: for perhaps two weeks I went to the library nightly and finally found <u>Petenera's Daughter</u> in.[74] And, my dear man, we had a wonderful time together. If I should read one more book by you I'm sure my mind should squirm into the big, bold letters: B-E-L-L-A-M-A-N-N. You have taught me a great deal about literary composition. In fact, you make me want to try my hand again.

Probably you have preserved the Penn-Dutch: you have certainly recorded the farmer—the small town folk that I know. These things are real—and even become beautiful—strangely—but true. I never liked these people—until now—you have helped me to understand. You see, my father and mother are of the soil and I have been thrown into its midst.

---

73. A radio quiz show aired by NBC.
74. Bellamann's novel *Petenera's Daughter* was published in 1926.

I was caught up immediately by Pa as an insect beneath the boiling sun. And the steaming, quiet meal! My father speaks seldom. The hot nights—that same daring of sleeping naked—even that gave a relief to a young body. I have shocked wheat with my arms scratched and stinging: found a rabbit crippled in the cutting: seen mice run: and have wondered at the pleasure my father found in this labor—and so, the pleasure my mother found doing the same. Such a perfect, earthy love exists there.

Probably what I enjoyed most was Mom's feeble mind for I have such a grandmother. A new feeling for her was born in me.

It is a remarkable writing.

I could go on and on: truly it is an overlooked work of art. Your novels should be collected as an historical presentation of an American People.

How strange that over these 20 years you should connect your works with St. Stephens, Kings Row, St. Louis, etc. It makes splendid connecting. The library does not have your other novels, and I regret not reading them. I have never followed an author so before: and I like it. One seems to gain a household item: a treasure for the mantle: to be seen often.

Now, to <u>Cups of Illusion</u>: also in my late reading. I hope you aren't bored by all this. I like best "A Sound of a Going in the Tops of the Mulberry Trees." I read it for 2-1/2 hours.[75]

I showed it around—it was poorly received—but to me it is sheer lyric beauty. I find myself mumbling it again and again.

I like the first of: From this tower room above the wall, etc. It is haunting in its realism. Of "High Trees" I keep remembering: "See how the highest leaf fingers a star."

"Homesickness" has interested me. Did you perhaps write it in France, then thinking of Missouri? Those "gaunt houses," I too have seen them. And when you speak of "a gentle tongue"—French?—I am taking you away, I realize, from high in New York,

---

75. Bellamann's *Cups of Illusion,* published in 1923, is a book of poetry.

from Juilliard, to tie you to "dull rocks" and "barren hills." You are coming even more alive to me.

Funny the strains in me that are touched by "God"—"I know, for I made him, put him there myself." I skip to "In the Wake." I was not at sea, but a "you" passed and ever since I, too, have strained to a far horizon.

If I have a moment tomorrow I shall type and enclose a few things I wrote—oh—way back in school. I won't call it poetry—just outbursts.

I enjoy poetry most when with people and everyone intensely begins quoting and philosophizing.

By this time I have wiggled through a number of psychology lectures. I cannot get used to my chair there! It is embarrassing. Not until this last class did I become interested. It is all so general but I realize I shouldn't be impatient. I have a habit of burning out my enthusiasm. I know one student—pre-medical. After <u>Of Human Bondage</u> I meet him—almost Philip—even with a limp. He is a nice person. I appreciate his kind friendship.

I've skipped around the usual outbreaks, haven't I? Just as well. Oh, I'm not content and all that—but I have school now, and the Pop Concerts, the swell attitudes of the men at work, and your welcomed mail.

Hope you found your way through this.

Most sincerely,
Tedd

65
HENRY

2 East 88th St.
New York City

July 5, 1944

Dear Tedd,

It's hot here!

I am always glad to know how you are. I am so glad you liked Petenera. I still have an affection for the story.

Your poetry came. I think you write better poetry than prose, though you could be taught; or could learn to write both.

I have forgotten; have you a copy of "The Upward Pass"?[76] Write when you can. I am sorely pressed this morning.

Faithfully,
HB

------

76. Bellamann's 1928 book of poetry.

187

2066 E. 77th St., Apt I
Cleveland, Ohio

July 17, 1944

Dear Mr. Bellamann,

I don't believe you'll mind my school pad for I like writing a straight line once. I especially liked your yellow paper letters. They were long, said much, and seemed awfully personal.

I have not meant to neglect you but I have been working from 7 AM to 7 PM quite a good deal. I go to my lectures and squirm with exhaustion. I wish these hours left before the too soon 5:30 AM would stretch far out.

Today I feel like it is a kind of birthday. One year ago today I was sent from my Dayton job. It scares me now when I think of it—the awful facing of things! For me it was like a terrible and painful end—to my mother, heartbreak. It isn't necessary to summarize for you the happenings for you are directly responsible for what I believe to be my rebirth. How can I thank you—I have tried each day—it just remains something glowing down deep in me.

I hadn't remembered this day as such until a letter came reminding me. It has stimulated much thought and considerations. Within a week I begin my 20th year. It has not been wasted, this life!—I hope it has not!

I did fight today—a depression that crept through me—how I longed for your aid—your words. The future was there, puzzling me. Whether to make the best and most of my job and get involved and entangled in its security as I have this past week: or strike out and taking [sic] a chance. If I could but sing there would be no question.

You know, for a long time a certain play has bothered me. I read the role for audition into the Dayton Y Players. Finally I got <u>Night Must Fall</u> and Dan became a part of me. I think of it all the time and am dying to play Dan. There has always been theatre in me. As a kid I built stages and gave one-person plays, gave impersonations, wrote plays for the neighborhood kids' club. I did that right up through high school. The Cleveland Play House fascinates me, but scares me, too.

But to you. You set me on fire with your few words! as to my poems. I think of them: they intrigue and I wonder if there is any hidden encouragement there. I don't want to be fooling myself.

No, I have not <u>The Upward Pass</u>. I have read all the library here has. I myself have <u>Floods</u> and <u>Victoria</u>.

I would like to read <u>Richest Woman in Town</u> and <u>Crescendo</u>.[77] What of the "shoes" story? Has it been printed yet? I don't want to miss it.

I shall be busy studying for a psychology test and must miss Greig's [*sic*] A Minor Concerto which I dearly love. Last week I heard an all Tchaikovsky and Gershwin program with Beryl Rubenstein at the Steinway.[78] Do you play still? It seems somewhat removed from our letters. I wish it weren't.

I am so tired I have made a sad mess of this letter. I wanted to ask you so much—now my mind barely functions.

It was just that I must come to you for answers. What to do. A course in history for the next six weeks. Or the Play House. Or the steel business. You see, my dad is like Peter Kettering and I simply cannot go there.[79] It is hard for mother, she is so eager and willing to help but not able to advise fully knowing only of my dreams as I tell her. She would want me to continue working at J&L, just as she took the Play House from me after graduation and sent me to Dayton to earn my living.

Mainly this is to let you know I'm still here, eager for one of your blue stationery letters.

Respectfully,
Tedd

---

77. Bellamann's novel *Crescendo* was published in 1928; *The Richest Woman in Town* (another novel) was published in 1932.

78. Beryl Rubinstein (1898–1952), American pianist and composer.

79. Fiercely self-sufficient and domineering protagonist of Henry's 1943 novel *Floods of Spring*.

2 East 88th St.
New York City

July 19, 1944

Dear Tedd,

I'll send you copies of the two books of verse. Some very bad poems in 'em! My other works are hardly worth your time. The condensed version of Red Shoes is terribly cut down. I'll try to send you a typed copy of the original.

Tedd: stick to your job. You are very young. Life hasn't begun for you. There will be rich things and good things if you'll study. You're still superficial. When I think of what I wished for when I was your age I can only thank whatever gods there be that I didn't get what I wanted! It would have been a lasting catastrophe.

I'm starting some work on the second KR. Sometimes I do a few very abstract experimental pieces. I play the piano a little. I always work on a few very difficult things to keep my soul humble.

You're a smart boy, Tedd. I've come to like you very much and to miss your letters when they don't come.

Try for a while longer to keep on an even keel—the theatre is unstable, unpredictable and cruel unless you have genius and/or a thick hide.

Tedd, there is a state called by psychiatrists <u>h.s. panic</u>.

It is a strange compound of frustrations, desire, hate of the world, fear of the world, loneliness, etc. It is a type of hysterical outbreak—tears, etc. Though it is the lot of sensitive people to cry. There's plenty in the world to cry about. But if there <u>is</u> such a state of mind for you sometimes, don't worry, H.S. or not—you're a good kid, and to hell with the rest of the business. Be yourself—and be happy.

Devoutedly [*sic*],
HB

2066 E. 77th St., Apt I
Cleveland, Ohio

July 22, 1944

Dear HB,

I just had to write this, so happy I am from your letter I just read. It's like having that age old lump-in-the-throat, and a fluttering stomach, and everything glows like a new sunburn or blond hair and blue eyes. I didn't know, I truly did not know you really liked hearing from me. I am grateful. I'm shy about writing more and more because the pages pile up and the content remains nil.

What you have sent to me are like guide posts. They pick me up, I reign in joy, and I feel like I have a helping hand in mine. For what I am today I owe to you. I have won much, Mr. B., my adjustment to a great degree has occurred for never have I been so happy in the company of my fellowman before. I hate leaving work at night because I miss all I work for and with. We have such good times kidding—which I didn't think grown men did. They do, all the time. That's just it: I've learned manhood. I know its simplicity. I always feared it. Now I know that everything they say is not important and serious. They're like me, too. I'm really not very different. I wonder about the same things as they—and gather many of the same conclusions.

At class I met a pre-medical student. Many evenings we sit on the school steps and talk of many things. We had dinner the other evening and I did like it. It was grand eating with someone again. I'm perfectly at home with Harry; he is not at all affected. His dream of medicine probably springs from his being a cripple. Perhaps I told you that it was like meeting <u>Of Human Bondage's</u> Philip—except that the persons are so distant. Harry is so decent and idealistic in every way that I admire him very very much. And of course his generous friendship makes me most grateful. I do like fitting in!

I have been working from morn til night. And with your words, I shall plunge in even more so. With my boss' vacation this week I am given the post of checking all material scheduled. I shake at the responsibility. Am secretly proud though! This week we receive the Army-Navy "E."[80]

If you do send your books of poetry they shall be treasured always. Nothing pleases me more than these personal gifts from you. It's quite a feather in my cap to have them, you know. Maybe you felt this way with Debussy. Do tell me of him sometime, please. Poetry—it only comes from me when painfully wrung out by something terrible like "Lost Love."

I shall plan taking a course in American history for the rest of the summer.

There is a story I should like to write beginning in 1914. Perhaps this late American history can help me with background thought.—I never knew I could enjoy a classic as much as I am Vanity Fair.[81] It is real fun and full of laughs. I'd like to write like that—it is masterful.

You're a real guy, aren't you? Sometimes I'd like to shake your hand with real gusto—then think of your lecturing on Modern French Music, and I retreat in fear of offending. But I can't help that certain feeling ... And, my dear man, how could you ever have had dreams of more than you have accomplished?

I don't want to seem silly in my weak position, but if ever I can do anything for you, I would be grateful for the opportunity.

And I agree with you,—"to hell with the rest of the business—" I am happy!

Most sincerely,
Tedd

---

80. The Excellence in War Production Award was granted to outstanding production facilities for the War and Navy departments.

81. William Thackeray's novel *Vanity Fair* was originally serialized from 1847 to 1848.

69

TEDD

2066 E. 77th St., Apt I
Cleveland, Ohio

August 6, 1944

Dear HB,

The books came—they are wonderful and I like hunting through them. I disagree with your notation, the first of <u>Cups of Illusion</u> is a remarkable word picture. Thank you so much for sending them; I'll be writing you as I read them.

It's difficult for me to find much else tonight for my mind is rather helplessly crowded with my surprise induction slated for Friday. I lean, a bit shakily towards the Navy.

Despite my "hot air" speeches about getting into it, this greeting gave me a start. The world became pretty unreal.

So I quickly called up the nurse Jeanne and rushed to her with my poetry books and had a fine evening.

I'll be needing your moral support. Sometimes I look at it as a wonderful adventure, the makings of me. Then, I'm not so sure.

I feel that a great hey-day is past. Several men at work saw Bernhardt—as La Tosca—and how I envy them. Would you tell me about her? I've read two biographies.

And Nijinsky—how he must have danced. I was so moved by his biography. Did you see him?

I'll send this disconnected bit. Finis!

Faithfully,
Tedd

HENRY

2 East 88th St.
New York City

August 8, 1944

Dear Tedd,

Do you mean you have actually passed exams and all and are "in" the service?

In any case you'll do your part like a man. Going to war is no child's job and if conditions didn't <u>ask</u> the sons of the country to come to its help no one would <u>choose</u> the business. But this is different, It IS one of the world's great and tragic hours. You will let me know developments.

… Yes, I saw Bernhardt many times. I met her once and had tea with her. She looked a complete <u>mess</u> at close range, spoke with unforgettable beauty of voice and was amusing. I saw Nijinsky also many times. Saw him do his sensational L'Apres-midi d'un Faune to the Debussy music. In Paris. I never saw Duse—failed to see her of my own carelessness. Nor Richard Mansfield. But I saw and heard nearly all of the great ones of my day.[82]

Had dinner the other night with Argentina: know her dancing?[83]

I never met Paderewski—could have, but didn't try. I loved his playing,—revered the man, tho he was peculiar.[84]

… Let me know all the progress of events now. I mustn't lose sight of you. You'll do a good job—whatever, I have faith in you.

Votre très dévoué,[85]

HB

---

82. Eleanora Duse (1858–1924), Italian actress; Richard Mansfield (1857–1907), English actor.

83. La Argentina (1890–1936), Spanish dancer from Argentina.

84. Ignacy Jan Paderewski (1860–1941), Polish pianist and prime minister.

85. Rough translation: Yours truly devoted.

161 Sheffield St.
Bellevue, Ohio

August 10, 1944

Dear HB,

I am home in Bellevue tonight, sitting down to something quite as I did last Sept., and under so much the circumstances. So you remember that first plea—I do—but I remember more that first answer, just received as I arrived home from another Army physical and so, one year ago, a new chapter began for me; what of now?

First to answer your, oh, so prompt and kind question. It is tomorrow morning that I go through the "mill" and it is so humiliating and more tense than any Hitchcock thriller.

I'm rather faced by problems to—most out of my reach so I am not bothering too much.

Naturally you can understand somewhat what faces me—the uncertainty of it all. Strangely I look forward to going to the Navy—often want to very much; then of course I have other moments, many selfish for it means leaving a promotion in the offering and my school, college what I've wanted so long and feared—now to end?

The Navy would be new adventure, people—there I cringe,—and a body builder. I would be proud in the service, but—

You know there is in the exam the psychologist who asks those straight forward and meaningful questions—they request you tell the truth—what am I to do. Truth, and I risk my entry. Lie, and God knows—.

If only I could have a few minutes to explain myself; my falling to the foul—my present struggle for rehabilitation—then let them decide—can they trust me; Can I take it!

Gee, what a mess. I shall late be going back to work—though they need me badly—but my pride! I want to be a man, like everyone. These things shall bloom in a few hours. I shall write you immediately.

Of course you'll not lose me: rather I shall cling to your coat tails the more; such moral courage I need, I become strong inside as if few hurts can really matter so far down-deep.

I was so confused in my last letter, so many things left unsaid. There are men at work who saw Bernhardt, Weld, Eagles, Reyes, etc—but they aren't the kind to "tell" me about that. I even have to describe the possible play to restore their memories. But more of today[']s artists—K. Cornell—M. Webster—M. Evans—E. Barrymore.[86]

Such a grand birthday gift from my sister "Kings Row." I saw the picture again last week. To that wonderful music published. The "KR" theme.[87] I shall tell you later of my emotions during those hours.

Sincerely,
Tedd

86. Margaret Webster (1905–1972), American theater actress, director, and producer; Madge Evans (1909–1981), American stage and film actress; Ethel Barrymore (1879–1959), American actress.

87. Erich Wolfgang Korngold (1897–1957), Austrian composer and conductor. *Kings Row* was Korngold's most gothic film score; in liner notes to the 1996 compilation CD of Korngold's film scores, *The Warner Bros. Years,* film historian Tony Thomas says the score "might well have been the basis for an opera or a grandly scaled symphonic poem."

HENRY

2 East 88th St.
New York City

August 16, 1944

Dear Tedd,

I cannot say that the psychologist was wrong. You <u>are</u> emotionally unstable. But I also know that a great many psychologists are dam [*sic*] fools, and once having an idea in their heads are unable to be elastic in their thinking. You are emotionally unstable. So, I gather, are great generals when suffering from combat fatigue.

Well, anyhow, that's that, and I wouldn't give it another thought. The past is dead as Egypt even if it is only four days past. The future is not yet here, the present is what you have. Use it, happily and as gloriously as you can.

Rose Bampton was a contralto. She made herself into a dramatic soprano and her top notes sound thin and forced. She had a beautiful voice, still has in part.

I saw Bernhardt many times in many plays. Someday I will tell you what she was like. One critic said she was a packet "de ficelles" — ficelles meaning either nerves or stage tricks. She knew all the latter, and for me was the greatest actress I ever saw. I never saw Ellen Terry or Duse. Sarah's voice was pure gold and it echoed in your emotions for long afterward.

I went to call upon her with an American lady who resolutely spoke very bad French. Bernhardt's eyes glittered with malicious amusement, but I could not help saying, "<u>You</u> don't speak English at all." "But I don't try" she said quietly.

You are still in the stage of emotional wallowing in your artistic experiences. That is all right. Better to be able to do it than to have <u>only</u> an intellectual approach. You can't it seems add the

---

88. There seems to be a missing letter from Tedd that informs Henry about not being conscripted into the military.

emotional to the intellectual if the intellectual comes first, but the reverse is possible. You will be a participating artist when you have a finely balanced blend of the two. You'll come out all right. I recognize so many of your stages of feeling and of being. I only fear you stopping short of complete realization and being superficial.

It is hot here, too. Favorable as the location of this particular apartment is, catching whatever breath of air stirs, it is still hot.

Be of good cheer. With good stuff in you you will make the better part of whatever happens.

Faithfully,
HB

2 East 88th St.
New York City

August 30, 1944

Dear Tedd,

You do seem to live in a more or less perpetual state of crisis which strikes me as being maybe not necessary. Certainly not so good for you, and I suspect, somewhat self-induced. Do I seem heartless? I do not feel so. I remember a good deal about the hysterical state of adolescence, but you are getting along a bit for that kind of thing.

So you like Miss La Gallienne [*sic*]? Good actress but a good deal like a harp with a lot of strings mssinh [*sic*]. Intellectual—but her emotions seem pretty synthetic. Probably due to her rather special emotional make-up. I used to see her in Paris when she was a little girl. She was, I think, the prettiest young girl I ever saw. Her mother had a hat shop and she used to deiver [*sic*] packages. Madame La Galleinne [*sic*] was already separated from Richard Le Gallienne. He was a sort of second rater I guess. I met Eva again in Philadelphia after she was so badly burned. She was the guest of Mrs. Bok and I sat in the box with her one night at a performance of Chávez' "H.P." ballet.[89]

I see, looking … at that paragraph, that my typewriter doesn't spell very well.

What kind of work do you do? Do you type well? Quickly? How much are you paid? I have a special reason for asking.

Do you have this wonderful fall weather in Cleveland? I have been in Cleveland several times. Went there to give some Juilliard

---

89. Eva Le Gallienne (1899–1991), American stage actress; Richard Le Gallienne (1866–1947), English author and poet; Mary Louise Curtis Bok (1876–1970), founder of the Curtis Institute of Music; Carlos Chávez's *H.P.* (*Horsepower*, or *Caballos de vapor*) premiered in Philadelphia March 31, 1932.

scholarships at the Cleveland Institute. All I remember is a Statler Hotel and a lot of penetratingly damp bad weather.

When the war is over I rather expect to go back to Paris to live part of each year. Not all year because of the climate and because I think it is a good thing to keep in touch with native soil.

Have you read the four "Joseph" novels of Thomas Mann? I find them only endurable in spots. Over written, verbose, turgid, and I'll wager not one of the world masterpieces some of the reviewers think them to be. If you run across a short novel "Absent in the Spring" by Mary Westmacott, do read it. It is a brilliant malicious study of a self-centered woman. A highly civilized piece of writing.[90]

Try to come down to earth, Tedd. You can't "suffer" all of the time. The earth has a lot of comfortable things in it, rewarding things. Food, going to sleep—etc.

Write when you can.

Always,
HB

---

90. *Joseph and His Brothers* (1933), a four-part German novel retelling stories from *Genesis;* Mary Westmacott (pen name of Agatha Christie), *Absent in the Spring* (1944).

2066 E. 77th St., Apt I
Cleveland, Ohio

September 2, 1944

Dear Mr. Bellamann,

Write when I can? I must, and this moment! Each letter received I think more exciting than the last. This one, today, was real. You see, I have been wondering about you. Most of the time you are a sort of myth or hazy shadow; then when I look at your picture or read a letter I become frightened. You are a person with two eyes that observe and behind which you calculate. My blood runs cold; how can I possibly expect to keep you.

You are not going to get that other letter, the morbid one, not this time. Perhaps I do bring it all on myself; I'm told I analyze every little thing and make something out of it. But here I am in a dirty mill (like that tree in Brooklyn) with all my excitement over a book, a recent play, a new thought. The men about are like machines and they look up at me as if I were mad! They have their homes; they drive on and on to that end and soon they eat and sleep steel until nothing else matters. And so I must try to cork up all my bubbling and be like a machine and wait until I can escape home: then I'm too tired, lonely, and unhappy for caring. Oh, I need someone with whom to go, to talk with, to laugh and to read. Someone to challenge my abilities.

I read plays on the street cars going to work. They are small and convenient and are finished before they become boring. So, theatre comes back into me. I had such plans when I graduated; to work and study, stabilize myself for later stage work … then I woke up in the midst of the world! I long for the Play House … but shake in my boots whenever I approach it. As a kid our neighborhood club gave plays in our basement. I always did a "hula" at the end and rated a few cents from extravagant parents invited. I was quite a boy soprano for years at home and performing was a weekly event. I always managed to be in church plays which I disliked; they seemed so stupid. I first remember teaming with Kathryn Tucker, a few years older than myself, and noted for her monologues. We were just kids then and cast in one of these church affairs. We were waifs. With a shawl pinned under her chin, she did a lot of talking. I had been bedecked with coal dust and merely agreed with her in everything by loudly wiping my nose down along my sleeve.

We were a great success. I remember a sumptuous lady with white curled hair, huge dangling pearl earrings, and a velvet dress, kissing me when it was over.

When I lost my voice—I had held two church solo positions—I turned solely to what drama there was about. In a "Chimes" sort of thing I merited most enthusiastic praise from a lovely hometown artist just visiting from her career. I still recall running the emotions in that play. But my costume was tight and I lived in a perpetual state of "ripping" fear. I had definite ideas as to the play's production and insisted on displaying them. It is well that my cousin was the director lest I should have been soundly slapped. In time I realized how stupid had been my suggestions.

I was asked once to read Patrick Henry's "give me liberty" oration for all English classes in the school. I have never gotten over the surprise of that invitation. I read "Macbeth" throughout the Shakespeare class, (I had practically leaped from a sick bed to keep this appointment.) and just about everyone in "As You Like It." I designed sets for "Macbeth" and gave a lecture with them too. For two years I had presented exhibitions of opera drawings in the library. I once gave the "Otello [sic]" "Purse and Honor" scene in the same Shakespeare class playing both the Moor and Iago. The class needed the sleep anyway. I was the Scotch soldier in the widely known play done in darkness by three voices. We had to repeat it.

I always drew character parts, mostly hen-pecked husbands with a straw hat resting on my ears at school; once a hillbilly in "The City Slicker."

"June Mad" had been chosen as the Junior-Class play and I was in a dither.[91] I fitted no part ... not one! It was rumored I was to play a father. I sobbed for days heart-broken. A father indeed! Suddenly I was handed the part of the wealthy college senior with a horrible superiority complex, a way with the females, and a way of hurting everyone. The director handed me my part and said, "It's the only one that needs any acting." I could have kissed her. And it did me no good to have the cast assembled in accordance with my height ... so short for a college senior! I was so proud then ... so embarrassed now.

I had to play and sing a love ballad ... I chose Ich Liebe Dich, imagine ... and in my frayed soprano ... a college senior! Could anything be worse. I still shudder ... I was certainly not ready for this assignment.

The next year we gave a '90s melodramer [*sic*] ... "Pure as the Driven Snow."[92] I slaved for one of its smallest parts, E. Z. Pickens. He was a character! I assembled an authentic costume, suspenders, striped shirt, watch chain and fob, a bulky straw hat, and parted my long coiffure down the middle and waved it away. With those exaggerated mannerisms, screaming voice, and flat-feet plodding they say I brought down the house. I was so intent on my walk I heard absolutely nothing. The next day my popularity with the class had jumped by leaps and bounds. It ended wonderfully, this play, but not before the fireplace burned and we were all little heros and heroines in putting it out and "going on with the show."

I gave two Carmen Miranda impersonations for the USO and went to Dayton. I joined the Y Players whom I do to this day dislike completely but for one, a poet busy being a mother and my good friend. They were a quarrelsome lot, overly dressed, overly smoked; sly men living with not such sly women. Such a group! And I traveled fourteen miles each Friday to be with them in hopes

---

91. Florence Ryerson and Colin Clements, *June Mad: A Comedy in Three Acts* (1939).

92. Paul Loomis (pseudonym for Wilbur Braun), *Pure as the Driven Snow: A Comedy Mellow Drammer in Three Acts* (1939).

they would launch a play and forget parliamentary procedures. I auditioned with the Dan role from "Night Must Fall." The president was pleased and told the poet so. The poet, Dorothy Engel-Payne, plugged with my ambitions then for playing female parts. The president closed like a clam (and I don't blame her) and I gradually resigned. I refused to be mis-cast in anything as the previous experience of "June Mad." The club had one grand actress, Ruby King, who tells me I wrote her her first fan letter. It was after her Birdie in "The Little Foxes." The Dayton critics had raved. But the club never gave her another chance. This whole contact has disillusioned me; they were such a petty crew, dragging their lives always with them.

I used to read Keats'"When I Have Fears That I May Cease To Be" with genuine tears. Once I did Birdie's drinking scene (Little Foxes) in a speech class, and had many crying. Two years has robbed me of much: mostly that confidence, that dream. What does the theatre mean to me now? I don't know. A lump in my throat often.

But this is what lies with me, these exciting memories: but I am not sure of anything now.

So I like Le Gallienne's voice: I read her autobiography, <u>At 33</u> and enjoyed it immensely. It's exciting that you know her. She will be here soon in "The Cherry Orchard." She is attractive! I look forward to her performance; your sketch was very odd and what do you mean, "her special emotional makeup?" She wrote so much of Hilda Wang[e]l in "The Master Builder" that I read this too and am completely puzzled. I can find no one who has read it and there is something about that play that will not leave me. Ibsen puzzles me to the core. I read "Hedda Gabler" in high school and was so taken by it that I'd stand in the wings of "The Driven Snow" production rehearsals "tearing up our child; burning our child," and then on cue would bound out as E. Z. Pickens. I wrote on "Hedda"; called it "Tale from a Norweigan [sic]: A Musing on a Play by Ibsen." Very impressive title I thought. I gave it as a monologue in a Speech examination. My own characters had once met Hedda and this was the way they had been effected [sic] by her personality. If I can find it and it doesn't seem too silly I'll send it to you. Kid stuff, you know.[93]

I didn't mean to go on like this. I'm so ashamed. But you shouldn't be such an untalkative person.

I spend my days filing a great many steel orders in a great many places; take the steel sizes and a heat of boiling steel and through a series of mathematics work up various rolling sizes. These are placed in a schedule which I type, duplicate in ditto and distribute nearly fifty copies over the entire mill. I type letters and memorandums, pick up the ends of many things, keep records and requisitions, work as a go between in several departments and do whatever falls my lot. I also mildly protest when the superintendent runs his hands through my hair and I lose my part until I get my next haircut. Yesterday, after this procedure, he sat down and laughed up at me, his eyes sparkling, "You know, some day I'm going to take you along with me over the entire mill and show you everything. I'll make a real mill man out of you. Then when I come in here, I can do my business straight with you." I was tremendously touched and grateful, but something inside me knew "No." I smiled and stammered, he laughed some more, pinched me and left. I'll try my best in anything as my father taught me, but I know I'll never be a mill man: I don't want that.

I hope this typing fares for it is the evidence in the raw. I seem to have good speed once the newness of a job is gone and my fingers cease to be thumbs. I average $50 a week, sometimes a slight margin more for overtime.

You did like Paris? I've dreamed of Europe so, quite determined to one day go there. The Globe Theatre at London, the Louvre, and on to Bayreuth. I must see those Wagnerian hills and skies. Are they as overwhelming as the Valkyrie? Perhaps Können Sie deutsch verstehen and Je parle en francais un peu would get me through Europe. I shall miss these letters when you go to France so much.

---

93. Anton Chekhov, *The Cherry Orchard* (1904); Henrik Ibsen, *The Master Builder* (1892); Ibsen, *Hedda Gabler* (1891).

I feel autumn coming, but not here. Only streets of dirt and noise are here. But I know that at home it is cool with a great warmth beneath a sweater; the trees sway all day and whisper all night; their leaves dry and crowd about one's feet as you walk. The garden is cleared and neat piles of bean plants are burned. Footballs threaten bay windows. There are scabby apples, popcorn, and cider; soon a fizzle of a Halloween as always. I like to walk down the railroad tracks (where snakes sun themselves) to the old swimming hole ... we actually had one. A street car line ran around it and how we would plunge our naked frames into its muddy waters when the cars passed. Another sport was climbing atop the corn shocks much to the farmers' fury. Oh, such fun I had. Then autumn came to mean loneliness when the evenings closed with mist and the air of my third floor bedroom was warm on my face.

The title "Joseph" would discourage me ... and four volumes! That great "American Tragedy" is the nearest I'll come to volumes. I have passed through "Outrageous Fortune," the play. So unreal, stagey, strained. Poophfffff. I admire E. Williams so for his very fine plays, for his talents. After Ibsen now, come Chekhov.[94]

This week we learned that my sister's husband was killed in action in the Pacific. I cannot bear Martha's suffering: I grew up with her, shared her life, love her so dearly. She had such a short time with him and they have the sweetest baby. He is blonde and tanned and wanders about with a most vivid imagination. She has been home since the baby arrived and I'm glad; glad too that she has my father and mother for she will not be faced with problems as to her son and herself. She can relax into their love and kindness. If only it does not twist her inside. She as yet cannot believe it. I feel most for her at night and in the morning when her world must really appear shattered to her. So I wrote a poem:

---

94. Theodore Dreiser, *American Tragedy* (1925); *Outrageous Fortune,* see note 46; Emlyn Williams, author of *Night Must Fall,* see note 6.

AUGUST 1944 ... WE REGRET TO INFORM YOU

All my little dishes,
Sitting on a shelf.
     All dusty, nearly mildewed,
     Unchipped, sky blue.
Sitting on a shelf in darkness,
     Unclinked, unsipped from,
     Untouched, full of tears.

Pretty little cloth[e]s,
To have mirrored their sky blue.
     Now faded, unwashed,
     Unsoiled, not worn.

Lying under moth balls,
In a lower drawer.

A perky little hat,
With a cookoo [sic] feather on the top,
     Wilted in tissues,
     Boxed and bound.
Dreams stuffed into a pillow,
     Now pounded, tossed.

A mate to that old pillow,
Quite as white as any ghost,
     Silently sleeping,
     Without a single dent.

Pale moonlight,
On that pillow,
     Cold,
     Blue.

Dear me, I hope this has not bored you. I am ashamed of such length. Forgive me. I am most glad for food and going to sleep, but at times this seems not enough. Only a waitress to greet me, an empty bed ... even in winter! No, life is too precious (though

I have often wished it gone), too promising for those who accomplish.

It is nearly a year that you came to me, the 25th to be exact. Such a momentous time that was. It ushered in a new life. I hope I have been worth this year: I am so happy today to be indebted utterly to you. Please accept all the love I can crowd into that word. I am a better man for it.

Faithfully yours,
Tedd

75
HENRY

2 East 88th St.
New York City

September 22, 1944

Dear Tedd,

I actually found the manuscript of your novel today! I <u>think</u> it will go off to you by express tomorrow.

I have been busy with no time to write. Have your letters and poem: more of these later.

These are beautiful days. Good luck to you in everything.

Faithfully,
HB

2066 E. 77th St., Apt I
Cleveland, Ohio

September 24, 1944

My dear HB,

This clear, bright and cold day is near its close: so swiftly it has gone: from the east to the west in one burning movement like the leap of a ballerina, sparkling.

These last two Sundays I have spent alone here in the city with great satisfaction. Despite the lonliness [sic] there was rest and happiness.

Early last week I wrote you a monstrous letter but never mailed it: I fear I bother you. I told you in it about the successful $14~ Opera stay here and mostly of "The Cherry Orchard." All week I have thought of little else. This play, like a snow crystal, so delicate—like a spider's web when the sun first strikes it and the dew sparkles and glistens. I could not stay its every moment but in my mind. I walked home that night, I don't know how many miles for the beauty of the piece lay so heavily within me. I stopped at an art gallery for they had several fine pictures in the windows. People can have their stamps and first editions, I shall want a few paintings: just a few that when I first see them, they talk to me. A picture of the sea: of Marie Antoinette's France when the gay court life gathered in the field and sang and flirted and loved. A picture which sings with plucked strings and happiness flows out—carefree, dreaming.

I believe I may understand what you meant of Eva Le Gallienne. She is lovely, white—very white, and so graceful. As Lubov she bubbled with an occasional pang of discordant sorrow. "I couldn't understand my life without that cherry orchard." The critics say the play is dated and of no consequence. How wrong they are. Can't they understand that Chekhov put down souls and not bodies? They say it is not realistic … if what graces our stages today is realism, I want none of it.

About me in that audience were lovely ladies with glowing hairdos and with them their puzzled men with polished nails and minds still in business schemes. They sputtered questions as to the play to their wives who shrugged and toyed with an earring.

Were these not Lubovs and Gaevs and Lopakhines? Oh, if they had but read the play, once, twice, learned it, lived it for a week. But their faces were as blank at the end as before the first curtain.

As a student I watched Joseph Schildkraut, a master of his art. Each gesture had a meaning, each blank look a musing beyond. There was so much to see—so very much more to hear—it was like fine, soft music.[95]

Now I've gone on for three pages. You see how I massacre your kindness? But there are so many moments that I want to share with you—I dislike warmed over emotions.

I listened today to the Tristan prelude and love death—cried a little for it left me broken in little pieces: such an unearthly composition.[96]

I hope you are busy and not ill in these weeks. They have been long in not receiving a letter.

Faithfully,
Tedd

---

95. Joseph Schildkraut (1896–1964), Austrian actor who had a long career in Hollywood films, including silent and talkie films.

96. The prelude to Richard Wagner's 1865 opera *Tristan and Isolde.*

77
HENRY

2 East 88th St.
New York City

September 26, 1944

Dear Tedd,

I <u>am</u> so apologetic. Your manuscript was sent today by express, insured, etc., but I was not here and the maid not knowing, sent it collect. Please be sure I wouldn't have done that: I am so sorry.

I am happy to have your letters—all you feel like writing. I quite agree with you about pictures.

We'll doubtless get around to a discussion of painters, too, one of these days.

Don't destroy your novel, even when you get to where you don't like it. Keep the record.[97]

Faithfully yours,
HB

---

97. Tedd did not take Henry's advice. Tedd tells us in the film *Letters to Uranus* (2000) that imagining himself as Ibsen's character Hedda Gabler, he took the pages of his novel and threw them into his apartment building's incinerator, dramatically speaking Hedda's words, "I'm tearing up our child! I'm burning our child!"

2066 E. 77th St., Apt I
Cleveland, Ohio

October 30, 1944

Dear Mr. Bellamann,

Somewhere in one of my books is a letter to you. Several beginnings lie unfinished in my stationery box. At least one other was crumpled and tossed away. I do hope this one makes it because long silences make friendships difficult. The letters I speak of have been unsuccessful because it was hard to say the right things in them. Not nice things … but, honest things. I rather feel it is my honesty that has held you and I want it to remain so. Yet I realize that when I approach you I'm taking valuable time and must make the most of it. So I try to sound intelligent and try to write well without being stiff. I'm an awful conversationalist that runs on and on for hours and find it hard saying and writing things simply and being done with them.

This course on composition has made me very self conscious. I've gotten to that point where I hesitate to write anything and lose many thoughts that way. So I've hatched many, many foolish theories resembling my excuses for the poor quality of "The Surf etc." My autobiography went over splendidly. The professor said that in all her years of teaching she had never received anything like it. It was read in place of the scheduled test. But looking it over this past weekend I lost my confidence. It lacks a great deal. I would like to send you a copy soon. The grammar was torn apart; I would like you to dive into the contents.

Meeting so many really nice people at school has made college quite worthwhile. I am having a wonderful time with a SPAR.[98] We see plays and talk and talk. She is kind and sensitive. I've been

---

98. *SPAR* (Semper Paratus, Always Ready) was a term for the U.S. Coast Guard Women's Reserve in WWII.

asked to concerts and all that for the first time haven't enough time to accept all. I want to hurry down to Springfield this weekend and visit old spots and old friends. I'm fairly nervous about it all. So much deep water has gone under the bridge since then. I've known many lovely dawns since.

Thank you. You mean so much to me that these silences hurt. I wish I could show you in some way my appreciation and affection. It is wonderful having you as a part of me. A deep rooted guide.

That was a fine push to Mary Westmacott. Her "ABSENT IN THE SPRING" was a treat I doubt will be equaled again. I read swiftly and breathlessly and thought of it a great deal. I suppose most of us can gain a great deal from that story. Yes, it is more than a story. I've lent my copy out.

"Othello" comes to town tonight and it has received a gala box office sellout welcome.

Of course I can't write you of the greatness of the Play House's recent productions. You would have to see them. Soon I shall be able to attend some rehearsals there. If nothing happens and royalties are secured, I am cast in Saroyan's "Hello Out There." A masterpiece. When I recommended it to the professor I had no idea she would hand it back to me with, "We'll do it. And you can have that part you want so badly."[99]

Just the beginning … already the end. I hope New York shows the autumn. "So many yellow sails are set. So many red."[100]

Sincerely,
Tedd

---

99. William Saroyen's *Hello Out There!* (1941) is a one-act play. Presumably Tedd played Photo-Finish, the male protagonist who is jailed when a woman accuses him of rape.

100. "So many yellow sails are set— / so many red!" Lines from Bellamann's poem "A Sound of a Going in the Tops of the Mulberry Trees …," which appeared in *Cups of Illusion* (1923).

2 East 88th St.
New York City

November 1, 1944

Dear Tedd,

You've been on my mind a good deal. I have not written because I've been ill. Nothing too serious—bronchitis, etc., and a devilish siege with eyes. I am better.

You sound happier. I hope you really are. I miss your letters when you don't write. Fall comes slowly here with little color. Out of the city I hear it is brilliant.

I'll be happy to see the autobiography … I'm trying to get to work—have been too long delayed.

Write often—and about anything you will. I am

As ever
HB

2066 E. 77th St., Apt I
Cleveland, Ohio

November 18, 1944

Dear Mr. Bellamann,

The rains have washed every bit of warmth from the sky and trees; now it is winter.

I have too long been silent. Actually I wrote several letters to you when in neurotic states to reveal my other self. I think I tore them up, or did I send one to you? I have a bad memory. Sometimes I dislike correspondence. It is so inadequate!

For instance, after class recently I wanted so for you to help me. I'm so confused about English applied to composition. When the professor says, analyze the paragraph you have just written, I do everything but count the number of words in a sentence, see if I'm using compound and complex sentences, and using which and that and whereas and as if, which are exactly what he means for me to do. It seems so awful to tear down what comes out of one. All this and much, much more goes buzzing around my head after each class. I can't write freely anymore. Oh, I'm so mixed up. I was hoping you might send me some advice as to how a writer sets about organizing his work, developing a style, and analyzing his work. I've decided to abandon good grades by memorizing what all is said, and thrash it out within myself. But this reminds me that anymore I am not willing to take anything said as is. I mix it all up inside until it is painful. Oh, dear, can you see what I'm aiming at? In other words, how did you come to write so beautifully as in <u>Kings Row</u>? Is it the material, or the composition construction?

I am sending a theme to you. I wish you would not spare me. I'd really like to know how it adds up. You see, I [was] quite proud of it when I first had written it. Now that it has cooled, I don't like it. Having copied it off in a rush during lunchtime, I hope it is readable.

Tuesday I attend a rehearsal at the Play House that I have mentioned so often. I shall see backstage too. Naturally, I can hardly wait.

Time goes so fast, and if I find one evening, I just spend it lazily lying on my bed. Life is fun, but it takes energy.

I must say that there seemed to be a time when I could write really important things to you. Now it is all the trimmings, the trivial. What has happened to me? Is it that I don't want to bother and bore you? Or have I lost a certain frankness and honesty? Of course, then we were going through a stage. I know that stage has not ended, finished. Twenty years mean more than that. And yet, there is nothing to say about it. Oh, if I could only reach you at those times when I need you so. When I don't understand the strange things in me. I want always to be a person with you.

I hope you are well, that you will write me soon and long, and that I shall send heaps of thoughts and ideas to you.

Sincerely,
Tedd

THE YELLOW LEAF[101]

"My way of life is fall'n into sear, the yellow leaf."[102]

Autobiography ... autobiography: all I am today are highpiled hours and days dashed upon days as the unknown sculptor twists and raps my common clay, then with deft fingers smooths away the clefts and my base grows firm. A goodly foundation is needed to withstand this adventure of living. For who are we? And what are we? Dare we explore this wide expanse of ourselves, search in its very recesses for the fearful psyches lurking there? Honesty with fellow man is such a "taken for granted" item; but honesty with ourselves—our diamond of life held before our eyes until the mirrors and reflections send us weeping to our shoal existences— is all too often permitted evasiveness.

I once wrote a poem of my "bloody soul," and such misery it caused me I care not to propound it again. W. Somerset Maugham wrote, "It is an illusion that youth is happy, an illusion of those who have lost it; but the young know they are wretched, for they are full of the truthless ideals which have been instilled into them, and each time they come in contact with the real they are bruised and wounded. It looks as if they were victims of a conspiracy; for the books they read, ideal by the necessity of selection, and the conversation of their elders, who look back upon the past through a rosy haze of forgetfulness, prepare them for an unreal life. They must discover for themselves that all they have read and all they have been told are lies, lies, lies; and each discovery is another nail driven into the body on the cross of life. The strange thing is that each one who has gone through that bitter disillusionment adds to it in his turn, unconsciously, by the power within him which is stronger than himself."[103]

This can cast disillusionment but consider youth as a collection of expanded dust—like specks of experience which shall

---

101. Tedd's autobiography, written for a composition class.
102. "Macbeth" by William Shakespeare. (Tedd's note)
103. "Of Human Bondage" by W. Somerset Maugham. (Tedd's note)

become personality and so, we are accepted, or rejected, by society according to our adjustment to its conventions and fashions of the moment.

Nevertheless, psychologists tell us that we are prone to remember the more pleasant aspects of life and with these I do prefer to deal. Let the morbid and the "bloody" real wait to be bound in black leather when I am cold and still in eternity. Rather then, I should like to cry, "Here I am when I was. And think not too bitterly on me. I tried." Oh, I should be very English and stodgy in my writing and most Thackerian if I could, for dear William has lasted strongly these many centuries.

Now let my life be drenched by the four winds—clean and sweet winds—that bring the distinctive seasons to hover over my small Ohioian town. The fields roll in upon it and emerge undisturbed on the other side. City folks speed through it and never see the little dramas lining Main street. The white bearded drunk who suns himself at the bay window with nodding, whirling head; the white house with green shutters that holds the lady with the crazed mind; the spinster in her dust cap calling her black cats for their treat of liver; the young dark haired cripple with the flashing eyes and temper; simple Albert who loves all little girls "a hundred bushels"; and the tall, lean poplars on which I had often vent my own unhappiness.

No, my town was never boisterous though speared from every direction by white ribboned roads. Huge locomotives lumbered through her center and cast waves of shadows with their smoke; but no one reprimanded too loudly. This was her life.

I am carried back to muse on the days that were long and often too numerous, when a year was a century, when memory was too unsubstantial to remember at dinner what had been eaten at lunch … and often, if lunch had ever existed that day at all. To be sure there were problems, but they were like the solitary pricks of a needle.

It is only fair and just to catch me in the throws of summer, for through nine months I had an angelic head bobbing over the Primer Reader, or slightly less simplified works.

I applied myself disgustingly well to the grades, but had la mistresse de la classe ventured after me when I left her care, she would have been quite surprised at the barbaric whoops that heralded my return to Sheffield Street.

No matter how quietly the dawn crept in my town and slipped down the deserted streets, I was there to greet her; but quietly for there were things to do that required utmost "undiscovery." I would dash across the street into the tall grass that was cold and wet on my bare feet and peer up at the old maple. There swayed the oriole's nest for which my soul thirsted. It was such a graceful work of art that I soon found I had acquired a taste for collections. Daily I dragged an auxiliary ladder to the tree and standing on its top stretched my hands fruitlessly towards the nest. I had stripped all available branches of their leaves long since, but that blessed bird had built with her heart miles up from the top of my ladder.

About this time the matron of our establishment would innocently peek from behind her bedroom shade with all good intentions of examining the weather for Monday's washing on Wednesday and hiss at me her first good morning well mixed with a sincere reprimand. I would totter on my ladder; a host, a crowd would pour from every house and the street would be a teeming metropolis. All the dewy, damp quiet would be trampled by carefree minds like my own and tired minds of those women in Sunday's best of three years ago wiping down their clothes' lines and conversing over rhubarb beds.

It was never too early for a trek to the old swimming hole a mile down the trolley track and under the overhead. Already the "snake doctors" whirled their blue bodies over the still water. One thing was required of all pleasure seekers; that the fear of water be conquered to the extent of a non-hesitant jump into any part deep enough to hide the nude at the first rumble of an approaching trolley and thus not cause embarrassment and blushing to the cheeks of fair maidens who might be viewing the more pleasant and aesthetic scenery. But we were such gentlemen that often we forgot and stood up to bow our respects.

The swimming hole was unsanitary and because there were those who must take every precaution to conceal their exercise from home governors, we slowly balanced ourselves back to town on the car tracks while our hair dried. If the tracks were unappealing one could venture through snake grass, pitch small stones at the telephone poles, or catch pollywogs and mud crabs. Once we found a dead muskrat.

I have since been back to the swimming hole under the overhead with woeful results. I don't believe it was my sophistication; the place had a terrible stench, it was choked with weeds and dying under an engulfing scum. Perhaps the younger generations don't know it is there.

I remember distinctly a distasteful gathering after a baseball game. Oh, the games were generally bad for me. When I listen to the world series' broadcasts and hear the shouts and applause greeting each strike-out, I wonder why I got such opposite treatment when I flourished with that ability. I didn't mind not being chosen for a team but merely accepted with shaking heads and shrugged shoulders in unison, but my pride would not permit my younger brother to out bat me. If I ever connected with a ball it was to send it gently rolling to the feet of the pitcher, and lacking all knowledge of diplomacy I never told him he was "just too good for me." When I found myself growing muscle bound I would swallow hard and consent to stand by while someone batted for me. The injustice of my sweating and panting down my homeruns that some generous friend had hit for me has left severe scars of misgiving for this all American sport.

On one particular day, when everyone but me was exhausted from a hard game (I had continually struck out by proxy that session) and were stretched out in the yard of a family who owned three cows, an old horse, and a remarkable mechanism called a cream separator, really important conversation about Mel Ott and Lefty Gomez had died and after fidgeting about I unwisely remarked, and meekly, that when school began that fall, I was going to wear long pants and I asked, "Are any of you fellers going to too?" In one thundering awakening I was showered by gloves and bats and took to my heels.

I was used to such exile having often been outlawed to the boundaries of the baseball field where I would squat on the sidewalks and draw nasty pictures and shout my resentment from beneath a furrowed brow.

Company came to our house Sunday evenings and then I had sweet revenge. I would generally be invited to play the piano and I would always hold out until my all-star brother was made to stumble through his one ivoried endeavor, "Jack and the Beanstalk." I knew he played the piano worse than I ever did baseball, and so my performance sparkled with malicious inspiration.

The afternoons were intensely still as if one sweep of death's cloak had waxed every lip. One might see a neighbor lady pulling her shades so as to cool the house and shield her from callers so that she might enjoy secretly smoking her cigarette. You see, it's an old fashioned town steeped in its own ideas on respectability, but not unruffled by occasional scandal. It is as if little people grow out of this little town, for ambitions wither and one marries, has children, talks a great deal, and dies. Those who leave disappear into obscurity over the horizon.

On the fields the heat steamed and the greens turned yellow and there was a buzzing as if one wore a crown of bees. But if you stole away into an oasis of trees, there could be found violets peeking from beneath damp, old leaves. The grass grew high and choked young trees. Somehow one must escape back into the light for it was if a million eyes were there and the breeze was the stir of an unknown's breath keeping a shady vigil. Childhood fears are soluble for they are gnomes, strange eyes and hands waiting behind every bush. After these years we grasp for understanding and cringe at philosophy and religion and fate.

Away from the town, across the pasture, through a woods wrapped in brush, into a cornfield and out, we would in single file march until we reached a drainage ditch which by mid-summer was generally dry. The floor of the ditch became a headquarters with the vegetation making a thick roof. The goldenrod was abundant and made the air heavy. Here we bravely ensued grown-up lives until wearied bodies sat about and stories of mystery and horror began the rounds. The trees grew more dense, the sky further away, and someone would tell of railroad tramps living down there and into each little mind would come pictures of kidnappings and knives and leering, unshaven faces. It took but one cry of fear to set everyone running. The cornfield shook over its trespassers and then became still in the oppressive heat. Once in later years I came upon the home of some rover and had my dignity permitted, I would have cut a new path back to civilization.

When evening came we would sit on the curbing and watch the bugs poke at the street light. A bat would dart back and forth over our heads and an owl would make soft, musical sounds from some distant, dark tree. Gradually the group would fall away, each to his bed, and I would be alone to lie beneath the four o'clocks and wait for a humming bird or a huge moth. The air was cool and the grass wet again.

The most beautiful moments of life were there, the night over me was the sky, far away and incomprehensible in its depth. And to this day I enjoy philosophizing into the night sky may it be on love under a blossoming cherry tree, or the tragedy of loneliness on a noisy city street car.

Sometimes in these years a pattern grew for me, unsolvable and incomplete—my autobiography. It is a story I hardly know within myself, lest put it down by pen. There is just no summing up of these thousands of days except for sprinkled remembrances of liking immensely a little girl with shingled hair and a green, silk dress loose over budding breasts, but loving hopelessly another who never knew. Ah ... here is the beginning chapter that counts. For life took on perspective and inadequacies and the helplessness of the situation transplanted my soul from childhood sunshine to the basement of realizations where it must live or die, bloom or wither. From that day on I was a person. I have a story, a story not for words but for the heart.

And as I walked over the paths of my younger years today in the bright autumn:

"There is a sense of journeying
Upon the trees.
So many yellow sails are set.
So many red."[104]

I found that everything so large yesterday to be small today. The distance between home and first base on the old baseball diamond is so slight to have meant so much. The sidewalks are washed clean of my pictures.

Now:

"When the frost is on the punkin,
and the fodder's in the shock"[105]

the ditch is dry and not at all mysterious, but beautiful with many colored leaves and bedecked with bittersweet orange. Where have the woods gone? Now there is only open space and new cement walks and gardens and houses. I found a tree stump amid a clump of brush and there I sit and look across the wide, open ground. It is no longer the end of the world. I rather imagine Keats stood at the ocean's edge when he wrote:

" ... now on the shore
Of the wide world I stand alone, and think
Until love and fame to nothingness do sink"[106]

Here in this brush as long as it thrives, the wind shall rustle and sigh, returning year after year as I never shall. Oh, to be a part of that wind!

---

104. "A Sound of a Going in the Tops of the Mulberry Trees" from *Cups of Illusion* by Henry Bellamann. (Tedd's note)
105. "When the Frost Is on the Punkin" by James Whitcomb Riley. (Tedd's note)
106. "When I Have Fears" by John Keats. (Tedd's note)

As I move from my brief abode back to civilization, I know one thing. All this that I am is a part of the wind, the trees and sky, the swimming hole under the overhead, and a bit of baseball diamond. Those pictures I had drawn in scorn have disappeared, but they ride on in my blood.

When Amy Lowell's poetic heroine asked, "Christ! What are patterns for?," I'm sure she learned her answer that after the greatest of soul's storms can be found a quiet happiness in the simple things of love and faith and conscience.[107]

Autobiography this? ... yes, for beyond the abstract, the sketch, is a story, more than a hint of my years, for I have searched my being and have found still youth and promise and not yet come to full acceptance of the reality of the future.

—TEDD I. BURR

---

107. "Patterns" by Amy Lowell. (Tedd's note)

2 East 88th St.
New York City

November 20, 1944

Dear Ted[d],

Just a line to say that Mr. Bellamann was stricken with Coronary Thrombosis on Thursday and is desperately ill.

Everything that specialists and nurses can do is being done and I can only <u>hope</u>.

He wanted me to say he will write you when he is able but it will be many weeks before that time. In the meantime he'll be glad to have you write him.

Cordially,
Katherine Bellamann

2066 E. 77th St., Apt I
Cleveland, Ohio

November 23, 1944

Dear Mrs. Bellamann,

I am so sorry that Mr. Bellamann is ill. I could but look at his picture and wish there were something I might do. Perhaps I can help in the only way I have. He must get well soon. He is a great man to me, not at all because he is a fine writer and musician, but because he took time out to listen and to help me. I shall be eternally grateful beyond words for all he has given me. For me he is the link from utter lonliness [*sic*] to happiness.

I have never ceased to marvel at each of his letters. I have always wanted more than anything to mean a little to someone. He made me feel that way. And now you have too by informing me so soon of his illness. If letters will not be a bother I shall write and write; forgetting my own troubles, I shall try to put down what I do at college, the city in the snow, things I think he'd enjoy.

It has never mattered that there are miles between us, that I don't know the tone of his voice, how and what he eats, his favorite painting. I have talked with him when I walk at night. He is across the table from me in every restaurant. We like good plays, the ballet, and pictures of stormy seas.

I never realized until now how really much he means to me. I should feel utterly lost without him for, I suppose, I work harder each day to please him, to show him that the time he gives to me is deeply appreciated.

Naturally I have thought of you a great deal. I've dreamed up not a few pictures of what you are like. Perhaps those pictures are not far wrong because you wrote me so simply. And although I'm not good at saying the right things, I don't find it difficult writing you. I'm hoping with you all the way.

Above all I don't want to be a nuisance, but if from time to time you might find it convenient to let me know how Mr. Bellamann is, I would be most grateful, for I am as concerned as much as, well, any son could be.

I will send letters, and I'll do my best to make them good ones.

Sincerely,
Tedd Burr

2066 E. 77th St., Apt I
Cleveland, Ohio

November 27, 1944

Dear Mr. Bellamann,

I cannot think of any new or profound way of saying I am very sorry you are ill. I have held up writing this several days because things like, "So sad to hear you are sick," or "Please get well as soon as possible" are really stupid. Of course I am not glad you are sick, and you certainly won't remain so if you can help it; so, I shall just skip over the whole business and hope you understand my sentiments.

Item 2. On the other hand, I can never quite stand that ray of sunshine in the sick room. That gushing individual who won't let you know that you aren't perfectly well. "Better go on as if it just isn't so," he smiles to himself and settles down to a discussion of aggravating, trivial things. But, woe, when she with a long face comes in and sits pulling down her skirts, frequently comments on the lovely, lovely flowers, and tries to hide her troublesome tears. The compensation is the bowl of chicken broth she brings.

Without any more much ado about nothing, I'm going to tell you about my eventful last week.

It started with a visit to the Play House rehearsal of "Uncle Harry" on Tuesday night.[108] I was there from six until one the next morning ... the only one that stuck it out and it was worth it. I went home in the new snow in a dream world. The long tiresome hours while the lights were being planned and adjusted were even exciting. I walked on the stage and saw flimsy and unglamorous sets; I was in the shop rooms where everything is made; I saw the prop girl set up the stage for that night's show; I peeked into tiny dressing rooms and saw actors studying lines; I saw the stage

---

108. Thomas Job, *Uncle Harry* (1942).

crew in overalls working very hard; I sat in the Green Room and talked and questioned and met some of the staff; and the rest of the evening I was on the edge of my seat watching. Mr. Fredric McConnell, the director, is nationally known.[109] There is only one Cleveland Play House!

I just can't cram everything I saw and felt in a letter. I must have fallen into a most happy and contented sleep that night for sometime that morning I snapped off my alarm, was awakened by the landlady, and flew to work a half hour late. It was a miserable day. I sat and figured just how I would work the future. When the war is over and there are many for my job, I will quit and work the early morning hours in some restaurant for my meals and rent money, and spend the rest of my time at the Play House. Oh, sometimes I'm carried away with the thought of building scenery, getting props, acting, doing just anything I could. Then I look at myself and think perhaps I should forget it. I wonder what 1945 shall decide.

Thursday I took my mother to the Ballet Theatre. It was superb, the best I have seen. I was truly moved to tears by its artistry. "Aurora's Wedding" was gorgeous in its traditions. But "Pillar of Fire" was to me the art of the evening. That wonderful Nora Kaye danced Hagar. Every muscle in her body seemed to convey an intense emotion. If you have never seen this work, you must. It was expression of emotions at the best. Drama, opera, or symphony could never do as well. The laugh was the third work, the new "Fancy Free" and it brought down the house. Ballets like this would gain a national audience. It was of three sailors in New York on leave. How fortunate I am to be in Cleveland where I can enjoy all this.[110]

---

109. Frederic McConnell (1890–1968), managing director of the Cleveland Play House for 37 years, directing 800 plays himself.

110. Nora Kaye (1920–1987), American ballerina. This program would have included a lot of variety: "Aurora's Wedding" was likely Act III of Tchaikovsky's 1890 ballet *Sleeping Beauty*; *Pillar of Fire* (1942) is a short ballet set to Arnold Schoenberg's *Verklärte Nacht* and choreographed by

Saturday night I was thrilled from top to bottom when I saw on the stage for the first time, Ruth Gordon in her "Over Twentyone." I was hypnotized by this actress just as everyone else. Her voice could "make" almost any play. To me, she is the finest comedienne I've seen. Perhaps you have seen her, and if so, I envy you.[111]

I'm dreadfully sorry I missed Otis Skinner, Bernhardt, Duse, Booth and Mansfield, but I thank the stars I'm in the generation to enjoy Cornell, Gordon, Bankhead, Massey, Le Galleinne [sic], Schildkraut, etc. What will the next generation be served? Yes, indeed, what plays will be written and how acted? I should like to study drama at the Play House here and then perhaps try to establish a theatre in some other city so that they might see O'Neil and the plays that they, and myself, just missed. The store of dramas is so full, why don't producers dust some of them off and stop hashing up such bad new ones?

Because of a research paper, I had to miss a concert by Dorothy Maynor. For compensation I saw the Play House's "Tomorrow the World." It is not a very good play, however, it was staged very well with two youngsters doing outstanding work. It is strange the way a child acts; so different from an adult. The child seems free of inhibitions and self-consciousness that the older actor is always battling. John Lee, the young blond boy playing Emil Buchner, was in the Green Room Tuesday night while I was there. How I wish I had talked with him. It would be interesting trying to find out how he can feel such an alien and matured part.[112]

I must have bored you outlandishly by now … it makes me sick just looking at this; but I do want to write you often so no barriers can spring up. Next I'll do a bit of soul searching if you don't mind. Those are the letters I like writing most.

Antony Tudor; *Fancy Free* (1944) was choreographed by Jerome Robbins with a score by Leonard Bernstein.

111. *Over 21*, written by actress Ruth Gordon (1896–1985), was a popular Broadway play in 1944.

112. James Gow and Arnaud d'Ussean's *Tomorrow the World* (1943) centers on a young German boy indoctrinated with Nazi ideology who comes to live in the United States.

I hope this siege will not last long. I'll miss your letters for they always made my days so right. But then, a silent pal is much, much better than no pal at all.

Faithfully,
Tedd

Portrait of Tedd, 1944. Photocopy included in Tedd's transcription of the letters.

2 East 88th St.
New York City

November 28, 1944

Dear Ted[d],

No change to report—
    Thanks for your letter—

Sincerely,
K. Bellamann

Card from Katherine to Tedd, November 28, 1944.

TEDD

2066 E. 77th St., Apt I
Cleveland, Ohio

November 30, 1944

Dear Mr. Bellamann,

There is a thick blanket of light, fluffy snow over Ohio. Dear old Ohio! … just farms and farms and farms. It is strange that in this age of transportation by cloud and life with plastics that you can get lost in Ohio. It is the oddest feeling of desolation to be driving through these hills. There are miles and miles of old corn fields. The stone bridges are strange. The trees are friendly. They seem to be laughing down at you very heartily. The weeds wiggle in the cold water of the ditches, but you don't touch them. It is Ohio, up and down, far and wide.

There are many little towns. I don't know how these people make their living. There are no factories. Just farms with old barns that let in drafts and snow. The hay seeps out of the doors. The barnyards are foul. But in these little towns, often hanging over a river, the houses squat on the open ground. Their porches are laden with old ice boxes and bags of rags and screws. Some popcorn hangs at the side along with the bacon. Oil cloth is thrown over some of the mess. The house steps are rotten and sagging. The cistern's heavy with moss.

But standing proudly above the network of mud roads and paths is that one house. It stands on just the smallest hill. It, the house, is old American with too many doors and little porches and windows. But it is queen and badly in need of paint. There is an iron fence of spears around it … like a corset, it holds the old thing in place. It creeks with storms, and stands chilled in the snow. Each year an eaten portion of it quietly falls without ceremony. Quietly.

Ohio is rich, unfound, loving of herself still.

I think I may be finding myself with this composition class. When I see people picking on this sweet professor, I rally to her aid. I can see now that she is trying to give you your money's worth. She knows what she is doing. That is what I've learned. I guess I just have to admire someone very, very much before I do as they suggest. That's the way she and I are now. She speaks of Goethe and anyone speaking of Goethe impresses me. My, she has just about read everything … and remembers it too. Quite a student on Milton too. So I do enjoy her sparkling wit now. She isn't really stuffy. Then too, she nearly always reads my compositions. This is what counts.

I'm being asked out to lunch and this has just about spent itself.

I hope your recovery is coming fast and steady.

Faithfully,
Tedd

The John Wright Mansion (built 1880–1882) inspired Tedd to write "The Surf." It is now part of the Historic Lyme Village Museum in Bellevue, Ohio. Photo by L. Pinna, 2022.

86

KATHERINE

2 East 88th St.
New York City

December 3, 1944

Dear Ted[d],

Our patient doing fairly well but still very ill.

Cordially,
K. Bellamann

HENRY

2 East 88th St.
New York City

December 25, 1944

Dear Tedd,

I am having special permission to do this.—The New Year always seems sad: anniversaries are depressing, often. But you don't belong to a <u>lost generation</u>. You belong to a generation who will have the greatest opportunities ever offered to human beings. Political chaos we have always had with us.

I'm sorry you hate your work. That is difficult, isn't it? But I should lament seeing you go with the Cleveland Play House. While I'm very ill I talked to a director about you.

I contributed to building the Keith Theatre at Columbia, S.C. and still own stock in it. It had a good director but it never did anything important. It just went around in circles. The Cleveland Play House is probably the best in the country, but still—the "little" theatres have sent very few people into the real theatre. I know the Pasadena one, the one at New Orleans, and I know the history of the Maurice Brown venture at Milwaukee. His artistic enterprise with a self-picked audience is never subjected to the crucial tests. They are too much like mutual admiration societies and they—these theatres—remain <u>amateur</u>. People who do <u>real</u> things in the theatre come into it by being in the vicinity of the real theatre.

I have yet to see a "little" theatre that wasn't arty and amateur.

I shall be so sorry to see you go into the theatre. It's a house of heartbreak for nearly everyone except the few top geniuses. You'll get more out of art—all the arts—of having a job and enjoying things on the side, fine music, travel, plays, fine picture[s], because you'll have the money to enjoy them.

I know some <u>for sure</u> fine and sincere people in the theatre, such as Ann Burr; but mostly they are shoddy and imitative. They generally have a shallow culture and pretend the rest. Nine out of ten people on the stage are not there for artistic reasons but because they are exhibitionists. Do some real soul searching, Tedd, and understand yourself first of all and above all.[113]

I hope this isn't turning into a sermon dotted with <u>don'ts</u>, but I am writing out of affection and concern. I have been very touched that you kept up your inquiries about me. I had a close call, but apparently I shall survive. I am still kept still and in bed, but my trained nurses are gone, thank God. They lived in my hair!

"<u>Never worry, you'll get to Moscow</u>."[114]

And I'm a good prophet. You have a lot of life ahead of you. There'll be time to go anywhere you wish. A wrong choice will land you in a deadend but certainly.

My affectionate feelings, and

all good wishes for the New Year.

HB

---

113. Anne Burr (1918–2013), American actress on stage and radio.

114. Line from Chekhov's play *Three Sisters* (1900). The three sisters yearn to leave their current provincial home and return to Moscow, where they were born. Moscow represents a place of sophistication and culture. Henry is trying to encourage Tedd, essentially telling him "Don't worry, you will arrive at the place you yearn for." Henry may even be hinting that Tedd's destination could be New York.

2 East 88th St.
New York City

January 16, 1945

Dear Tedd,

I seem to be definitely better this morning. I think of you and your
problems even when I can't write. I am still ridiculously weak.

I hope all goes well with you. It will be well with you.

You have a lot of time. You will "go to Moscow" if you want
to. Thank you for your affectionate letter.

Faithfully,
HB

2066 E. 77th St., Apt I
Cleveland, Ohio

January 24, 1945

Dear Mr. Bellamann,

Why is it I disagree with so many people on so many things?

I see "Fumed Oak" as such a subtle and heart-breaking piece; the director wants it drunken loud. My Henry Gow comes from inside me—he is not mere lines. Rather, he is a man caught up in a pool of circumstances. For 15 years he has lived with a woman who loathes him, a child with a running nose, and a mother-in-law steeped in suspicion. He has lost youth. He's never known freedom or love. He's buried himself in Fergueson's Hosiery while his heart climbs up to the sunlight and tastes salt air as put down by Joseph Conrad. He drinks now and then, tragically trying to understand life. He creeps home one night with 2 whiskies and sodas under his belt and almost before he knows it, the lid is off. He finds he can say things to his wife; she can't really touch him. He loses his soul in a deluge of hate. And when he reminds her of the night she seduced him, the night their child was to have been conceived, he says "Three years and a bit after that wonderful night our child was born." This comes from me with all bitterness, sarcasm, hate, loathing, as I believe it would come from any Henry Gow.[115]

But the director—"Come in smirking—you're dead drunk-wabble—smile that dead smile—look silly—now then, 'that wonderful night ...' boy, oh, boy it was something. Come on with that smile—'that wonderful night' ... ummmmm."

I shake inside because I'm trying. She is the director but it's imitation. It's not real. I'm not Henry Gow then. I'm awkward trying to say some awkward lines. No one seems to understand.

---

115. Noël Coward, *Fumed Oak* (1935), part of a series of short plays titled *Tonight at 8:30*.

"Play it up—Play it up!" Here is a slice of life in Noël Coward's best style—and they walk blindly through it. Or am I wrong?

See here, sir, don't think on these problems of mine too much. Just get well. One of those "smiling" letters from you and all my troubles disappear for awhile. Why do I get into such mixed up messes? I wonder why I don't take life with a shrug and laugh laugh laugh. My friend Jeanne says I insist on complicating everything I see, do, or hear. My only excuse is that I think that I think; but mostly about me.

The professor of English sat with me on the street car after class last night and since our conversation about D. H. Lawrence, James Joyce, and Stephen Vincent Benét was so interesting, she asked me to her dorm for a coke and chat. She is real, relaxed, and friendly. But me? I'm stiff, and awkward, and stumble around correcting my grammar. I like our letter relationship. I can be myself—as I wanted to be with her.

It doesn't make me twinge realizing I write very badly. I can let tumble out of me all sorts of bothersome things. To me you are like some guy the likes of whom I have never seen or found really. No artificialness [*sic*]. Just sincerity. A willingness to listen over and over. How different it would be having dinner with you. I should be tongue-tied for fear I was using the wrong spoon or wondering if my vegetables were going to slide through my fork. (I've always meant to read a concrete book on things like that.) I'd certainly spill my water or choke on some dry bread. I'd end up with a wet brow and indigestion.

She and I talked about many things last night. She spoke of her Ben. Maybe I looked lonely because she wished awfully I had someone to live with. Yes, so do I. It would be someone different from myself; quiet with a great knowledge of life someone who would look out the window when talking, laugh, and at times, just sit staring and the stillness would be welcomed because I would know that I wasn't alone, there was Someone, another personality I'd never know completely. Someone who would be a challenge with quotations from Keats or Milton. We would like music and books, and scrambled eggs and cold milk. We'd never get tired of thinking. Someone who would be strong where I was weak.

Yes, I dream: dream of a home of my own with furniture in deep, rich colors. It would be regal and a bit stiff, and far too polished. There would be a large piano, a Baldwin or Knabe or Steinway. I would write flowing letters with a quill pen. There would be a picture of a stormy sea rushing over cutting rocks. An alcove, there would be, lined with nice books and an ivy by the window. I'd listen to Gershwin when happy, Tchaikowsky when sad, and Wagner when lonely. I would have a copper haired span-iel. He'd tag me all over and I would talk to him in French and scold him in German. He'd bark when I came home and look up from sad eyes. He'd have a damp nose.

Such a hazy future makes my head whirl. You keep writing that I'll get to Moscow. I don't know if it's a prophesy or a philos-ophy. I have enclosed a layout of the Play House (—and not to an-noy you—) along with a page showing the early American rooms I told you I had seen last week at the Art Museum. I hope you don't mind; clipping is a habit of mine.

Write when you can, I like being a recipient.

Faithfully,
Tedd

2 East 88th St.
New York City

January 27, 1945

Dear Tedd,

I think I agree with you in what you say of "Fumed Oak."

Only I don't think it's subtle. I think Gow is sly. The whole business is pretty sordid, isn't it? He's a kind of poor thing, and stages at last a sort of poetic justice revolt reminding one of what Balzac said about nothing being more terrible than the revolt of a sheep. I saw Coward play this piece along with two other short plays. I think of Coward as a sort of entertainer who has seldom in his life seen anything much in life, or even in his life, below the surface. He has a brittle texture and plausible surface of his kind—and he's not to my mind a very admirable kind at that. I suspect you of having talent. I don't know what kind or where it will lead you but you are not ordinary.

One thing you must learn well and that is that the greatness and richness of humanity lies always in the common man. It rises to expression in the uncommon man. The <u>Oh, so special</u> kind of man usually isn't anything and seldom does anything of importance.

I tire too easily to write you fully what I mean, but I shall eventually get around to it. I am up for a few hours every day, but I don't seem much like myself.

… Tedd, I could bop you for talking about such things as the right fork—etc. I am sure you know all you need to, and if you didn't you could learn in five minutes—<u>if it were important</u>. <u>Inner</u> qualities of heart and mind: simple kindness, simple unselfishness, little concern with appearances, full concern with motives and intentions—such things matter. Don't be an off-stage actor. I am sure that what you really are is good. Don't make it over into anything modeled artificially after some appearance. Develop <u>what you are</u>.

You are a bewildered and troubled boy, and that is what is appealing. You'll find yourself if you don't go after false and superficial ideals.

Faithfully,
HB

91

TEDD

2066 E. 77th St., Apt I
Cleveland, Ohio

February 13, 1945

Dear Mr. Bellamann,

I hope you have noticed my not writing. I've been really busy—so much so that for a week I had not one dinner and got by on a minimum of sleep. I always keep hoping that next week brings me much leisure, but it never does; and, besides, I'm miserable with time on my hands. The plays for the veterans' hospital, Crile, took nightly rehearsals for the girls of the casts had been existing in a dream of meeting the boys.[116] When they were informed that it was not a social visit and that unless the plays were super the audience would hiss them from the stage, well, they got down to work. Exhausting work began with everyone furnishing his own costumes and bits of scenery or props. Being in two of the three plays, I was thrown back and forth enough to end up like a drab dish cloth.

The performance day finally arrived and after work we met at the college and with the aid of a huge army truck, were off! There was so little time to set up the stage for the first play and to get into costume that we were on stage almost before realizing it all. This play, "A Florist Shop," we had given before the college's Women's League.[117] It is a comedy, but from them we got not a single snicker. At Crile it was immediately evident that our audience was alive. It was also a treat acting the play before stacks of gorgeous flowers contributed by a late funeral.

---

116. Built by the U.S. Army and opened in 1944, Crile General Hospital (a sprawling complex) cared for American military veterans and housed German prisoners of war during WWII.

117. Possibly Winfred Hawkridge's 1926 play *The Florist Shop: A Comedy in One Act.*

The curtains come down. There is a mad rush to reset the stage, and up goes the curtain on "Undertow," an all girl show with a dark psychological theme.[118] While this play is on, let me comment on attitudes. We had no committees; everyone was to do his bit. When it came to these quick scene changes there was hardly a single person to aid the director. The casts had forgotten everyone but themselves. Although they all appeared in but one play and had come to Crile already in costume, they were packed in dressing rooms doing their hair instead of for one moment thinking: "The show's the thing—as a whole." And when their performances were "fini," they disappeared into the soldier audience.

Now, with just one half hour before the boys must return to their wards, came "Fumed Oak." Even though time was short we wanted to try the play at least, so the meager cast pushed on their furniture, piled out their dishes, and sat down to the breakfast table. The director told me later how she had almost fainted at seeing the would be nagging wife of Henry Gow come out in a clinging black gown, low cut, with roses at the waist. The girl had her hair up, softly waved about her face. My heart sank too. Then I looked to Elsie, the brat, (she was a riot) and to the trooper who was doing the mother-in-law … they looked their roles at least! There was something to analyze. It came back to me that Nancy (Dorrie Gow) did a good role when we rehearsed alone; but when in the recreation room, a handsome student sat watching us, she turned the rehearsal into a hopeless lark. (He dated the mother-in-law actress.) The night before Crile, she had brought with her an old Marine friend. The rehearsal went badly. For the first time we had all our props and in using them, I spilled tea over her, nearly knocked out her teeth, tossed her about for fair in our mad scenes, and generally ruinated [*sic*] her. I was so sorry for her—she forgot her lines, did everything badly, and the director, not thinking of the Marine, really put her through the hoops. Nancy disappeared early with that Marine and "Fumed Oak" threw up its hands and hoped.

---

118. Anne Weatherly, *Undertone* (1936).

Now the curtain was going up; it was too late, the black low-cut would have to do. I played mostly to a coy-eyed, lovely woman and it was enough to frustrate any Henry Gow trying to pull up stakes. But once the fireworks were off there was no stopping the play. As the worm turns, some soldier yelled to me, "Give her hell, fella, give her hell!"

Oh, they were alive and it was glorious fun—as I remember now. At one place as I said a line, I noticed the chair had been set on one side of the stage and the bewildered character stood on the other side. I made no particular deductions but found myself improvising dialogue while I set things right and the character gratefully fell into the piece of furniture.

"Fumed Oak" was the hit. It far surpassed the other productions, t'was said. I think because it was Coward. Nancy and I had unintentionally cut speeches in a few places which was fine for we ended on the dot for the soldiers to leave for their wards. Mutual congradulations [*sic*] began flying around and at times like that I want to creep away and not be seen or heard. I don't like meeting the public.

The ride back in the bus was noisy and bumpy. I was so tired I didn't care if I never saw or heard another play. (Funny how each day removes that from my mind.) At the college the soldier driver pushed the props into my arms. I staggered into the building with them and distributed them thus. I was met by a host of glamorous girls already changed and heading for Fred Harvey's.[119] Not me! I tried covering my corn-starched hair with my pork-pie (dear ol' hat), gathered up my suitcases and coats, and in a daze of weariness, stumbled home to bed. Every muscle, tissue, and thought ached.

Since then, appearing at Crile has been a pleasure and delight to think of. As put down, there were things to analyze; things that I learned—about people who want to be actors and actresses. I learned give and take—as written before. I was one of that class

---

119. Fred Harvey's English Oak Room, a chain restaurant in Cleveland's Union Terminal Building.

who really had a lesson in the technique of acting. Remember how upset I was over playing Gow? How tragic he was to me? After the director and I had drawn swords, I had coffee with one of the girls and a long talk. This talking ourselves out, I believe, kept me from brooding and made it possible for me to alter Gow to happier lines and actually enjoy doing him that way. It was not long until I knew that I wouldn't want to play him tragically. Perhaps they were right that he wasn't. I could never do him as drunken as Prof. Stewart wished, but I like to think she perhaps went to the extreme in order to balance me. All in all I had many directors. Nancy didn't want my speech to suffer from intoxication, so with Nancy it wasn't. The director would come in and on would go the defective speech. Nancy's mother, who turned up at every rehearsal and the actual performance too, had her ideas too—about my posture, etc. (You see what I mean in give and take? I just clenched my teeth and thought, "This won't go on forever. Courage!") I was kept hopping to please everyone—really became too busy to think about my own Henry Gow. Now that it's in the trunk I can feel I have played at least one good role (how I dream of things like Oswald of Ibsen's <u>Ghosts</u>) in Henry Gow of "Fumed Oak" from TONIGHT AT 8:30 by Noel Coward. My … my![120]

I'm surprised if you have gotten this far for I must bore you. But I can't let the theatre dangling here. You see, I am to study with George McCalmon, guest director of the Play House, at college this semester.[121] I'm looking forward to it. I don't know what it is about the stage that keeps tormenting me. I know few ever accomplish anything; I feel utterly limited and untalented; and I'm awfully thin. I am not gay nor clever. When I'm on the stage it's like a nightmare of unrealities—without my glasses everything is strange and indefinite. I get awfully warm under the collar. I don't

---

120. In Henrik Ibsen's 1882 play *Ghosts*, Oswald is a young man who suffers from syphilis and unknowingly starts a romantic relationship with his half-sister.

121. George McCalmon (1909–1965), theater director and teacher. He later became the director of theatre and chair of the theatre department at Cornell University.

see how I can study drama and live too because at times I'm very impracticable [*sic*] as when I buy eight books because I have always wanted to read them and I know full well if I prop myself up in bed and begin on a book, in five minutes I'll be sleeping. However, when I read something like <u>Ghosts</u>, I'm about to burst. I look at the mill men around me. None of them have read it or even heard of it. Though my life seems often wretched, I'm so fortunate to have been led to it. Furthermore, I think I understand them … these Ghosts' people.

Perhaps something will happen soon to give me things more exciting of which to write. For instance, I might discuss Mencken's <u>Treatise on the Gods</u> but the men of the mill say, "Don't discuss politics and religion with anyone, not even with your wife."[122] Cowards! What is marriage anyhow? Every female I have ever known well has talked with me about everything, with no subject too delicate. What is marriage? A polite living together? I thought with one's wife one dared to be himself, let fall every barrier and could really say, "This is me." I have funny ideas about many things, they tell me.

Getting back to Mencken. I don't know why I relish his book, regard it as amazing literature. In my younger days I went to church every Sunday and sat in the second row of pews so that two ladies in the choir could smile at me. One was a beautiful school teacher—the other, her impressive mother. There was a man in church who echoed the minster always with an Amen. He said an angel had appeared to him and had written the date of the world's end on his bedroom wall. He never revealed that date. He wasn't a very pleasant man as I remember, but fierce and fanatic. I believe he died in an insane asylum.

Mencken made me think and remember a great deal about my Methodistic [*sic*] childhood. Very distinctly I recall my church offerings. Usually they averaged four pennies. There was a Gulf gas station on the street to church and there was a spacious candy

---

122. H.L. Mencken's best-selling *Treatise on the Gods* (1930) surveys philosophy and religion.

case in that station. At first I spent only two of my pennies on candy; but in time it seemed to me that two for church was an extravagance. Besides, if I dropped my money into the collection plate carefully no one could see that I left only one cent. There came the day when I convinced my mother that I was too mature for four pennies and she increased the amount to eight. I was on top of the world then. I gladly and with much show gave the church its three cents; the other five went for a Milky Way after church. I could buy these carmel [*sic*] bars at that Gulf station, you see. But my spirit wasn't hard for there were always fears of someone seeing me buy that candy or perhaps the station 'tendent would become suspicious. Besides, the candy was so rich it choked me and spoiled my appetite for dinner. My conscious [*sic*] suffered in the end more than my stomach benefited. I knew God looked over my shoulder everytime I pointed to those Milky Ways.

And the poor church. They just recently burned their mortgage. I've never told my mother. Perhaps if I do now the whole business will never bother me again.

Sincerely yours,
Tedd

92
KATHERINE

2 East 88th St.
New York City

February 13, 1945

Dear Tedd,

Henry desperately ill—a series of heart attacks. He's under oxygen tent and doctors and nurses doing everything possible but it looks hopeless. Keep "pulling" for him.

As ever,
Katherine Bellamann

2066 E. 77th St., Apt I
Cleveland, Ohio

February 15, 1945

My dear Mrs. Bellamann,

I am heartbroken that Mr. Bellamann is so ill when from his letters he seemed to be getting on so well. This is a great shock—I can but stare at the ceiling and feel utterly lost. If only over these states I could give him what strength I have. He is a fine man; his books are great literature.

Of course to me he is something—infinitely more; quite undefinable. My own father is a splendid man and parent but a sort of Peter Kettering. My two friends are as immature as I. Mr. Bellamann is the iron chain holding me to this world. I need him so.

It is not only in such a selfish manner that I am concerned, but with his being such a part of me, it is as if I am sick too.

He must get well—for his sake as well as for all of us indebted to him. Pulling for him?—every fibre in me.

Thank you for taking the time and effort to write at such a crucial moment. I shall be thinking of you always.

Faithfully,
Tedd

22 East 88th St.
New York City

March 3, 1945

Dear Tedd,

He is improving we think—very slowly. Thanks for your letters.

Cordially,
K. Bellamann

2066 E. 77th St., Apt I
Cleveland, Ohio

March 29, 1945

Dear Mr. Bellamann,

I have too long been silent; how good it is to write again. I never realized what writing to you means. I hope you are getting well and will stay that way.

Spring is here in warmth and color. Have you ever sat in the park to read poetry? And are there white haired ladies there with sun umbrellas feeding the pigeons?—or has Quintero's Sunny Morning fooled me?[123] There are plays about couples meeting fifty years after a love affair in sharp contrast to the modern short stories of tragedies in Central Park. Parks are fine! Cleveland is grime and smoke until one comes to Wade Park that goes on and on. It has an art museum, a garden center, pools, trees, a Shakespearean garden, winding roads, benches, and green. I like getting lost in its cool and quiet.

A few weeks ago I saw my first French movie, "Un Carnet de Bal," at the Art Museum. I was thrilled and listened carefully. Since it was about a frustrated widow I picked up often my favorite phrase:—with a shrug of the shoulders—"je ne sais pas." Raimu and Harry Bauer [sic] who are both magnificent were in it.[124]

I am sending along a few pictures. I like the Sarto because there is so much signified in the child's neck—the thrill of having a portrait done! I like the picture—I generally like portraits for one can dream stories over them. I always make a pilgrimage

123. Joaquín Álvarez Quintero and Serafín Alvarez Quintero's *A Sunny Morning* (1914) is set in a park on a beautiful, sunny morning.

124. *Un carnet de bal* (1937), directed by Julien Duvivier; Raimu (1863–1946), popular French character actor; Harry Baur (1880–1943), prolific French stage and film actor.

to the Turtle Baby. He is so spontaneous in his innocent laughter. Perhaps I want a boy like him—but innocence lasts for only a short time and he would soon have his world. If that abyss could only be bridged.[125]

Don't you have a collection of Japanese prints?

(After visiting the galleries I want to get out my pastels and water colors and paint. If I only knew of some group doing charcoals from (live) models. But then, if I only had time for workouts at the Y—time for records—time for books on theatre—! It is the economic set up! We need a revolution to gain fewer working hours. One's job should support one's life—not consume it.

Wanted: more time. I like effeciency [sic], a schedule. Have an appointment book to keep me from worrying about forgetting engagments [sic]—I have a bad memory. Besides not being able to spell. I'm awfully stiff; want my day planned to the minute; time on my hands and I am miserable; like a place for everything and everything in its place—except closets and drawers (which I pack in disorder).

El Greco puzzles me with his drawn faces and shapely hands. Dali fascinates me and I'd like to see more of his works. The <u>Times</u> recently pictured his "Tristan and Isolde" at the Whitney Museum. I do not make snap judgements on surrealism.[126]

Recently I was invited to join Mr. Zelinski, his neice [sic], and the Professor of English Composition at Western Reserve, in attending a private showing of the "Portrait of America" exhibition. It was a gala occasion with the Governor and the Mayor present. There were a number of admirable paintings—I would like to have Clarence H. Carter's "Tech Belle"—.[127]

---

125. Andrea del Sarto (1486–1530), Italian painter, sketched and painted many portraits of children. *The Turtle Baby* is a sculpture of a young child located outside the Cleveland Museum of Art.

126. El Greco (1541–1614), Greek painter and sculptor of the Spanish Renaissance; Salvador Dalí (1904–1989), Spanish surrealist painter.

127. Patricia Vettel-Becker writes of Carter's Tech Belle, "In his 1940 Tech Belle ... an artist's mannequin is clothed in a dress decorated with a bow and roses, markers of femininity. She is seated before a table holding

In this cross section were some abstract works which I viewed seriously—at least quietly—but my companions could not tolerate them, laughed at them with disgust, and said they could paint <u>that</u> well. Thinking of Wagner, Tchaikowsky, Zola, Ibsen, Galileo, Bernhardt, one realizes that so many accomplishments and their authors were ridiculed. How can one be sure that these paintings are not contributing to a new expression of the art? I would like to know an artist—a surrealist—and watch him paint and listen to him, try to understand what and why he is painting as he is. Then, perhaps, I shall be able to comment on them. Now, I'm pleasantly puzzled and interested. If I ever get a flat I want to have in it a few art objects—an oil of the sea, a portrait, several water colors, and a semantic—there was one at the May Show years ago called "Samson." I have never forgotten it.

Now that I have broken the ice at the Museum, I hope to go there often. I want to take a gallery at a visit—too many paintings have the same effect as too much champagne, I suppose. Over paintings, my senses grow numb. My work here at J&L is decorated by sketches of stage sets, costumes, characters with large eyes. Perhaps my energies can be used more wisely in looking at Van Gogh, Rembrandts, Michaelangelos [*sic*].

And now that I have broken the ice twice by writing you, I hope you won't mind if I repeat it often. Let them pass unread if you wish. Just getting all these things out of my system, down on paper where I can see them, then away, does wonder[s]. I feel less like Atlas.

It's foolish to write "do get well quickly." Of course, you are. The days are glorious and I wish the seasons would get stuck.

Faithfully,
Tedd

---

a glass of wine and a book, which, of course, she cannot drink nor read. The painted face with raised eyebrow insinuates life, yet she is clearly dead, machine-made. There is no chance that she will move on her own. She is at the mercy of the male artist whose signifiers surround her—easel, frame, canvas and brush." ("Clarence Holbrook Carter's War Bride and the Machine/Woman Fantasy," *Genders*, May 1, 2003.)

22 East 88th St.
New York City

March 31, 1945

Dear Tedd,

I was so glad to hear from you. I have dull days. I am up and dressed some days, but I still see no one. The portrait of the little girl by Renoir is a beauty and it is one I have never seen. Will you find out if there is a color reproduction of it—if there is it should be on sale at the Museum. Though sometimes New York has the best stock of things.

Don't be confused by Dali. He <u>can</u> paint, but <u>doesn't</u>.

Perhaps to try to humbug a public. Of course by any test the man's cuckoo. Lots of stranger painters and worse ones are not, but there's no doubt about him. Cuckoo—and fake.

No, I have no Japanese prints, never did. One biographical note on me speaks of my interest in Japanese art—an assumption based on a few verses I did in Japanese form—<u>hokhen</u> and <u>tanka</u>. I don't understand Japanese prints and don't particularly· like them. The same goes for Chinese painting. I don't know what they're doing, and life is too short to absorb a whole new and different culture unless one has some purpose in view. There's a lot of cooing about Chinese paintings that is phony.

Once I was looking for some square Chinese vases of the "hawthorne" type to make lamps. After a long time a dealer sent me a pair marked <u>$2300. Each</u> on the bottom. But he forgot to send his address, so there they sat on my mantel. My artist friends exploded in frenzies of delight saying, "Oh, but they are that rare inlaid porcelain of such and such." Eventually the dealer got in touch with me. He couldn't explain the price mark, didn't know how it got there. The vases were cheap imitations and were priced $5 for the pair. You should have seen my art expert friends deflate. Eventually I got tired of the vases and gave them away. I have two

Chinese ginger jar lamps for which I paid $3.50 each. A long time resident of China [who] was here last summer clasped hands over them (they're in a room with a lot of fine furniture) and decided he'd never seen more beautiful ones! So I'm wary of Oriental art appreciation unless it's a real expert doing it. There are some Chinese vases at the Frick Collection just down the Avenue which are beautiful. Even I can tell them from the ones I had!

Like what you really like—what you recognize as having a relation to the line and color of life. Art helps you to see Nature, but Nature is a good check on art, too. Just look—don't analyze too much, and like what you like. You'll change tastes some as you grow. But you're on the right track.

No one can be a judge of tapestries, paintings of all periods, Egyptian art, Chinese sculpture—etc, etc. There will be a few fields where you can be more and more sure of yourself. Enjoyment is the real purpose—not to be an art critic. The critics are so often wrong. So it goes with music, the theatre, poetry. There is so much. Our capacities are not equal to the whole of the human spirit.

(I wish you'd put your address on your letters, it is so hard to remember!)

Perhaps someday when this global unpleasantness is over we can see some of these things together and talk about them.

I am still very ill and still wonder sometimes if I'm going to get well at all.

I don't feel like reading, I'm too weak to do anything else, so I just sit or lie down when I can—the latter is difficult most of the time.

Write when you can. I like to hear from you and of what you are doing. During this long acquaintance I've gotten very fond of you.

Sincerely,

HB

97

TEDD

2066 E. 77th St., Apt I
Cleveland, Ohio

undated, likely April 1–4, 1945

Dear Mr. Bellamann,

I had misgivings about going home, having forgotten how lovely spring is there. Streets of brick with grass choking in the cracks which run down the hill from the town under an arch of green, green trees. The houses are banked with white spiraea. Every year a collection is taken to redecorate the Methodist parsonage. All it really needs is more spiraea.

To Bellevue I had carried a letter for you in a copy of <u>Candida</u>.[128] When I mailed it in our polished and quiet post office with its mural of industry shaking hands with agriculture, I remembered the thousands of days I had come here. And whether spring or winter it was always polished and quiet. Across the street is the <u>Gazette</u> office—the paper that never prints articles correctly. Now only its night light was burning. It is deserted until Monday. Town paper offices are funny places with old desks of many scars and frosted windows for partitions and with the banging of linotype in the next room. The paper gets printed between four and eight p.m.— And the paper carriers sit mournfully seeing the rest of their day fade and darken. I know—for years I was with them, reading by a solitary bulb dangling from the ceiling of the basement. We had rare times for which we were lectured and shut out to stand in the rain. The railing with its top of tiny spears is still there. For initiations new paper carriers were bounced up and down on the spears. I always felt sorry for the victims because it wasn't as bad as it looked. For want of amusement some quiet night, some boy would light his face with, "Hey, it's time we had an initiation!" Poor kids, they would go white and try to be brave. The leader of

---

128. *Candida* (1894), a comic play by George Bernard Shaw.

this torture looked like Mickey Rooney. I wonder where they all are.

Many of them went to war. Some made up the basketball team of Bellevue this year that won the state championship. But, where are they? Will their faces ever be young again? Kids carrying paper sacks while your day slips away; young men carrying the weight of the world while your life slips away, where are you? Have you found love?—you were shy boys then with dirty stories. Have you grown up to learn the folly of banging little backs upon an iron spear? Do you remember bouncing balls against the side of the Methodist Church while a western shadow crept up its side?—and the minister coming out to ask you to come to catechism while you waited for your wares? Do you remember the kind lady who on a hot day treated us to an ice cream cone? We never knew who she was. A lady with a white powdered face and filmy dress. All this and more: snow, rain, and sun making the bag about your neck heavier until your shoulders became round and your back bent. For this they said you learned economy and business. You also learned about people. I learned to talk to myself an hour every night as I wound along dark streets and through alleys where apple trees grew. The last of the town's weary working men going home.

My mother says I am a terrible sentimentalist. Is it bad? At home I discovered immediately a long iron pole. Dad was being dad again—building a new bird house to replace the one that crashed down in a storm, breaking its ornaments. Dad never made ordinary bird houses—they weren't for ordinary birds.

Purple Martins only and every now and then we would clean out the ragged nests of the sparrows and burn them. I felt it wasn't quite right. Dad would sit beneath the cherry tree with mother, both of them with bare feet having just come from the garden. And while the sky blazed quietly herding its tired sheep like clouds to be tucked in bed, and while we whirled about playing "statue," they would watch the Purple Martins throw their young to the winds. There were always little birds crying in the beans.

Dad was himself again—his birdhouse—his garden—his hour's nap in the afternoon—. Where has he been for the last few years?

Our home is on the edge of town with other people who cannot decide whether to live in country or town and so, spread in both. I looked down the lawns and gardens and fields to the houses that sheltered the kids so important to me a very long time ago. The houses are banked by spiraea. Down there is where the Geigers lived. Don't live there now—moved down the street further. But this red brick house with two living rooms—one with a piano kept for good—is still there. I used to watch that house to see when Chick and Don were up. (What would we do—play ball—or swim?) Today there is not that hope. The Geigers owned a hatchery. I used to test eggs for them for my fun and watch the chicks all wet and ugly being taken from the incubators on trays. We played hide and seek under the long rows of warm incubators.

The front of the hatchery smelled of farmers' cigar smoke and was noisy with laughing and bargaining. Further back was the feed that had a heavy odor in its burlap sacks. At the back were the egg shells reeking in decay. It was a long, stone building with a hot attic.

They had three sons and an orchard. Don is a school teacher now. (Who would have guessed it!) I saw him last at the draft board. He is stodgy now; no longer the guy we camped with in summers. Harold's in the Navy and married—he stopped in to see me once:

"Hy—a!"

"Hello, Chick!"

"How are ya?"

"Fine. And you?"

"Can't complain."

"Ummmmmmmmm."

"Well, gotta go. Have to leave for Trenton soon."

"So soon? That's too bad. Glad to have seen you. Thanks for stopping in." (Oh, God, Chick, what's it like to be married? Grown up? You used to tell me about your affairs. They sounded wonderful. And now you have to go back to Trenton? Oh yes …)

"Goodbye."

Our lives were closely knit with trips to school each day—and sitting listening to the cold water in a ditch—or teaching you to ice skate and swim—the only things I learned first—and in high school seeing you in love with the girl who had been my girl in grade school. She belongs to someone else now.

But here is Bellevue—and where am I?—and lawns are green, gardens plowed, air fresh.

One of the hounds just had a pup to satisfy the wish of little Davey who had sat on the top step of the stairway and sighed, "I wish I had a little dog to take to bed witz me." Much to everyone's surprise, so he has. I call him Rodolfe—(or Rodolphe)—they call him Bing! Such a common name and dogs with common names are uninteresting. Once we had an Adam, Hester, and Emily.

I was clawed by the cat—that old alley cat, Miss Sarah. She has kittens as fast as nature permits and leaves them to die. There is no affection with her. She lies in the best chair and is nasty in refusing to share it.

We strolled across the street to see Dick—(the earth was drying)—and to be shown his mount, Goldie. She crossed her legs, stamped out her age, and gave us the horse laugh.

I looked over the fields that were changed in their hue according to the crop or last year's rugged weeds. Beyond was the ditch, that thrilling hideaway where one dreamed away summers under heavy goldenrod and light canaries.

The two Hass spinsters with their father stumbled past us with their baskets on their arms. In turning to smile on us they could not watch the uneven sidewalk. They moved on in single file up the street.

I ate great slices of pork with tomato sauce and a frozen salad. I saw my grandmother across from me, her white hair wildly encircling her wrinkled head. She is dying. No, she died some years ago. This is a shadow—a persistent ghost … My dad and I spoke our few words and the well between us echoed its depth and was silent. He asked me the same questions about steel; I gave him mechanical answers. About my theatre appointment mother had told him and he had answered, "If that's what the boy wants, it seems a good beginning. In such things you have to work up." He and I said nothing. What does this man know of us? He was not told that his younger son was engaged for, said mother, "Tony's too young. Maybe it will wear off. We needn't upset Dad." And dad builds his bird houses and looks into the sky and feels the soil and is a great, good man—silent like an autumn stream through a crumbling corn field.

Soon it was time to go. Late afternoon was blowing cool shadows into the town and the spiraea was snowing on the ground.

I changed in my old room beneath the roof. It is low and dark there and the attic warmth aches in my legs. The curtains flap and pink shines on the walls. The varnish looks, as ever, polished. I never come here but that I feel passion as I knew it while my body grew—here beneath this roof—the slanting roof—little windows—pink curtains.

It was time to go. But I didn't want to leave. This jewel, would I ever find it again? As I come here through the seasons and the fields grow from green to purple and white, and the wheat shocks crackle, will I find it again, this water lily pond that waits for the stone that will mar its top?

I left them standing in the shadow of the depot—their red faces smiling—waving, come back. My jacket was rich rust on the seat. The coach was freshly painted.

Faithfully,
Tedd

2066 E. 77th St., Apt I
Cleveland, Ohio

April 5, 1945

Dear Mr. Bellamann,

Last night I came home late from a class and a two hour rehearsal. I was feeling quite low with either the flu or grippe which meant backache, headache, sore throat, and just pains. I switched on my light and there was a familiar envelope, the same yellow paper, and that handwriting. I was surprised and delighted. I had no idea you were well enough to write. Your pages were devoured; and then, in the darkness of my room, I composed long, inkless letters to you about things I knew I never could remember to put down. I got up this morning well and full of energy. I should call you "Doc" Bellamann.

I suppose you do get dreadfully discouraged. Being sick and secluded is a morbid business, but I, for one, am very anxious for you to get back on your feet and into the groove.

I'm sending you themes I have written for college, but don't let me take advantage of your kind nature. If they are a bother toss them away. They are in the original without the corrections and suggestions made by the professor so you will find errors of all kinds. Please disregard them and look upon me as a "Morgan Evans" just out of the mines.[129] The only reason I bother you with them is that the professor has taken a special interest in them and has gone over them with me at her dorm—that is, some of them. She is a brilliant woman and what she points out is often important really; but there are other times when we disagree (especially on content) and I don't like to think I may be just stubborn.

---

129. Morgan Evans is a character, an illiterate teenager in a Welsh mining town, in Emlyn Williams's 1938 play *The Corn Is Green*.

I have never found your "Red Shoes Run Faster." Perhaps I have been looking for it in the wrong magazine, <u>American</u>. I try to get things read, but it is forever 11:30 p.m. Fowler's "Goodnight, Sweet Prince" is giving me quite a jolt.[130] It certainly is a frank biography. One of the men at work said John Barrymore was a drunk and even played Hamlet in a stewed condition. I knew John liked his bottle, but to play Hamlet while drunk seemed impossible. I got Fowler and began reading. Barrymore did heave often into the wings while in Hamlet's attire. I can't understand the man; I shouldn't have liked knowing him; I don't want to be stuffy, but I think he let many people down with his selfishness; and I can't feel too sorry over his sad end. Did you ever know or see him? To my generation he was only that buffoon on the radio and I did not know when I laughed at him who he <u>really</u> was.

I'm also plowing through "Early stages" by John Geilgud [*sic*]. I've listened to some poetry records made by him also. I like reading poetry aloud. Lately I've been spouting Browning's "Home Thoughts from Abroad"—"Oh, to be in England now that April's there."[131]

At school we shall start Benet's "John Brown's Body" and Hardy's "Tess." Now we are in the midst of some fine short stories like "Innocence" and "Trip to Czardis." Have you ever read W. D. Steele's "Beautiful with Shoes" or "The Occurrence at Owl Creek Bridge"?[132]

---

130. Gene Fowler's 1944 biography of actor John Barrymore (1882–1942), *Good Night, Sweet Prince: The Life and Times of John Barrymore.*

131. *Early Stages* (1939), autobiography of English actor John Gielgud (1904–2000). The first stanza of Robert Browning's 1845 poem "Home-Thoughts, from Abroad": "Oh, to be in England / Now that April's there, / And whoever wakes in England / Sees, some morning, unaware, / That the lowest boughs and the brushwood sheaf / Round the elm-tree bole are in tiny leaf, / While the chaffinch sings on the orchard bough / In England—now!"

132. Stephen Vincent Benét, "John Brown's Body" (1928); Thomas Hardy, *Tess of the d'Urbervilles* (1891); Honoré de Balzac, "Innocence" (1837); Edwin Granberry, "A Trip to Czardis" (1932); Wilbur Daniel Steele,

Generally when people just know me they think I am quite well read which is not so. I make great use of the things I have read by quotations and references, but actually I haven't even made a visible nibble on the book shelves. I seldom waste half an hour on a street car or at lunch, but still books keep rolling out and I can't plow through them. I like modern works, but knowledge of the classics is so important, though Milton makes me shake my head.

I shall investigate Renoir as to the sizes available. I should be most happy to get you the print and will try to be most professional in viewing it from every angle.

Going to a museum with you would be a delight and something I dream of. Your letter this time was not the sage to the adolescent. I learned things, felt things about you I didn't know before. I still can't realize that this exciting friendship exists. I feel so wonderful inside when I connect thoughts with you.

I have quite an eventful few weeks coming up. The college is planning a Shakespearean festival for May with "A Midsummer Night's Dream." Saturday the college shall be popping with the annual Penny Carnival. For this all the clubs and organizations erect booths and fares and trades are made in pennies. The Square Players are giving a good old fashioned mellerdramer [sic]. I am the villain. The heroine is played by a girl once in Hollywood, Pasadena, and the Reinhardt theatre. She and I get so emotional over some of our lines that we always break up and go into spasms of laughter. Her eyes just sparkle when she turns on me to say, "You cur!" It is lots of fun and we are playing it straight and seriously, so that adds to it. I find I have one thing in common with John Drew. I forgot my grippe on stage just as he forgot his rheumatism.[133]

"How Beautiful with Shoes" (1932); Ambrose Bierce, "An Occurrence at Owl Creek Bridge" (1890).

133. John Drew (1853–1927), American actor and uncle of John Barrymore. Tedd likely read this account of John Drew in Barrymore's biography; see note 130.

I have lots more to tell you but my time is up. You can expect another letter very soon about a recent concert.

I am certainly glad to know that they can't keep a good man down.

Sincerely,
Tedd

HENRY

2 East 88th St.
New York City

March 11, 1945[134]

Dear Tedd,

I read your pieces with a good deal of interest, first because they are yours. I don't know whether you have a talent for writing, or if you are just a talented boy who happens for the moment to be writing.

You know I never take time to pay you compliments. I have time for so little so I have to devote myself to criticism.

You do over write, too dramatic for the material, but still there is something in it. The first version of the Euclid Ave. Church is overwritten, but I kept reading. The revised version (was that after teacher got hold of it?) was correct and <u>terrible</u>. Terrible, no life, no interest, no faintest corpuscle moving. Of course I know you have to learn to write correctly, but in correcting, teachers usually gut the writing completely.

You have a nice feeling for nature, and some of your best lines have to do with just the appearance of a wayside ditch, the color of leaves, the feeling of a season. You probably have no important stories <u>in you</u> at present except your own which you are not ready to write.

But anyway <u>keep on writing</u>—it's like exercises, scales and arpeggios at the piano. They aren't piano playing but you can't play the piano without them.

… Yes, I saw Jack Barrymore often, at his best he was wonderful, at his worst pitiful. Alcoholics aren't a pretty spectacle. What Lionel says about acting and actors is true. Ethel B. is

---

134. Postmarked April 11, 1945.

probably more of a person. She lives close to me here in the Eighties somewhere.[135]

Actors spend their lives being so many people that they end up in having no self. Exceptions? Yes. Helen Hayes for example. [136]Most lessor actors are impossible. The near artist in my field is apt to be rather shoddy and cheap.

What I am trying to talk at you all of the time is a simple sincerity, a high personal integrity, no pose, no make-believe. Be yourself first and build on that afterward for whatever you wish to be.

The danger of people of your temperament (and mine, I guess!) is to be trivial. When one is at all sensitive it is hard to pass over the small everyday pinpricks (which feel like saber thrusts) and think of broader, more important things.

The fault of our whole country in this century is that it is trivial minded.

... Old Clemenseau [*sic*] said: "I admire failures: they are the men who strove to surpass themselves."[137]

Affectionately,
Henry B.

---

135. Henry is possibly referring to this quote attributed to Lionel Barrymore (John Barrymore's brother) in Fowler's *Good Night, Sweet Prince:* "The Great Actor always must act.... Every last second of his life must be pose and posture." Actress Ethel Barrymore was the sister of John and Lionel Barrymore.

136. Helen Hayes (1900–1993), American actress.

137. George Clemenceau (1841–1929), prime minister of France during WWI: "A man's life is interesting primarily when he has failed, I well know, for it's a sign that he tried to surpass himself."

2066 E. 77th St., Apt I
Cleveland, Ohio

April 11, 1945

Dear Mr. Bellamann,

I went to Severance Hall alone. Music is much nicer that way, more personal. When sitting with friends one must keep emotions steady; when alone, let the eyes drip, drink all the power and beauty; become dissolved. Vladimir Golschmann, a favorite, conducted. He is not only a splendid musician, but a showman. Frank Black, colorless, leaves me cold; Szell is brisk and business like; Reiner and Leinsdorf labor and sweat; but Golschmann is the artist whose deft strokes mold from notes and tones an emotional experience. Do you know him? I admire men who have accomplished such as he but I shouldn't like to know them.... I mean: I saw <u>Othello</u> with a SPAR friend. We decided to go backstage and compliment Mr. Robeson and Mr. Ferrer. Once inside the stage door we realized we could think of nothing but "you were wonderful"—so trite! Terrified, we left without seeing anyone. Whenever I come into brilliant company I am awkward, use bad grammar, and wish hell's doors would swallow me up. I get home sick, knowing I lack charm, poise, and personality.[138]

But it was of the concert I wished to write. It opened with Weber's Overture to "Der Freischütz"—it was like an overture to

---

138. Severance Hall, concert hall in Cleveland, Ohio that opened in 1931 and is the home of The Cleveland Orchestra; Vladimir Golschmann (1893–1972), French conductor of the Saint Louis Symphony Orchestra, 1931–1958; Frank Black (1894–1949), American conductor of the NBC Symphony Orchestra in the 1930s and 1940s; George Szell (1897–1970), Hungarian conductor and composer, conductor of the Cleveland Orchestra from 1946 to 1970; Paul Robeson (1898–1976), American bass-baritone and actor; José Ferrer (1912–1992), Puerto Rican actor.

our spring and all the things it promises: love for some, despair for others.

I had really gone to hear Debussy's "L'Après-midi d'un Faune." Debussy caught what no other composer can touch—clouds, seas, the sunken cathedral, and, I think, love in Clair de Lune.[139]

Even wanting to watch Golschmann, I could not for the Faune. Physically I was hemmed in by strangers around me, but my emotions sailed out. I was waking in the deep forest green with the sun sending dusty ribbons of light down through the foliage. On the ground the white spots were like jewels, lustrous green stones. It was warm, moist and I stretched and nearly floated about searching the green. I blinked into the sun and felt warmth. The atmosphere was sensuous. The quilt of the forest was still but for the buzzing of the awful quiet. I was yearning, not sad, but there was no one there. Alone, I danced to the sunlight and the mist rose from the green and slithered over me. I crumbled to the ground, into the warm leaves to fall asleep. I was a faune.

It was a delightful experience. I must have quite an imagination. I don't think that the stern man over there was playing at being a faune. Or that captain. The bald headed husband yonder, I wonder what he thinks of—the one that squirms, leans forward, tires, lunges back. Is he hearing Debussy? Or is he thinking of the fifty dollars flown for these season seats? Or of the office and the big deal on tomorrow?

Or do the notes of Debussy fit into a pattern for him? Does he know harmony, counter point? Is he thinking of planting an early garden—"it ought to be in. These showers would sure make radishes pop up!"? Is he watching that woman down two rows and over? She that was smoking in the lobby as he came in—she in the black gown and ear-rings. He had walked close by her. She wore delicious perfume. Has a husky voice—something strong and vital in her body. Sees her every concert. Can't help looking

---

139. Claude Debussy, *L'Après-midi d'un Faune* (*Afternoon of a Faun*) (1894), poem for orchestra; Debussy, *Clair de Lune* (*Moonlight*) (1905), piece for piano.

at her. Who could she be? and—And does the flute as it skips and trills awaken dormant desires in him, as in the faune? What lies behind the eyes of men and women?—eyes that soon lose free life and become pinched and desperate and confused. What thoughts seethed through Sever[a]nce as the faune stretched his languid legs? How many minds added up the tones of Debussy or dreamed of green, smoky forests or were blank and unattentive. I wonder.

Schönberg's "Ver[k]lärte Nacht" was played. If this letter were not already too long, I would dwell on the work. It is based on the poem "Wei[b] Und Welt," by Richard Dehmel:

"Through the cold forest fare two mortals.
The moon paces with them; they look only within.
No cloudlet dims the radiance of the sky,
At which grasp the black spires of the trees."

The poem has great depth in simple words. There is something terrifying about the strings—as in life—passionate, but terrifying. If you have never seen Tudor's ballet "Pillar of Fire" with Nora Kaye as Hagar you have really missed something! This ballet caught every *fibre* of emotion from the music "Ver[k]lärte Nacht." It represents a new field for ballet—it combines sure-fire theatre with music, and how the two fit. Wonderful effects could be gained if the classics (Shakespeare) could be supported by orchestras in the wings. Truly Schönberg's composition stands as a masterpiece.[140]

The splendid evening ended with Sibelius' 5th Symphony in which I got lost. It was a river overflowing, had unusual endings, and a final movement that sounds like "Casey would waltz with the strawberry blonde" that got stuck. I walked all the way home and felt good; proud of having been there, and just happy.[141]

---

140. Arnold Schoenberg, *Verklärte Nacht* (1899), a string sextet; Kaye and "Pillar of Fire," see note 110.

141. "Casey would waltz with the strawberry blonde" is a lyric from John F. Palmer and Charles B. Ward's popular 1895 song "The Band Played On." Jean Sibelius (1865–1957), Finnish composer, was known for

I have investigated Renoir's Mlle Lacaux [*sic*] and can not help you. I am sending you the only print the museum has. It is cheap and quite worthless, simply not catching what is in the original. Something was lost—the eyes? well, the entire realness. At Vixseboxse, Higbee's, Strong, Korner & Wood, and the museum I was told that a reproduction has never been made for the trade.[142]

This was one of the most exciting things I've ever done. At first I was bewildered as where to begin, but found I progressed splendidly. I knew my bit of French was flashed outlandishly. But being in the galleries, telephoning, describing, and questioning gave me great happiness and satisfaction. I was grateful for an extra opportunity to get to the museum. The garden was a paradise with the trees holding great armfuls of blossoms. Sometimes I want to go into such a garden and build a wall around it. Escape, that's my middle name. Once in the museum I came upon a work, in oil, "Wisdom and Destiny" by Davies.[143]

Mr. Bellamann, I regret that another visit with you has come to an end. It has been such fun even though much has gone unwritten, and that which is down came out so awkwardly. If ever there is anything more I can do for you, please let me know. We are good friends, aren't we?

Faithfully,
Tedd

---

incorporating popular and folk music into his classical compositions. He composed his 5th Symphony in 1915.

142. Establishments in Cleveland: Vixseboxse Gallery, art gallery established 1922; Higbee's, department store founded in 1860; Korner & Wood, bookstore founded in 1900.

143. The Cleveland Museum of Art does not hold an oil painting titled "Wisdom and Destiny" by an artist named Davies. Tedd may be thinking of Arthur B. Davies's *Hermes and the Infant Dionysus* (1900–1905), which depicts ancient Greek gods Hermes and Dionysus in a garden. The museum does hold in its collections an oil painting by Henry Keller titled *Wisdom and Destiny* (1913).

Pierre-Auguste Renoir (1841–1919), *Mademoiselle Romaine Lascaux*, public domain, via Wikimedia Commons.

HENRY

2 East 88th St.
New York City

April 20, 1945

Dear Tedd,

You are very thoughtful to have sent the Renoir print. I didn't mean you to get one, but just to find out if one was available. Anyhow I shall value it because it came from you. The coloring looks light for Renoir. Is that what's wrong with it as a print?

I think I am better, but it is all so painfully slow. I can't write much—if I could I'd be at work over the new volume of Kings Row.

Best luck to you—and many, many thanks for your trouble.

The little girl is a darling, isn't she? I wish I could own a Renoir.

Affectionately,
HB

102[144]

HENRY

2 East 88th St.
New York City

April 30, 1945

Dear Tedd,

Your letter came on my birthday and thereby added to that day for me.

I always like to know what you have liked and what not because I shall continue to belabor you in behalf of greater catholicity of taste. To: <u>Meistersinger</u>. I never heard a Wagner opera that wasn't too long but it's hard to say what you can cut out. Of course we seldom hear an uncut version of any of his operas. But <u>Die Meistersinger</u> is one long sustained lyric and contains a lot of the finest music ever written. I find the humorous sections a little hard to take. In fact humor on the operatic stage is about the poorest variety of comedy there is though I've seen some first rate comedy in performances of <u>The Barber of Seville</u>. You're a little too hard on tenors though in general they are as Von Bulow said: "not men but a disease."[145]

But it is probable that the most generally perfect singing done in my life time was that of John McCormack. The greatest tenor performances were really those of Caruso and I've heard all of them. The <u>most</u> dramatic and interesting interpretation, the most eloquent singing was that of Chaliapin.[146]

---

144. I suspect there is a missing letter from Tedd before this letter. Henry seems to respond to a discussion of operas and singers that Tedd may have reported to Henry.

145. *Die Meistersinger von Nürnberg* is almost four and a half hours long; Gioachino Rossini, *The Barber of Seville, or the Useless Precaution* (1816), an Italian opera; Hans von Bülow (1830–1894), German conductor.

146. John McCormack (1884–1945), Irish tenor; Enrico Caruso (1873–1921), Italian tenor; Feodor Chaliapin (1873–1938), Russian tenor.

In general I don't like opera, but one couldn't do without a lot of the great music that has been written for opera. How much poorer one would be without <u>Tristan</u>.

In general I dislike arias from Italian opera because the emotion is always slopping over on all sides. I sort of think, <u>Pace, Pace</u> is not too good. Whereas the arias, such as "Si, mi chiamino Mimi" from La Boheme is beautifully within bounds. Do you know the aria—Air de Lia from Debussy's <u>L' Enfant Prodigue</u>? Interesting.

Of course it is all right to like a lot of music that pins its heart on its sleeve and howls amain. The Tchaikovsky symphonies do this, but who would have them do otherwise? A great deal of Brahms held up by anti-Tchaikovskyites work as openly, looking up quietly as if to say "see how I weep." That always make[s] me mad. Much German lyricism is open self-pity done with excellent compositional craftsmanship which misleads the listeners into thinking he is listening to something more restrained. But the Brahms symphonies are really something. So are the concertos.

Bigness—amplitude of means, great sweep of concept, depth and richness of ideas, good solid craftsmanship (just good carpenter work)—look for these and expect them in the best of all the arts whether English, Finnish, German or Russian (Czech included). But if French look for originality of concept, subtlety of ideas, economy of material and means.

The total effect of French—all the arts is (to us) a bit over intellectual, a little bit <u>dry</u>—but there are exceptions. Notably the painting of Renoir.

... I am better it seems, up today and dressed for part of the day, but not going anywhere or seeing anyone.

Take good care of yourself.

Don't over work—rather,

don't over try. You have time.

You'll grow.

Faithfully,

HB

TEDD

2066 E. 77th St., Apt I
Cleveland, Ohio

undated, likely April 20 to May 11, 1945

Dear Mr. Bellamann,

> "Sleep—the innocent sleep,
> Sleep that knits up the ravel'd sleave of care,
> The death of each day's life, sore labor's bath,
> Balm of hurt minds, great nature's second course,
> Chief nourisher in life's feast,—"[147]

All the things that cried out in me last night until I could not think or read seem small today and far away except for a dull pain left. I remember I could not concentrate on Mr. Benét's poem, his Windgate [sic] Hall and Sally Dupres [sic].[148] My eyes wandered up and I saw your picture and I knew I could have courage to face tomorrows as long as you had faith in me. I want only a corner of this world in which to live my tiny life until it's spent. I want no strange eyes or voices at me. I want to sink down into some bottomless rhapsody that is so beautiful that the emptiness where a love should be shall heal and disappear. I am not always a very nice person, but I have a great capacity for loving. And with this Dali painted desert in me I've turned to other things, but they are cactus flowers, pink and sweet for a season. I am out of joint with this world for when I seem to walk most happily I stumble and all my confidences are dashed. Eyes haunt me with their bursting thoughts though I ask for the smallest corner, wanting to hurt no one.

---

147. Shakespeare, *Macbeth*. Act 2, Scene 2.

148. In Benét's epic poem *John Brown's Body*, Wingate Hall is the southern plantation home of Clay Wingate. Sally Dupré is the love interest of Clay Wingate.

This was the beginning of some other letter to you and though it never got finished, it was started in great sincerity. I remember feeling bad—things seemed to be piling up. Pushing everything from me, I slept. When I rose I felt better and so, ever since. ("Balm of hurt minds.") But I know this still: please, stay with me. There are times when only you, and your picture keep me going over the hurdles.

Fairly important things have happened to me, but instead of bubbling I have been made to think. Our largest radio station, W T A M, signed me to their dramatic staff. I can hardly believe it even now. A few days later Director MacConnell [*sic*] gave me an apprenticeship with the Play House.[149] And yet, I am not giddy over these. Because local broadcasts are rare, one shall be smiled on and be requested to give his efforts without charge. That is alright with me. But inasmuch as I must work to live here, my Play House apprenticeship can amount to only work—work—work—and mostly on scenery. Unless I can disengage myself from this steel mill by next September I cannot read for parts since the cast rehearses in the afternoon besides giving matinees. I am at J&L until 5:00! Apprentices are not paid—they work for the love of it. Actually I am chasing my tail:

"Now that you have all you have wanted for years why don't you feel different? instead of serious and scared! (It's so important) Isn't this what you want? (I don't know) can you act? (So often I think not—not a bit.) Are there any parts for your type? (There have been such parts written—but what of tomorrow. And how can one get near a Marshbanks [*sic*], a Dan, an Oswald?)[150] Are you going to quit your job? (It means gambling my savings … on what? … a faint chance.) Are you just being foolish about the theatre or in dead earnest? (How can I find out) Do you want to act … act… act? (Only, sometimes … so many fail, and I dream such lovely dreams) …"

---

149. Frederic McConnell, see note 109.

150. In George Bernard Shaw's *Candida*, Eugene Marchbanks is a young poet who falls in love with the wife of a clergyman; Dan, see note 6; Oswald, see note 120.

Then last night I saw Elisabeth Bergner and I was enraptured. These actresses fascinate me and I lose my reasoning again. What a divine artist, this tiny Bergner![151]

———

Last Sunday afternoon I went to the art museum with a new sketch book under my arm. I was hoping that this summer would see me recapturing my old sketching technique. For hours I sat near "The Thinker." I didn't know how to begin. My first attempt was dreadful. I started over again, slowly, doing an arm, a finger, an eye, trying to rebuild my ability to put down what I saw. Next I tried a complete sketch once more. It went a little better but the finished sketch was still weak and badly proportioned. It held none of the power in the statue. I had lost what had been so strong in me before, what I had taken years to build. Gone! Sick, I did a few trees, far off buildings, church spire out of the mist; my pencil wabbled, and I went home.

———

How really lovely is the Coda ending—the second movement of Rachmaninoff's 2nd Piano Concerto. I play the album at the library whenever I can; that one record, dozens of times.

———

Not having been with the company for a long enough time, I get no vacation, but I do dream: To the North for me where I could wear a leather jacket, a big woolen shirt, and checked trousers. I walk beneath spruce and pine and see mountains, blue sky with drifts of clouds, and hear cold, deep water. I would get out my fly rod and cast poorly and fish. There would be eggs and bacon to fry and canned beans to heat with huge chunks of butter in them. I would get hungry to the odor of strong coffee. During the day I would dream while sitting in the cool sun; while it rained there would [be] moose trails to walk. There would be a fire to read

---

151. Elisabeth Bergner (1897–1986), Austrian actress.

by—unimportant books. The radio would play softly. The night air would be sharp and my bed, deep and white. Mosquitos [*sic*] and gnats could not discourage me.

Truly, bitterness nips my bones while men about me plan their freedom for two weeks.

In a few hours I shall be on my way home for the week-end. I can't decide if I am glad or not. That town haunts me. Every tree, every street. I remember nights and blossoming cherry trees. Even the ant hills on every sidewalk crack mean something, lonliness [*sic*]. Lonliness [*sic*] that I knew there every moment. It is far better to just think of that little town from here.

You are very kind to write so regularly. In fact, I am ashamed that this has taken me so long. You see, I try to keep myself in check. I don't think it's nice to bother you every time I have a twinge.

I hope New York has been touched with this first glorious May day. It's hard to be ill in such light.

Faithfully,
Tedd

2066 E. 77th St., Apt I
Cleveland, Ohio

undated, likely May 8, 1945

Dear Mr. Bellamann,

The news of V-E Day has been flowing through here this morning and I have a great empty feeling as if looking into a fog. It is huge, this moment, and full of meaning with much lying in the balance. The last few months I have not been one for prayers; but this day I do pray. I don't quite know to whom—perhaps to the arts that have given me happiness. Are they my gods? At least they are beauty, and peace certainly is beauty in its highest form.

I wish I could be with someone—my mother, rather than these men who talk so loudly about the saloons. I am quietly happy today because it means men can come home; that our lives are turning to a more normal passage.

I am very sad because there can be no happiness in the hearts of those that have lost their loves. I know how terrible it is to have a heart full of love and no one there to receive it. These whistles must echo coldly for them. My sister. Her husband was killed a year ago. She has a son three years old; a darling child with fair hair and blue eyes and oceans of affection. What of them? I'm glad she has my mother and father—they are so dear. But her problem remains … and bigger than any I have ever known. I wish I were with her. I think of my brother, somewhere in Germany. The old bachelor has had gifts sent to "a lass in Scotland" … he has seen France … the Rhine … and the empty faces of a crushed people. I think also of my other brother, young Tony in his new sailor suit and his first romance. And at my back I feel the weary faces of Germans who don't know what shall happen to them.

And I am ashamed that this day was necessary; that we, all of us, have failed so utterly and have made war, hate, intolerance, and misunderstanding big in us. I am ashamed that I have lived through it all so coldly. I was in junior high school when Hitler marched into Austria. I didn't understand. I have never understood. I've grown up in a strange atmosphere of conflict. But I was selfish and took all these years in growing while others quietly accepted and moved on.

I wish I were home, or in a church, or maybe in a woods. I don't want to hear whistles and people talking about the saloons and laughing because it is as if a great and wonderful accomplishment, like a tide is slipping back into the sea.

A part of <u>John Brown's Body</u> runs through me.

"What do the souls that bleed from the corpse of battle
Say to the tattered night?
Perhaps it is better
We have no power to visage what they might say."

Mr. Bellamann, what a masterpiece this Benét work is. I have never read anything so beautifully dramatic. I read it aloud; I repeat passages. This book has lain on shelves for years and I might never have read it!

"Here was October, here
Was ruddy October, the old harvester,
Wrapped like a beggared sachem in a coat
Of tattered tanager and partridge feathers,
Scattering jack-o-lanterns everywhere
To give the field-mice pumpkin-colored moons.
His red clay pipe had trailed across the land
Staining the trees with colors of sumach:
East, West, South, North, the ceremonial fume
Blue and enchanted as the soul of air
Drifted its incense.

Incense of the wild,
Incense of earth fulfilled, ready to sleep
The stupefied dark slumber of the bear
All winter, underneath a frozen star."

I thought you would like this because you wrote "There Is the Sound of a Going in the Tops of the Mulberry Trees." So that they won't get laden with dust, I keep your books in a drawer. They have now a companion in "John Brown's Body."

Although it seems rather unimportant now, I want to tell you of my really fine week-end. A week ago at a tea, Max Ellis of the Play House asked me to be his model-guinea-pig for a lecture-demonstration on stage make-up at which he is an expert. Masterfully his hands turned me into a very very old man. Max is a charming person, warm with friendship and unaffected. He told me to go backstage to see him whenever I come to the Play House. I may watch him make-up for the "Squire" which he is now playing in "The Corn Is Green."[152]

A year ago I dared touch the bricks of the Play House as I walked down 86th Street. Now I am already inside, and in a wholesome way. How fortunate I am to have left behind me a sordid life for a promising one. There are times when my happiness is too great. I have met at school fine people. I have learned new subjects. I have been in on splendid conversations. My life seems to be putting on a meaning; perhaps later, a purpose.

After the lecture, Bob Jones of the Drama Department asked me to join his date. I had just met him, but something rose in me and I said yes. I rounded up a girl and the four of us started out on a swell evening. It wasn't much ... but real and good. Barbequed beef sandwiches and talk ... a bad movie through which we laughed ... a walk through the art museum's gardens as evening fell and the birds took to the bushes ... a milk shake on the campus ... lots more talk ... and then we walked home ... Bob and Ethel their way ... Patty and I, ours. It was new to me and delightful. I had laughed and they had liked me. It seemed as if I had torn down a few more bars of my own prison. Look at me, Mr. Bellamann, I'm coming along!

Not knowing about your birthday, I'm glad the Forces looked out for my letter. I hope you are getting well ... better and better as these May days get brighter and brighter. I want to tell you so

---

152. *The Corn Is Green*, 1938 play by Emlyn Williams.

much; and I want to thank you for your letters which are very rich and must take time and thought. I hope that Mrs. Bellamann is well. I shall always be grateful to her for writing me while you were ill.

You know, I'm very bad at farewells. The other night when I took Patty home, I was on her doorstep for half an hour. We both were tired and wanted to go to bed; but when I have a hold on happiness, I am reluctant to let it go. So it is here.

Faithfully,
Tedd

2 East 88th St.
New York City

May 11, 1945

Dear Tedd,

I am always glad to hear from you. This letter of yours sounded happy. The words had a shine in them. I think you have made great headway just in human development. I am afraid that I often sound parental and admonitary [*sic*]. One friend of mine said once: "When I get one of your letters I run this way and that through it dodging the 'don'ts.'" I don't mean to be a check rein. I think you must and should have fun—laugh.

It is the time for testing life, savoring it, and the time to squeeze rememberable juices out of it. I see you so often going through the same processes I remember going through myself. Once in a while I want to say, Don't go <u>that</u> way. But I also remember that experience has to be your own and not a second hand warning.

I hope you are being happy. There is much that is well to see, hear and follow even if it is not always congenial. You can be too "ree-fined" you know, and so let life and its experiences pass you by on the side. I fancy Shakespeare listened to everything, to everybody. Nothing was beneath his notice, or too commonplace.

It is still cold in New York after a too early budding and flowering. The lake under my window looks wintry.

Faithfully,
Henry Bellamann

2 East 88th St.
New York City

May 21, 1945

Dear Tedd,

I should be very happy to know that I have indeed been some sort of crutch or support for you in bad days. I remember what it was like to go thru bad days alone when I was just a bit younger than you are. I poured out most of my distempers in ink, but that's a lonely business, too. You recall the ancient story of the little girl who didn't wish to be left alone in the dark? Reassured by her mother that God was with her, she said: "But I want somebody with a meat face!" I sympathize with that little girl. But I also understand so well the little girl in New Orleans who was always allowed to see the table decorations whenever her mother entertained—candles lighted and all. But one day she behaved badly and was sent upstairs. (Do you know the story? I suspect I bore you sometimes.) When the guests were all seated the folding doors rolled quietly apart and a tiny figure in night-gown looked balefully in and remarked: "Everybody in this room 'cepting me is bitches." There are time[s] when we have to even up with the world by such wholesale denunciation.

Tedd, I think I understand these tragic outbreaks of yours. I read pretty well between the lines. You won't ever have easy times all the time, but I think I can assure you life will be much easier in some ways. Sometime we will meet and talk a lot of these things out. Writing takes so long.

I see your letter was mailed from Bellevue. Was that somewhere on the way home? If you can remain attached to the best things of home and still emancipate yourself from the hard memories it would be good. But you must be careful that you do not carry about with you the whole corpse of the past. Past is past. Only the future is ours, and that only so far as we modify it with the present. Things will be better for you. You have a lot in you. I feel sure of this or I would not be writing this letter, and so long as you need my friendship and interest—here I am.

There is a new novel called "The Folded Leaf"—I have forgotten the author. I wish you would read it. Oddly enough there is a magnificent story in the current Cosmopolitan. It is by Eliz. Enright—never heard of her—and is called "The Maple Tree." It is a superb story. Wish I had written it.[153]

I feel that I know you very well and that I understand a lot about you. Apropos of that photograph, I'm going to send along a couple of others not so accusing and severe.

I'm so afraid for you to give up your present work until you can lay hand on something else and have it secure. Gambling with chances is all right, but these <u>are</u> precarious times. Be as patient as you can.

Faithfully,
HB

---

153. William Keepers Maxwell, Jr.'s *The Folded Leaf* (1945), a coming-of-age story of two friends, set in Chicago; Elizabeth Enright (1909–1968), children's book author and illustrator.

250 Park Avenue
New York 17, New York
American Editorial Rooms

June 5, 1945

Don't miss Henry Bellamann's novel, "Red Shoes Run Faster," in the July issue of The American Magazine to be published June 5.

The Editors

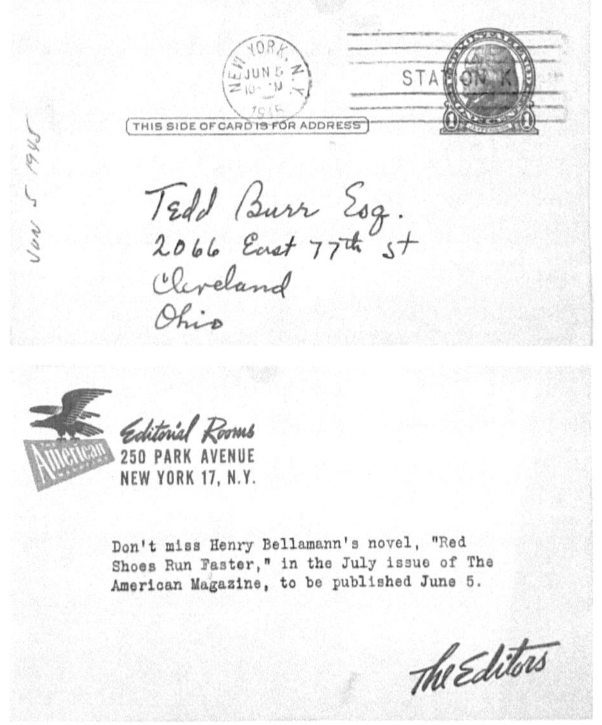

Publisher's notice for Henry Bellamann's novel "Red Shoes Run Faster" in the June 5, 1945 issue of *The American Magazine*.

2066 E. 77th St., Apt I
Cleveland, Ohio

June 6, 1945

Dear Mr. Bellamann,

I have not neglected you in my thoughts. Perhaps with this end of exams I shall be able to breathe and collect myself. I want to spend the next few months in some hidden corner of the library. There are so many good books with something important in each one. Now I am reading "Red Shoes Run Faster" for which I waited a long time.

I am enclosing something to you. I don't know what to call it—hardly a poem.

I see few movies because the general run isn't worth the time. A few evenings ago I did go see "A Song to Remember" with Paul Muni. It was the story of Chopin and his love for George Sand. Although it was glamorized certain qualities remained, namely this love and Chopin's music which was set against some of the most gorgeous technicolor I have seen. I could not forget the experience and the next day I was wading through a sort of happiness that I tried to put down in a few spare moments at work—or perhaps I stole them; I don't remember.

I shall be writing you within the next few days about many things.

I hope you are feeling as sharp as these spring days.

Sincerely,
Tedd

SOLILOQUY

A mood like Dresden china—
So delicate if it were broken I should cry.
It is a fluttering in my breast
With tears filling my eyes and falling on every word,
Making me wish to live within a minute …
A Chopin nocturne … deep blue velvet.
I would be a white stream running through another century
Of candles … soft words and rustling silk …
A Debussy poeme [*sic*] … lyrical … realized.

They are all gone.
The years are between,
Not as a solid block, but as a veil,
A veil that quivers at my breath.
Could I touch their hands beneath the musty covers of their
     books,
Could I feel wet ink and say,
"She wrote this; here is his music."?
Are they shut away in portraits … dead smiles …
Or would they come to me at silvered petaled midnight
And take me with them to some moonlit tryst
If I could find a silver petaled midnight?

Or is it the wilderness stone I seek?
And he that looks for the wilderness stone
Should never marry or beget.
In what realm of unreality rests my heart …
In what pendulum of fading jade?

Ugliness I am … on ugliness I exist
But for moments when some part of me
Can soar on a chime to the leafy past.

Let me be loved in someone's memory
At evening when the four o'clocks grow damp
—and the moths and humming birds—
When the bees guard their gathered sweetness
—and little children lie on wet grass
To watch the stars.
May I be loved
When the white petals fall from cherry trees to the ground
Where I stood alone
And my naked feet felt every solitary blade of grass.

Paint me on a canvas and spill red wine upon its frame;
Then let me gather dust.
Touch me only with old winds that have dipped into a salty
    sea,
And wherever there is heather,
There let me be.

109[154]

HENRY

2 East 88th St.
New York City

June 12, 1945

Dear Tedd,

Of course you ought to be punched in the jaw for this nonsense about ancestors. If you <u>could</u> trace all of your ancestors back to say the year 1200 you would have more ancestors listed than there were people in all of Western Europe. In other words you would have in your family tree every king and queen there was. You would also have every pig-stealer, pickpocket and horse-thief extant of the time. You probably wouldn't actually because there was naturally much overlapping. Nobody who is anybody in himself gives a damn about ancestors. To bring that up is to concern yourself with trappings. Trappings are external. Externals are for display to impress someone when you can't impress otherwise. And there is the show-off standing before you. Only <u>what you are</u> by <u>intelligence</u> and <u>character</u> mean anything—of these character is the greater. All of us (unhappily) are related somehow to all of the nobility (which was seldom noble) of Western Worlds, and to all the European peasants (which is good).

Forget this stuff. I expect you to be more sensible.

I think in your reading you should follow your bent. One thing leads to another. I never could keep history in line either. May be not important. One should learn a few things well. As for most matters we <u>can only</u> know them superficially. There's too much. And so much one doesn't wish to know. Read some old stuff, but read new stuff, too. Steinbeck and Hemingway are of our day after all.

The poem had a good idea in it—homesick for a <u>time</u>, not for a place—it wasn't bad, but there was too much of it.

---

154. There seems to be a missing letter from Tedd sent between June 7 and June 11 that garners Henry's response in this letter.

I think you may have a talent for writing. Anyway most any-one could learn to write.

Some days you spell well—others you don't. Why can't you spell? But I like your letters.

I can write but a little. Write when you can.

Faithfully,
HB

Western Union
New York City

June 16, 1945
4:45 p.m.

Tedd.

Henry died today thought you should know.

Love,
Katherine Bellamann

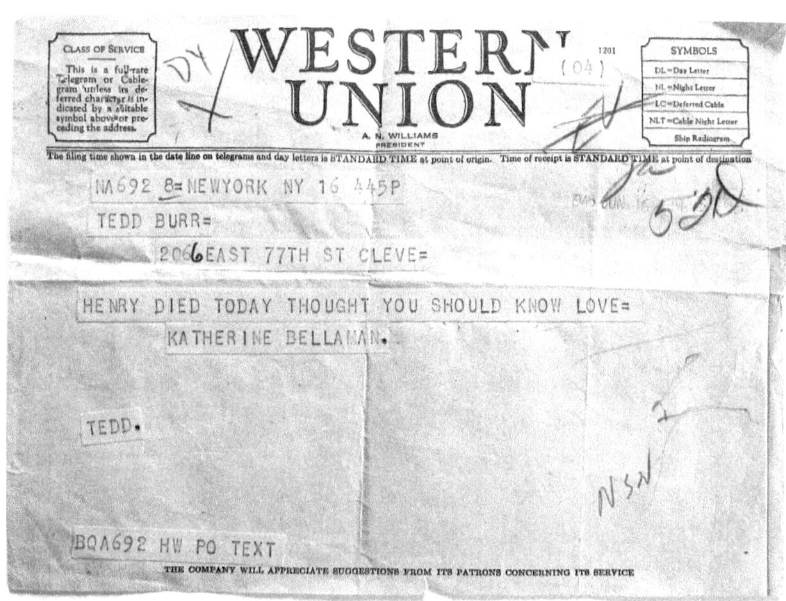

Western Union telegram from Katherine to Tedd, informing him of Henry's death.

2066 E. 77th St., Apt I
Cleveland, Ohio

June 20, 1945

My dear Mrs. Bellamann,

I cannot clearly write the many things that have flooded through me in the past days. My sorrow is great; my sympathy is with you. Although I knew him briefly, I felt his warm affection and greatness. There will always be an emptiness in me for he was my courage and ambition. I must rely now on his words in the past.

I had gone to my home Bellevue Saturday and there heard his death announced on the radio. Having just received a letter from him, I was greatly shocked. Having thought he was almost well, by Sunday evening I was convinced I had misunderstood the radio. Monday morning in Cleveland, I got a N.Y. Times and my fears were confirmed. It was not until evening that I had your message. Thank you very much for that kindness. You have always made me feel close to you. How I wanted to tear away the miles between us and come to you, but could only think of you.

Mr. Bellamann was an inseparable part of me. In my mind was a constant relationship. He walked with me, sat with me, and all my thoughts were directed to him. In letters I took to him my happiness and sadness and he accepted it all with quiet care.

Yes, I dreamed of meeting him too. A short time ago he wrote, "Sometime we will meet and talk a lot of these things out. Writing takes so long." And again, "Perhaps someday when this global unpleasantness is over we can see some of these paintings together and talk about them." I had great plans for that time and was frightened too.

Surely one knows such a friendship but once. I'm sorry he wrote so little of himself, but I selfishly kept him busy and he was patient.

I have treasures in his books, his picture, his letters which I read again last night and realized what he really did for me. In two years he built happiness around me, helped me grow up, made me strong, taught me living. O I shall never forget him. His picture, which I love, with its character and manhood is a challenge and a comfort.

Please forgive any indiscretions that may have crept through. Thank you again for thinking of me and if you will, count me as your friend.

Faithfully,
Tedd

2 East 88th St.
New York City

July 6, 1945

Dear Tedd,

You will forgive my not writing when you remember that I am living in a bleak, desolate, lightless world. When I orient myself a little I shall write at length. Keep thinking of me as your friend. Both you and I lost what can not be replaced but <u>we must keep him alive</u> by remembering.

He kept most if not all of your letters—and there are some Mss. also of yours. Would you like me to return them to you? Your photograph I should like to keep if you allow. Would you like a memento of some kind—one of his desk pencils he used in writing Kings Row? I kept those things for sentimental reasons and perhaps some little thing like that you'd like—or cuff-links he wore—or <u>anything</u> you suggest. Did he send you copies of his two volumes of verse?

Please ask for anything you'd like. He was so fond of you and would want you to have some little "remembrance."

I wish you were here to help me close up this phase of our life—there might be something from his library you'd particularly like.—But please let me hear from you. I'm very <u>low</u> in spirits.

Affectionately,
Katherine Bellamann

I saved every letter (53) from Mr. Bellamann; returned to me were those (46) he had kept. The correspondence was then stored in a trunk, along with the last composition sent to him:

A spirit within me having also died, I shut the trunk and wrote no more.

—Tedd Burr

2 East 88

Dear Tedd:
          You will forgive my
not writing when you remember
that I am living in a bleak, desolate,
lightless world. When I orient
myself a little I shall write at
length. Keep thinking of me as your
friend. Both you and I lost what
can not be replaced but we must
keep him alive by remembering.
          He kept most if not all of
your letters — and there are some
Mss. also of yours. Would you
like me to return them to you?
Your photograph I should like to
keep if you allow. — Would you
like a memento of some kind —
one of his desk pencils he used
in writing King's Row? I kept
those things for sentimental

First page of letter from Katherine Bellamann to Tedd Burr, July 6, 1945.

TEDD'S AFTERWORD

Tedd Burr followed Mr. Bellamann's advice and continued to work in the steel and railroad industries for forty-four years, until retirement at age sixty-three in 1987.

In 1945, three months after Bellamann's, death Tedd turned down the Play House apprenticeship. After college, he continued acting in community theater (playing Oswald in Ibsen's *Ghosts*), and in 1951 the Play House engaged him as guest actor in Maxwell Anderson's *Anne of a Thousand Days,* followed by Jean Anouilh's *Antigone* and a series of minor roles through 1954.

In the theater he acted in classics by Ibsen, Shaw, Wilde, Chekhov, Moliere, Sophocles and Shakespeare and modern plays by Brecht, T. Williams, Albee, Pinter, Mamet and McNally until retirement at age seventy-five.

After a dinner conversation in February 2000, actor/director friend Lenny Pinna asked to film Burr in an unscripted, real-time docudrama in his home remembering his teenage years and leading to the correspondence with Bellamann. For the first time in fifty-five years, Burr took from the trunk the letters and read briefly from them.

Ten months later the film *Letters to Uranus: The Hidden Life of Tedd Burr* was shown to an invited audience at the Cedar Lee Theatre in Cleveland Heights, Ohio. In March 2001 it was selected for showing in The Cleveland International Film Festival. Audiences expressed a desire for the correspondence to be published.

Tedd Burr lives in Cleveland Heights, Ohio, in his house full of art, still attends the theater, continues to read and listens to opera.

—Tedd Burr, 2000

Portrait of Tedd Burr, taken in the early 1990s as an actor's headshot for a production of Terrence McNally's *The Lisbon Traviata*, in which Tedd played Mendy, at the Dobama Theatre in Cleveland Heights, Ohio. See "Introduction" (xi). Photocopy included in Tedd's transcript of the letters.

Katherine Bellamann was asked by Simon and Schuster to finish writing the second volume of *Kings Row*—published in 1948 as *Parris Mitchell of Kings Row*, by Henry and Katherine Bellamann.

Tedd and Katherine continued to correspond with letters and cards for the next eleven years. At Katherine's request, Tedd visited her in Jackson, Mississippi after she moved back to her family roots.

Katherine Bellamann died November 10, 1956. She was buried at the Church of the Heavenly Rest in New York City, alongside Henry Bellamann.

Tedd Burr died August 29, 2012 at the age of eighty-eight.

—Lenny Pinna

In the Name of Jamie Wakefield

As noted in the introduction, my primary interest in Tedd and Henry's story has always been in its dramatic possibilities. They never met in person, but I have been compelled and inspired by the psychological and imaginative realms in which they did meet. I believe that with an unconventional narrative structure and visual style, a modern audience will easily comprehend and appreciate the dynamics of their "virtual" relationship.

From their first letters, I felt the dramatic poignancy of Tedd and Henry meeting through an intermediary fictional character, Jamie Wakefield. Tedd refers to Jamie six times in his initial letter. It's clear that he personally identifies with Jamie, internalizing and integrating the character within his own psyche. "I am writing to you on the strength of Jamie Wakefield," he tells Henry. He specifically cites the instance he felt his complete embodiment of the character: "Last night I read a scene between Drake McHugh and Jamie Wakefield ... it was not of Jamie I read, but of myself" (3).

Given his dramatic sensibility, Tedd instinctually heightens the stakes with the line, "I beg of you in the name of Jamie Wakefield" (1). These imploring words are made more powerfully persuasive by their obvious allusion to the divine invocation—in the name of Jesus Christ. He then conveys a sense of urgency: "If you can picture Jamie waiting for a coming day ... which would decide his possible army induction ..."(3). By projecting himself as Jamie in his own circumstances, Tedd reinforces their oneness, while signaling a coded message to Henry: Imagine an effeminate and possibly homosexual young man entering military service and surviving the realities of a predominantly hyper-masculine, heterosexual culture.

Throughout the letter, Tedd builds his case of identification with Jamie until he can ultimately express what he really wants from Henry—to be seen, heard and known by someone who might actually care about someone like a Jamie Wakefield. He pleads, "[P]lease send me an address where I might write you personally, a story of a Jamie" (3). Tedd offers himself to the author as an alluring subject of interest—a real-life version of a character the author created.

In Henry's first letter of response, he immediately acknowledges Tedd's real-life kinship with Jamie: "Jamie is one of my favorite people because he is one of the most misunderstood" (5). "People." It's significant that Henry refers to Jamie as a real person, not a fictitious character that he had created. He also offers Tedd warm sentiment with his compassionate understanding and appreciation of Jamie. So what is it about the character of Jamie Wakefield that immediately bonds Tedd and Henry?

I first learned of the character Jamie Wakefield during the evening that Tedd and I filmed *Letters to Uranus*. At one point, Tedd wondered aloud, "What was it—that led me to write to him in the first place—this little kid—writing to this famous author?" He then picked up the book *Kings Row*, which was lying on his bedside table; he had recently begun rereading the novel after seeing the film on TV. He opened the book and thumbed a few pages to an opening scene, indicating that this was the passage in which he first identified with one of the characters in the novel. He proceeded to dramatically interpret the scene, which was narrated with limited third-person omniscience from the perspective of the grade-school teacher Sally Venable:

> She stirred in her chair and sniffed audibly. The windows were open—those tall, narrow church windows, but they afforded poor ventilation. The room smelled abominably. Sweaty bodies, most of them infrequently washed; winter clothes that had seen a hard season; the harsh odor of small boys verging on adolescence—she closed her eyes for an instant and thought of the hour of dismissal, still thirty minutes away. When she glanced up again she saw Jamie Wakefield looking at her. Almost she could believe he wore a look of concern—of sympathy, even. She nodded at him, and the boy flashed back his quick, brilliant smile.

"He's pretty, that boy," she thought. "Too pretty for a boy. But all the Wakefields are good-looking."

Jamie's attention had returned to the reading, and Sally Venable watched the play of expression on his mobile features. He was affecting, now, a sort of disdain—a precocious expression for a boy of twelve—that pursed his full red lips and narrowed his wide over-bright eyes. His hair, soft and black, swept back picturesquely from his wide blue-veined forehead with its exquisitely traced brows.

"I wish they'd dress him differently. That ruffled collar now—"

That very ruffled collar spread out over his blue jacket did get Jamie into trouble sometimes. Boys called him "sissy," but he never resented it and usually this proved a good defense.

He was interested now in spite of himself. He had forgotten that Miss Venable was looking at him and his lips parted in a half-smile—an enchanting smile.

"He looks like a girl—like a girl in love," his teacher thought. "He's as beautiful as Cassandra Tower." (7–8)[155]

As Tedd ended his recitation, silence and stillness permeated the room. I sensed a direct connection between the elder Tedd Burr, his younger self and the character Jamie Wakefield that transcended the bounds of time. And for some reason, I felt that I had been called to bear witness to their timeless connection.

When Tedd gave me his copy of *Kings Row* to read, I was particularly attuned to the plight of Jamie Wakefield. I was quite curious about the author's personal sensibilities as he described Jamie Wakefield's "too pretty for a boy" fine features in such sensuous detail, and I became suspicious that he used a woman's gaze as the narrating perspective. I couldn't help but wonder, was the author really a "heterosexual" male? It seemed plausible that

---

155. Henry Bellamann, *Kings Row* (Simon & Schuster, 1940), page numbers noted in text.

Henry Bellamann could have been voicing his own personal perceptions of Jamie through a female perspective as a sort of literary disguise—one that Tennessee Williams often employed in voicing himself through female characters.

Subsequently, I learned that one of the reasons *Kings Row* was considered a controversial novel when it was first released was because it contained overt references to homosexuality. There are a number of instances throughout the novel that deal with homosexual leanings or wonderings. The most typically virile male character in the novel, Drake McHugh (played by a young Ronald Reagan in the movie version), offers Jamie Wakefield a ride in his horse-drawn carriage. (This is the scene in which Tedd wholly identified himself as Jamie.) Drake brings up a conversation about Jamie not liking girls, and turns to him, staring at his sensuous features, telling him, "[Y]ou look like a girl yourself." During this scene, the author makes us privy to Drake's inner stirrings.

> Drake did not question further. Once more he gave Jamie a quick, keen, scrutinizing glance. Jamie was much as he had always been. He looked no more than sixteen, Drake decided. His face was as soft of contour and as warm and lovely in coloring as ever. He was incredibly good-looking. Drake thought he looked a good deal like Poppy Ross. Jamie had the same yielding look—the same sensuous roundness, and the same silky-looking mouth.
>
> Drake slapped the horse with the reins, and half-whistled under his breath. He would not have liked for anyone to know just what he was thinking at that moment, or how Jamie actually made him feel. (383)

The other major male character in *Kings Row*, Parris Mitchell (modeled on the author himself), often has mixed thoughts or feelings about masculinity and sexuality. Parris is both fascinated and perplexed by Jamie's overt femininity and developing homosexuality:

> ... He liked Jamie. Yes; he was sure about that. But why was he always a little embarrassed about it? The other boys didn't seem to dislike Jamie—they, well, they merely seemed to push him aside somewhat. They called him girly names. Certainly, he was girlish, but he was really all right.... (122)

And

> Jamie had strange hands ... His fingers left a tingle where they touched.... Jamie leaned forward and kissed him on the mouth. Parris was too amazed to move, too amazed to think.... He was not too clearly aware of anything for awhile except Jamie's caresses and his flattering hands which carried both violence and appeasement in their touch. (127–128)

In the introduction to the recent reprinting of *Kings Row*, Professor Rachael Price discusses the ambivalent feelings that Parris Mitchell seems to have about Jamie. Professor Price surmises, "while the town as a whole rejects [Jamie] on some level, the character of Parris reacts to the situation with a much more nuanced and understanding approach. He does not invoke the homophobia often associated with hegemonic masculinity; not only does he not dislike the experience but, as we see via syntactical choices such as fingers that 'left a tingle' and 'flattering hands,' he does enjoy it on some level."[156]

If the younger Henry Bellamann indeed had similar experiences to those of his fictional counterpart, Parris Mitchell, it would speak to Tedd's intuitive knowing about Henry's past. Tedd writes, "It was that conversation between Drake and Jamie that made me turn to you. I felt it must come from some experience of your own. It was so true, like something from my life. I know a Drake and he

---

156. Rachael Price, Introduction to Henry Bellamann, *Kings Row* (Hastings, NE: Hastings College Press, 2022), xiv.

has said some of the same things contained in those pages, but not so eloquently" (25).

In Henry's second letter to Tedd, he discloses the origin of the character, Jamie Wakefield. "Now, I'm going back for a moment to Jamie Wakefield. There was a real Jamie Wakefield. He was a friend of mine. 'Jamie' has missed all boats, although he was talented" (21). Henry again confirms that his childhood friend was the model for Jamie. "You see, I knew Jamie Wakefield. He was my good friend, and the later days of Jamie are not pretty" (53).

While working on the dramatization of the letters, I became increasingly preoccupied with questions about Jamie Wakefield. Who was this childhood friend of Henry's that served as the model for Jamie? What really happened in his adult life that caused Henry to describe him in such unflattering terms? I also wondered about Henry's motives, either conscious or subconscious, in conveying this information to Tedd. Henry seemed to use the information about his friend's life as a cautionary tale—as a deterrent to Tedd's underlying desire to present himself as a "pretty boy" (30). I thought Henry was quite manipulative in his attempts to persuade Tedd to stop wearing make-up, to cut his luxurious hair shorter and to learn how to conform to living a life within the norms of society. Henry seemed to encourage Tedd to live out an existence that I would call a *half-life*, helping Tedd to cut off half of his life so that the other half could live.

When Tedd died in 2012, I felt a stronger motivation to bring young Tedd's story out into the light. However, at that point in time, I realized that my various creative attempts to dramatize the material had been too protective of Tedd's younger image and too disparaging of Henry's influence upon him. Dramaturgically I knew it would be necessary to balance the positive and negative qualities of each character for the story to feel more essentially true. I was cognizant that I needed to research Henry's life so that I could better understand his motivations within the context of his time.

My initial research led me to Professor Harry McBrayer Bayne's dissertation, "A Critical Study of Henry Bellamann's

Life and Works," which was completed at the University of Mississippi. I tracked down Professor Bayne who was then teaching at Spartanburg Methodist College in Spartanburg, South Carolina. Professor Bayne replied to my initial email with enthusiasm, telling me that he had tried to find me ten years earlier; he had caught wind of my film about the elder Tedd Burr and his correspondence with Henry Bellamann. Bayne informed me that while he had been conducting his research on Henry Bellamann in the University of Mississippi Archives, he had come upon two of Tedd's letters among Henry's papers.

When Professor Bayne and I decided to schedule a telephone conversation, it seemed that each of us had preliminary curiosities. Professor Bayne first asked me whether Tedd and Henry had consummated their relationship. I was surprised by his question. From reading just two of Tedd's letters, Prof. Bayne got the impression that Tedd and Henry were engaged in an intimate relationship. Although I believed that the two were deeply enmeshed in a uniquely complex psychological relationship, I had to reply, "No, they never met in person."

My first inquiry was to confirm Henry's statement that the character Jamie Wakefield was based on a childhood friend. Prof. Bayne responded matter of factly, "Yes, Jamie Wakefield was based on his childhood friend, Albert Berghauser." I next wanted to confirm Henry's later statements—that this childhood friend "missed all boats, although he was talented" (21) and that "the later days of Jamie are not pretty" (53). Surprised by those statements, Professor Bayne contradicted them emphatically. "That's not true at all!" he said. "Albert Sartor Berghauser became a respected professor of French and German at Furman University in Greenville, South Carolina."

Aha! Henry had misrepresented the life of his childhood friend, the real-life Jamie Wakefield. Bayne's words were like a dam breaking, unleashing a torrent of thoughts into my imagination, lending credence to my suspicions about Henry's underlying motives. Professor Bayne proceeded to disclose information about Henry and Albert's respective childhood—a series of revelations that completely rewrote the entire dramatic narrative for me. Bayne was aware that Henry held conflicted feelings about Albert, because Albert Berghauser had come from a well-to-do family; Henry was considered to be "from the other side of the tracks." He then divulged information about Henry's questionable paternity and how, basically, he had been raised by his German immigrant grandmother, Matilde Ausfahl. It was rumored around the town of Fulton, Missouri that Henry was "illegitimate." Thus, he was looked down upon, whispered about, and marginalized by polite society.

Professor Bayne was also able to compare and contrast the narrative of *Kings Row* with Bellamann's actual background. In fiction, Henry placed Parris Mitchell in much better circumstances—equal to those of Albert Berghauser. Like Henry, Parris lived with his German, immigrant grandmother, but she was a highly respected woman of much greater means. The author also made interesting transferences of facts in his fictitious version of events. Henry's grandmother was a seamstress and made fancy ruffled collars and cuffs for the high society folks in the town. Coincidentally, she dressed Henry for school with fancy ruffled collars and cuffs, giving him an appearance of proper respectability and covering up his lower economic and social standing. It's quite telling that in *Kings Row* Bellamann ascribes the fancy ruffled collars to Jamie Wakefield and even voices the ramifications that arise from wearing such clothing. The teacher, Sally Venable laments, "I wish they'd dress him differently. That ruffled collar now—" The narrator admits, "That very ruffled collar ... did get Jamie into trouble sometimes. Boys called him 'sissy'" (8).

Although Henry's childhood friend Albert Berghauser was the feminine-looking boy that became the model for Jamie Wakefield, it was the author himself who as a child wore the "sissy" ruffled collars. Notably, the author did not give Parris ruffled collars to wear; he transferred that seemingly feminine attribute to the character that appeared feminine—Jamie Wakefield! Bellamann did maintain the similarity between Albert Berghauser and Jamie Wakefield when it came to family respectability, though. Albert Berghauser's family maintained its social status as successful business owners of the town's hardware store; Jamie Wakefield's family garnered their social status as well-respected bank owners. Albert actually worked at a bank while helping with the family hardware store.

Still, the author undermined Jamie Wakefield's character with other attributes that were thought less desirable within society—like a boy who wants to be a poet instead of a banker, and who has questionable associations with men who are thought to be having sex with men. Bellamann burdened the character with socially undesirable attributes until Jamie became somewhat deadened within—almost a walking corpse—unhappy and unfulfilled—quite unlike the life of the real Albert Berghauser. According to Professor Bayne, not only did Albert Berghauser become a respected professor, but he later married a woman from the prominent Powel family of Rogersville, Tennessee. This fact disproves Henry's statement that "the later days of Jamie are not pretty." In actuality, Albert gained higher social status.

Bayne's further revelations brought everything into sharper focus. He divulged that misrepresenting or embellishing the truth was something Henry had done in his earlier adult life. Bayne's research uncovered that after high school Henry began to misrepresent his educational background to gain initial teaching positions. For example, Henry stated that he had studied piano and organ with masters in Europe, when in fact he had studied in Denver. Henry also claimed he attended the University of Denver, where in fact there was no record of him. Henry did study with a famous organist, an Englishman, Henry Houseley, who happened to be teaching at the University of Denver.

Apparently, Henry continued to pad his resume each year as he dotted his way across the South, securing various teaching positions. At one point, Bayne concluded that the credentials and dates Henry listed on his resume would make sense only if he had entered college at the age of fourteen—which he did not. It was while teaching at Tuscaloosa Female College in Alabama that Henry met and married Katherine Jones, another music teacher. It bears mentioning that Katherine was five years older than Henry. In one of our ongoing conversations, Professor Bayne shared with me that he had been told during his research interviews with several of those that knew the Bellamanns that Henry had been extremely insecure about Katherine being older than him. Professor Bayne speculated that this insecurity might have contributed to Henry padding his resume to make himself seem older. Together, Henry and Katherine achieved a certain level of notoriety as an academic "power couple" when they both secured teaching positions in the music department at Chicora College in Greenville, South Carolina.

Early in their tenure at Chicora College, the young newly-wed professors lived in campus housing. It wasn't long before "a childhood friend" of Henry's visited the couple seemingly out of the blue. Yes, the childhood friend was the very same Albert Berghauser. Evidently, Katherine knew nothing of Henry's childhood friendship with Albert Berghauser before his arrival at their home. Henry invited Albert to live with them, and as chair of the music department at Chicora, Henry was able to secure Albert a teaching position in the music department. Professor Bayne's knowledgeable sources informed him that Henry hired Albert as a piano teacher—"a job he apparently wasn't qualified for." Henry, Katherine and Albert lived together for five years until Katherine decided that she could no longer tolerate the arrangement. During one of those five years, Henry and Albert took a sabbatical (without Katherine), to live together in Europe to study piano and organ with Isidor Philipp and Charles-Marie Widor. Sources confided to Professor Bayne that after five years, Katherine finally gave Henry an ultimatum saying, "I married only one of you. The other one of you has to go."

During his entire correspondence with Tedd, Henry only once mentioned that he had a wife, and he did so only because Tedd had specifically inquired about his personal life. Henry never even mentioned her by name; he merely states, "I have a wife." (133). Tedd did not know Katherine by name until she wrote to him on behalf of her ill husband. I think it speaks volumes that Henry said nothing about Katherine's personal qualities or anything about her highly successful career as a vocal coach for professional opera and Broadway singers. Henry is quite verbose throughout the letters, expounding the virtues or heaping criticism about a myriad of singers, composers, conductors and performances, yet never once mentions that his wife, Katherine, is also connected to the music world. She actually gave voice lessons in the living room of their apartment, where the couple kept their two grand pianos.

Ironically Henry chose to share only one story about his wife, a story that actually referred to him: she had published a novel that he claimed had almost ruined his reputation (133). Indeed, in 1931, Katherine Bellamann published her first novel, *My Husband's Friends,* a semi-autobiographical account that centered on the private suffering of the wife of a famous scientist, Gene Perryfond, who has a sequence of affairs, primarily with women. In the early chapters of the novel, the character Victor Sayre, "a childhood friend" of her husband's, arrives at their home and is invited by her husband to live with the newlywed couple. It has already been written about that Victor Sayre was based on Henry's friend, Albert Berghauser. In a list of characters preceding the novel, Katherine describes Victor Sayre: "His gay chatter was like an impalpable dust—a fine sift of inimical dust—a drying, obstructing, sterilizing, killing dust."[157]

Victor Sayre lives with the Perryfonds for five years until Nina, who could no longer bear the situation, concocts a plan to push Victor into a marriage with a spinsterish woman. Nina, who speaks in the first person throughout the novel, reflects near the very end, "I summoned up the long-laid spectres of my old disquiets. I answered them one by one…. There was Victor Sayre. Perhaps he had been the nearest of all to a genuine threat. He endangered too many beginnings. He had been unimportant, but Gene and I were young then. Even so I had understood little enough" (276). I suspect Katherine (through Nina) was expressing the hurt and pain that she had felt during her early years of marriage to Henry, which included Albert's abiding presence.

---

157. Katherine Bellamann, *My Husband's Friends* (Century Co., 1931), page numbers noted in the text.

While researching Henry's life, I did find compassion for him, primarily because of the unfortunate circumstances of his childhood. I visited Henry's hometown, Fulton, Missouri and stood outside of the little stone home that had belonged to his Grandmother Ausfahl. It is plain to see just how marginalized the Ausfahl house was from the rest of the social life of the town. One reaches the outer perimeter of the town, then crosses a little stream to enter a sparsely wooded area where a half dozen rustic homes are tucked away; the Ausfahl home is the furthest removed, sitting alone at the very back of a tiny enclave—on the frontier edge of a rocky and wooded hillock. By comparison, Albert Berghauser's family lived in one of the large Victorian homes near the center of town where they enjoyed their respected status within society.

When imagining myself in young Henry's childhood circumstances, I begin to understand some of his internal struggles and possibly the core of his psychological pain. He was a highly intelligent and gifted being, yet was marginalized and made to feel inferior in society by the mere circumstances of his birth and socio-economic class. As an adult, he had an affectionate bond with another man that could not be acknowledged publicly, knowing privately that their bond was a threat to his marriage, and possibly to his livelihood. To have this unaccepted relationship end so abruptly and so completely could only have compounded his wounds.

I have thought a lot about Henry's ending years as well, dealing with chronic infirmity and becoming more and more reclusive. I pondered often, what was it that kept Henry committed to his correspondence with Tedd? Whether true, or whether Henry was conscious of it, the answer that makes the most sense to me is that for Henry, the young Tedd Burr represented an opportunity to re-engage his psyche again with his childhood friend, Albert Berghauser. I imagine he carried unresolved feelings about his relationship with Albert throughout his life, so that in some ways, while he thought he was helping Tedd he was also helping himself work through those complicated feelings about Albert—the real Jamie Wakefield.

—Lenny Pinna

Ausfahl house in Fulton, Missouri—Henry Bellamann's childhood home. Photo by L. Pinna, 2022.

POST-POSTSCRIPT

I am grateful that Tedd kept his and Henry's letters intact for all those years, and I'm humbled that he entrusted them to me. I'm even more grateful that Katherine Bellamann sent all of Tedd's letters back to him; I deem it an act of compassion on her part. Over a span of many years, there seems to have been several improbable or serendipitous events for this story to have occurred, to have been preserved, to have been uncovered and to now be shared with a wider audience.

—Lenny Pinna

Since the initial publication of *A Face from Uranus* in 2022, Ecclesia Arts has established a YouTube channel where Lenny Pinna and collaborator Bonnie Diczhazy have produced the series pilot (as a dramatic reading/performance) for the proposed limited TV series, "In the Name of Jamie Wakefield: Too Pretty for a Boy." The subsequent five episodes of the series are offered as dramatic readings. Additionally, Lenny Pinna presents dramatic readings of a number of Tedd and Henry's letters from *A Face from Uranus*, and the original docudrama filmed in 2000, *Letters to Uranus: The Hidden Life of Tedd Burr*, can be seen in its entirety.

inthenameofjamiewakefield.com serves as the portal for all the works and media affiliated with Tedd and Henry's letters, including a producer's demo reel.